Transitions and Transformations

Life Course, Culture and Aging: Global Transformations
General Editor: Jay Sokolovsky, University of South Florida St. Petersburg

Published by Berghahn Books under the auspices of the Association for Anthropology and Gerontology (AAGE) and the American Anthropological Association Interest Group on Aging and the Life Course.

The consequences of aging will influence most areas of contemporary life around the globe: the makeup of households and communities; systems of care; generational exchange and kinship; the cultural construction of the life cycle; symbolic representations of midlife, elderhood, and old age; and attitudes toward health, disability, and life's end. This series will publish monographs and collected works that examine these widespread transformations with a perspective on the entire life course as well as mid/late adulthood, engaging a cross-cultural framework. It will explore the role of older adults in changing cultural spaces and how this evolves in our rapidly globalizing planet.

Volume 1
TRANSITIONS AND TRANSFORMATIONS
Cultural Perspectives on Aging and the Life Course
Edited by Caitrin Lynch and Jason Danely

Titles in preparation:

FOUR DAYS OF LIGHT AND IT'S DARK AGAIN
Dementia Care in India
Bianca Brijnath

AGEING AND THE DIGITAL LIFE COURSE
Edited by David Prendergast and Chiara Garattini

WALTZING INTO OLD AGE
Redefining Aging, the Life Course, and Eldercare in China
Hong Zhang

TRANSITIONS AND TRANSFORMATIONS

Cultural Perspectives on Aging and the Life Course

Edited by

Caitrin Lynch and Jason Danely

berghahn
NEW YORK · OXFORD
www.berghahnbooks.com

Published in 2013 by
Berghahn Books
www.berghahnbooks.com

Library of Congress Cataloging-in-Publication Data

Transitions and transformations : cultural perspectives on aging and the life course /
edited by Caitrin Lynch & Jason Danely.
    p. cm.
    Includes bibliographical references.
    ISBN 978-0-85745-778-3 (hbk. : alk. paper) — ISBN 978-0-85745-779-0
    (institutional ebook)
    1. Aging—Cross-cultural studies. 2. Aging—Social aspects. 3. Life cycle, Human.
I. Lynch, Caitrin. II. Danely, Jason.
GN485.T73 2013
305.26—dc23

2012024974

British Library Cataloguing in Publication Data

A catalogue record for this book is available from the British Library.

ISBN 978-0-85745-778-3 (hardback)
ISBN 978-0-85745-779-0 (institutional ebook)

To the generations in our families:

Robin, Auden, and Isla. And to the memory of my grandmother Benita Hermano (1920–2008). —JD

Generations from my grandmother Esther to my daughter Nicola Esther, and to all in-between (especially Nick and Cormac).—CL

CONTENTS

ILLUSTRATIONS

ACKNOWLEDGMENTS

WE THANK THE CONTRIBUTORS TO this volume, who have not only impressed us with a wide array of fascinating and thought-provoking chapters, but who were also instrumental in articulating the grander vision of the volume as a whole. We extend our gratitude to *Life Course, Culture, and Aging: Global Transformations* Series Editor Jay Sokolovsky for his tireless dedication, guidance, and passion for this project from the very beginning. And we thank Jennifer Cole for the Afterword in this book and for her critical comments on a draft of our Introduction to this volume. Emily Wentzell came through at short notice with feedback on the Introduction; we are grateful for her speed and smarts. We are also grateful for the support of the other members of the Series Editorial Board, and the anonymous reviewers for all of their comments and suggestions. We also thank Alice Kehoe and Anthony Paredes of the Association for Senior Anthropologists, as well as the members of the Association for Anthropology and Gerontology (AAGE) and the American Anthropological Association Interest Group on Aging and the Life Course. Finally, we are indebted to Marion Berghahn for the confidence and vision that she has shown in leading life-course studies in anthropology, and to Senior Editor Ann Przyzycki DeVita and the staff at Berghahn Books with whom we have enjoyed the privilege of working.

SECTION I

FRAMEWORKS

Introduction

TRANSITIONS AND TRANSFORMATIONS
Paradigms, Perspectives, and Possibilities

Jason Danely and Caitrin Lynch

THIS BOOK IS THE PRODUCT of a general shift in perspective among anthropologists interested in aging. Rather than an earlier "geroanthropology" that focused exclusively on the lives of older adults as if they constituted a distinct and easily bounded category of persons (Cohen 1994: 138), anthropologists are moving towards a more inclusive, multigenerational, life-course approach that better captures the dynamic complexity of how humans grow older in ways that shape values, institutions, and social life for all of us.[1] A life-course approach to aging recognizes that as individuals age, their lives unfold in conjunction with those of people of different ages, and that all of these actors, who occupy different and changing positions and multiple cultural and physical environments over a period of historical time, are shaping and influencing each other in important ways.[2] A focus on the life course, therefore, helps us to see not only the possibilities for individual development and maturity, but also how intergenerational conflict, cooperation, and contact can reconfigure values and redistribute roles and resources. Together, anthropological and life-course perspectives help us to realize that although social structures and practices appear to exist in the ethnographic present, they are embedded in the pasts and futures that make up cultural models and personal identities.

The "transitions and transformations" of our title are about the changes that people experience and those that they create. As our section headings suggest, they are not only changes to bodies, spaces, temporalities, families, and economies, but also changes in how people imagine what they want to become and where they have come from (cf. Cole and Durham 2007: 15). Studies of the life course in the social sciences, ranging from those on infancy to old age, commonly employ the term "transition" to describe changes accompanying different kinds of social and psychological development. A life-course transitions model is generally applicable to a number of conceptual frameworks and perspectives, and implies neither abrupt disjunctures between a uniform set of stages nor an assumption of steady progress or decline. "Transformation," in contrast, is more commonly used for large-scale, radical, and dramatic changes (be they local, national, or global) that affect people's daily lives.

In this book we examine the dynamic interplay of transitions and transformations: when the individual's life-course experiences and the social, cultural, and historical structures and meanings that shape the life course interact with and permeate each other. Couching our examination of aging and the life course in terms of the dynamics of transitions and transformations advances our analysis in two ways. First, it allows us to point analytically to the wider range of inquiry in the social sciences in which life-course studies are embedded. Second, it allows us to situate an individual and her/his experiences and understandings in wider contexts—contexts that are intimately experienced by that person, and contexts that are not.

While contributions to the anthropology of youth have led our understandings of the ways that the life-course perspective can be utilized within anthropology (see Cole's Afterword in this volume), we also recognize that questions about aging hinge upon the idea that the transitions and transformations that occur, even at the most intimate level of the body, are discursively and practically linked to a broader social context. The contributors to this book demonstrate the insight that anthropological approaches can bring in the context of grounded ethnographic description and analysis. A lens on old age enables us to see how the transitions of aging are a matter of entangled horizons of transformation. To study transitions and transformations of aging and the life course is to study the webs of relationships and possibility that unfold through lives as they are embedded in social, economic, and political contexts.

The ethnographic encounters with transitions and transformations in the life course described in this book produce a number of analytically important anthropological questions: How does historically unprecedented longevity affect personal identity and social relationships? How are cultural pasts and futures revised or forecasted in light of changing age-compositions of family and community? How do social and cultural institutions that organize labor, political power, and care respond to demographic changes, and how does globalization affect these responses? Do changes in *how* we age change *who* we can think we are? How do these changes disrupt some forms of social cohesion and create opportunities for new forms of sociality to emerge?

These questions do not exhaust the possibilities for integrating aging and the life course into anthropological inquiry, but they do illustrate both the complexity and urgency for greater work. Aging, and old age in particular, is a primary focus of this work, since, as Baltes (1996: 367) reminds us, in the grand sweep of the history of humanity, "old age is young" and its architecture is still incomplete; the effects of global longevity cross borders and generations. As generations work through and adapt to the resulting social transformations, they are, in effect, reshaping the life course. Old and young alike are implicated in this process of life-course shaping that involves the reconfiguration of relationships of care, conflict, recognition, and exclusion. Not only do we recognize the value of seeing aging as a dynamic process, and older people as important social actors shaping the life course, but we also see fundamental questions concerning aging and culture leading us to paths of inquiry that enrich our overall understanding of society.

Anthropology of Aging and the Life Course

Although there are threads of aging and the life course in diverse work throughout anthropology (and we will discuss examples below), these concepts have not yet acquired a foothold as central to anthropological thought. We hope this volume will be a move toward braiding these threads together, bringing the transitions and transformations of aging and the life course into a more central focus in the discipline. Here we situate these threads in historical and cross-disciplinary perspective.

Aging in Context

Similar to other volumes on the anthropology of aging (Amoss and Harrell 1981; Fry 1980; Sokolovsky 2009b), this book begins with the challenge to the assumption of universal, transcultural models of aging and the life course, be they social, psychological, or biophysical, by highlighting the importance of cultural diversity and plasticity. This approach contrasts with reductionist uses of cultural diversity as points on a scatter-plot by means of which we reckon a line of "best fit." Cross-cultural studies of aging in other disciplines seem to be particularly prone to this kind of treatment, and the result has been a field that is comparatively data rich and theory poor.[3] That is, we understand how cultures deviate from or conform to our general models of "best practices" for "successful aging," but we have much less understanding of alternative models that are driven by cultural influences. Anthropologists, who are familiar with the dangers of essentialism and understand the importance of multiple modernities and identities, have a long history of engaging cultural difference, and our empirical findings and conceptual insights can help us recognize the uniqueness of the transitions and transformations of aging and intergenerational relationships in the current historical moment, without reverting to zero-sum scenarios or alarmist demography.[4]

While "old age" remains an important focus of life-course studies, cordoning off old age as a discrete category of analysis limits our ability to accurately portray aging as a context of interactions among and between generations, including the imaginative landscapes of memories and aspirations (cf. Cole and Durham 2007). Just as the anti-racist humanism of the anthropological pioneer Franz Boas has come to inform the fundamental principles of the discipline, such as cultural relativism and social constructedness, and feminist thought has broadened well beyond its original scholarly goals to enrich our general understanding of gender, sexuality, and identity, geroanthropology is making a transition to a larger project of life-course anthropology.[5] As the chapters in this book show, the importance of aging and life-course perspectives in ethnographic writing is becoming not only more prevalent across all geographic regions, but it also has potential for identifying and addressing some of the most important challenges for anthropology in the twenty-first century. These challenges include engaging anthropology with problems that people face worldwide—though with different contexts, meanings, and effects—including economic inequality, global climate change, human rights violations, and the spread of disease. All of these problems impact, and are impacted by, how we make sense of and experience the transitions and transformations of aging and the life-course. In taking up these challenges, the anthropology of aging is moving through one of its central aims—deconstructing cultural taboos and ageist assumptions to advocate for and strengthen the voices, perspectives, and rights of older persons—with the result that it is able to have a more balanced and productive interchange. This interchange is not only with other anthropologists under the umbrella of the life course (such as childhood and adolescent studies, medical anthropology, public policy, and psychological anthropology) but with other disciplines as well.

Disciplinary Perspectives

Anthropology is a latecomer to the study of the "life-course" as an object of knowledge (see Bateson, this volume), as it has been adopted by scholars in fields such as demography, sociology, and psychology. Sociologist Karl Ulrich Mayer's review of the empirical studies and research trends in life-course studies mentions anthropology as a contributing discipline (2009: 414), but does not list a single study or publication from a major anthropological journal. In his conclusion, Mayer notes that one area that has "not

yet fully lived up to its potential" is "the interaction of psychological processes of development and socially embedded processes of the life course"
(2009: 426), an area in which anthropologists have traditionally excelled.
The fact that anthropology has only recently begun to emerge as an influential area of life-course studies need not be a fault; anthropologists now
have the opportunity to benefit from the work of these other disciplines and
generate new levels of critique and analysis. It does mean, however, that
anthropologists will need to eventually reshape life-course studies in a way
that reflects its unique research methods and empirical data. Longitudinal
studies of the life course, for example, have been utilized with impressive
results in psychology and sociology, but similar studies are far less common
in cultural anthropology (Mayer 2009: 416–17). Similarly, anthropological fieldwork methods do not typically employ the same kinds of rigorously
validated standard measures and metrics used by specialists in geriatrics,
sociology, and developmental psychology, such as those that have been developed to assess levels of resilience, healthy adjustment, and even identity
and purpose in life over the life course (see Setterson and Mayer 1997).

Despite differences in styles and methods, anthropologists are not averse
to or ill equipped for life-course research, even if this is not always the explicit analytical framework of their work. Ethnographers usually revisit
their fieldsites, following key informants and close friends over years or decades, keeping detailed records of the changes that occur over these periods. Additionally, anthropologists often collect observational and interview
data from people of many ages and generations, from children to elders,
even if these age cohorts are not the primary focus of the intended study.
In other words, anthropology has exactly the kind of information needed to
describe and analyze societies in terms of the life course, but it has moved
away from viewing the life course as a principle means of organizing and
understanding this information. How has this shift away from life-course
studies occurred? What are the implications of this shift for the approach to
aging and the life course exemplified by the contributions in this book?

For anthropologists and other social scientists conducting qualitative
ethnographic research on aging and the life course, it has been important
to speak the languages of other disciplines, since the topic at hand encom-
passes such a broad spectrum of experiences, relationships, and macro-level
forces. Life-course researchers in anthropology, as well as in other disciplines, have benefited from the interdisciplinary contact that is often necessary in order to gather together not only concepts, approaches, and data,
but also institutional support, research funds, and opportunities for presenting and publishing work. However, interdisciplinary approaches also
pose numerous obstacles, not only for anthropologists, but also for other
social and behavioral scientists (Levy and The Pavie Team 2005). Reengag-

ing with anthropological ideas through cross-cultural life-course research not only strengthens anthropology's ability to collaborate and contribute to other disciplines, but it also shifts aging studies from its peripheral role in cultural anthropology, placing it squarely within the foremost concerns about social, economic, and political change in the twenty-first century.

Multiple Lenses

Anthropologists have long recognized a correspondence between maturity, the timing of significant life-course events, and the ways social groups redistribute statuses, roles, and obligations. While these processes sometimes operate according to temporal structures of chronological age, anthropological investigation has revealed that transitions and transformations of the person occur as a result of social distinctions that might be based on any number of additional factors, such as gender, kinship status, and economic or political position (Fortes 1984; Hareven 1982; Maybury-Lewis 1984; Sokolovsky 2009b). These observations have gone far in initiating a much-needed critique of earlier philosophical or psychoanalytic perspectives on life-course development, which sought to uncover a kind of ontological ground or universal sequence that could describe underlying processes common to all human experiences of aging, from birth to death (cf. Freud 1961; Kierkegaard 1967).

Anthropologists have certainly not ignored the importance of life-course processes that appear across history and cultures. Indeed, one reason the life course has been such a compelling subject of investigation for anthropologists is because it deals with fundamental human experiences (birth, aging, death) that display considerable cultural diversity in their interpretation and organization. Theories based on the anthropology of human evolution, for example, have enriched our understanding of the life course by asking questions concerning the development of our extended period of infant dependence and its relationship to the perpetuation of cooperative bonding with parental and alloparental figures (Hrdy 2009). At the other end of the life span, the "grandmother hypothesis" has helped us understand how sometimes culturally devalued aspects of aging have benefited early human social development and survival (Gibbons 1997; Voland, Chasiotis, and Schiefenhövel 2005). Thus, it might be argued that social interdependence between individuals at very different points in the life course might have supplied conditions necessary for certain social and biological achievements that further contributed to our capacity to create and transmit cultural knowledge and practices. This kind of anthropological work links the biological and social heritage of human beings, showing just how profoundly important bonds between both agemates and individuals of different ages have been throughout our history as a species.

The life course cannot be fully understood by examining universal processes to the exclusion of its social and cultural diversity. Despite its biological origins, the life course has proven to be incredibly plastic and adaptive to different social structures, exhibiting, for example, variations in the range of social roles or identities occupied at different times over the life span. Structural-functionalist anthropologists studying this phenomenon focused on societies based on recognition of age grades, sets, or ranks (Evans-Pritchard 1940; Fortes 1953; Fortes and Evans-Pritchard 1994 [1940]; Wilson 1951). These forms of age-based distinctions not only identify and encourage social bonds between agemates, but also order the distribution of statuses, obligations, authority, and expectations between ranks in ways that crosscut descent-based groupings. In these models, the individual life course is characterized by the movement through various roles, ranks, and statuses, usually signified by ritual rites of passage, grounded in cultural perceptions of natural biophysical change, and socially designated through institutionalized customs.

The institutionalization of age-related changes accommodates perceptions of what social scientists have come to call the "life cycle," or the process by which people fill the social positions vacated by senior members as they age and move through the life course (a process that links individual development to intergenerational dynamics and social reproduction) (Dannefer and Falletta 2007). The life cycle of a group describes the means through which knowledge, skills, authority, property, wealth, and other resources attain a degree of continuity by processes of socialization and the maintenance of stable cultural institutions that outlast the individual. Life cycles commonly operate through descent (such as in matters of succession, inheritance, and ancestor worship), again grounding cultural norms in analogous processes of genetic reproduction and affective bonds. While anthropologists often think of the descent-based life cycle as operating vertically, age ranks cut through the life cycle laterally, organizing discrete sections of the life cycle. From this perspective, the study of the life cycle and life course describes the way "society copes with the stream of individuals" (Mandelbaum 1973: 177) rather than the role of individual agency in the aging process.

The risk in thinking about the life course primarily in terms of semi-discrete grades or ranks is that it becomes easier to mistake the social role for the person (we think of the role of grandmothering, but not the person who is experiencing grandmothering). What is much more interesting is how individuals come to occupy those roles and how they make transitions to the next role by interacting with a world full of cultural meanings. As Mary Catherine Bateson notes in the first chapter of this volume, it was the students of Franz Boas and others trained amidst the rise of both psychoanalytic and behaviorist theory who looked at how the social roles over different phases of the life course are learned, internalized, and expressed in distinct cultural practices. The study of techniques of child rearing and socialization became important to better understand the development of adult personality and cultural institutions (Benedict 1934; Gorer and Rickman 1950; Mead 2001 [1928]). Anthropologists influenced by Culture and Personality theories understood that while the life course was strongly shaped by cultural structures, just as important was a psychological component rooted in the emotionally rich interactions between and among generations as one ages.

Where is the Anthropology?

Very little of the cross-disciplinary discussion between anthropologists and gerontologists in the mid-twentieth century has had a lasting impression on either field, despite notable contributions of pioneering anthropologists like Bernice Neugarten and Margaret Clark (Neugarten 1968).[6] The outstanding exception to this, however, is the work of Erik H. Erikson (1963 [1950]; 1997]), which presents one of the first systematic attempts to merge developmental psychology principles with anthropological insights on cultural variation and historical change over the entirety of the life cycle (see chapters by Bateson, Danely, and Rodríguez-Galán, this volume). Erikson worked on his theory of the life course throughout his life, refining and expanding its implications for the transitions and transformations brought on by adulthood and old age.

While Erikson's model has been taken up, elaborated, and critiqued in the field of psychology, it came under particularly harsh criticism from cultural anthropologists who found it to be too firmly lodged in Anglocentric assumptions and overly deterministic processes that produce narrow visions of what constitutes healthy and even ethical characteristics of adult human development (see Hoare 2002). Similar critiques of Culture and Personality studies, and consequently the psychosocial developmental approaches they had become associated with, created a need to rethink the anthropology of the life course. This process of rethinking aging and the life course in anthropology led to many landmark studies, including Barbara Myerhoff's *Number Our Days: A Triumph of Continuity and Culture Among Jewish Old People in an Urban Ghetto* (1976), David Plath's *Long Engagements: Maturity in Modern Japan* (1980), and Sharon Kaufman's *The Ageless Self: Sources of Meaning in Late Life* (1986). These works are notable not only because of their insights into the complex interweaving of culture, aging, and the life course, but also because they showcase the range of innovative research methods, theoretical perspectives, and forms of writing that have advanced the rethinking of aging and the life course in the field.

Lawrence Cohen's 1994 essay on aging in the *Annual Review of Anthropology* offers a poignant evaluation of why, despite the large number of high-quality ethnographic works on aging, there remains a struggle to articulate a "contemporary anthropological theory of old age" distinct from the institutional history of gerontology, applied sociology, and social work (1994: 139). In the nearly twenty years following Cohen's challenge, however, new works, including Cohen's own monograph *No Aging in India: Alzheimer's, the Bad Family, and Other Modern Things* (1998), have created innovative spaces for studying and theorizing age in anthropology. Other recent ethnographies on aging and the life course in anthropology have also reflected Cohen's concerns, initiating a revived discussion with the trends within the discipline as a whole. These include engaging with theories of illness, embodiment, and subjectivity (Kaufman 2008; Lock 1993; McLean 2006; Solimeo 2009); gender (Lamb 1994); political ecology (Cliggett 2005; Rasmussen 1997); migration (Oliver 2008); digital technology (Prendergast et al. 2009); and the impact of neoliberalism on families and social life (Cohen 1998; Lamb 2009; Lynch 2012). The authors in this volume build on this trend but also emphasize the importance of placing age in the context of cultural and institutional structures, meanings, and processes by adopting life-course approaches and multigenerational frameworks.

Whereas the works cited above explicitly address aging and the life course, scholars not focusing on these topics per se also have done important work in the area. For example, Margery Wolf's *Women and the Village in Rural Taiwan* (1972) presents an ethnographic portrait of how culture shapes women's identities from birth to death, with each chapter organized around a different stage of life reminiscent of those in Erikson's model. Renato Rosaldo's work on the Ilongot (1976, 1980) and Paul Willis's research on working-class youth in England (1977) similarly assume a degree of continuity over the life course and between generations that reproduces key symbolic distinctions. Even Pierre Bourdieu's concept of *habitus* (1990) and its power to structure temporal orientations invokes a theory of life-course development.

As we reflect on the trends in anthropological thinking about aging and the life course, we are able to better recognize where we stand now, at the beginning of the twenty-first century. There is not only a greater convergence with other disciplines, but also with the broader trends and problems within anthropology. The contributors to this volume illustrate the variety of ways that these valuable convergences of life-course theory ultimately advance our ability to understand cultural experiences of transition and transformation across the world.

Transitions and Transformations: This Volume

We have divided the chapters of this book into five sections: Frameworks (this Introduction and Chapter 1), Bodies (Chapters 2–4), Spatiality and Temporality (Chapters 5–7), Families (Chapters 8–10), and Economies (Chapters 11–13). These sections are followed by an Afterword by Jennifer Cole. Bodies, space, time, families, and economies: these are arenas of social life that have both intimate and individual experiences, meanings, and dimensions, but also are deeply structural and contextual. The dynamic interplay of transitions over the individual life course and social and historical transformations can be seen within each of these chapters as well as across them; each is intended to be part of a conversation rather than lecture.

Mary Catherine Bateson's chapter expands on this Introduction and addresses many of the key issues of this volume while providing a bridge between past studies of aging and the life course and current work. Noting the importance and theoretical depth of anthropologists such as Erik Erikson and Margaret Mead, Bateson also recognizes the need to expand and adapt their insights to the increasing generational complexity of today's societies and to worldwide changes in longevity and health. Building on Erikson's and Mead's contributions, Bateson's formulations of "Adulthood II" and "multifigurative" societies represent ethnographic and conceptual turns that many of the contributors take up in this volume when describing relationships of care and dependence, subjectivity, and newly emerging patterns of global aging.

The chapters in Section II investigate how life-course approaches offer insight into the interaction between mind and body in three different societies: the United States, Mexico, and China. Each chapter shows how intimate experiences of the body are situated within cultural and historical narratives involving age, health, and gender; as such this section illustrates the impossibility of drawing stark lines between the experiences of bodily aging, emotions, cultural values, social relationships, and gender identity.

Lindsey Martin (Chapter 2) uses a case-study approach to examine the role of the life course in therapy for patients coping with chronic pain in the United States. Martin offers ethnographically rich examples of how illness narratives interact with life-course narratives to produce a meaningful sense of continuity and disruption within the therapeutic context. By focusing on women in two different life stages, Martin demonstrates the importance of a therapeutic life-course approach to a person's sense of self after a life-altering event. Martin's analysis is not just about an experience of "old age," but of how positions on and perspectives about the life course affect the experience of bodies at different ages. We learn that chronic pain patients who seek an understanding of their new lives are best considered within both the process of seeking continuity and also within the process of developing age-related identities.

Jeanne L. Shea (Chapter 3) and Emily Wentzell (Chapter 4) focus on transformations of gender as experienced through the body. In both chapters, gendered experiences of the body become not only markers of physical aging, but also of changing identity within a wider social context. Shea shows how middle-aged Chinese women experience emotional frustrations generated over a lifetime of deference. She focuses on Chinese women's feelings of irritability and anger during the period of *gengnianqi*, a Mandarin Chinese word usually translated into English as "menopause." As Shea demonstrates, women's narratives resist characterization of *gengnianqi* as simply a biomedical or social phenomenon. Instead, women understand their midlife bodily changes and their midlife anger as arising from both bodily and social processes—in their narratives of *gengnianqi*, women work out complex feelings about both getting older and about the waves of social transformation that have overtaken modern China.

Wentzell's chapter examines how age- and illness-related changes in sexual function shape Mexican men's ideas about, and practices of, masculinity. We read of young Mexican men who embody values of modernity by denouncing the masculine sexual aggression of their fathers' generation; young men see their performances of masculinity in relation to their nation's hoped-for shift from a bastion of machismo to a more "modern" society. Wentzell's work enables us to appreciate the centrality of intergenerational interactions to performances of gender.

Over the life course, bodies transition and transform through space and time not merely as the stuff on which culture is written, but as the context in which meaning is made. Spatial and temporal contexts are also contingent on complex historical and generational dynamics that produce meanings and possibilities. Section III includes: Jessica C. Robbins's (Chapter 5) analysis of Polish understandings of aging in institutional settings, Frances Norwood's (Chapter 6) work on meanings of in-home illness and dying in the Netherlands, and Jason Danely's (Chapter 7) exploration of changing orientations towards temporality over the life course in Japan. These contributions on space, place, and time remind us that not only is physical location important to how people make sense of life's transitions and transformations, but also that the physical is always embedded in a temporal space. We co-construct spatial and temporal experience as we wrestle with what is in front of us on the one hand, and what we imagine, value, and dream, on the other.

Robbins, as with others throughout the volume, shows how an individual's experience of aging is set in the context of national imaginings and histories. Focusing on older Poles who are aging in the displaced context of institutional settings, Robbins examines how people place their own personal suffering in the context of national suffering. When older Poles attempt to make sense of the anxieties of their institutional lives, they situate themselves within a wider social context of national anxieties about Poland's membership in the European Union. Robbins offers a powerful example of how individual experiences of aging and transitions in the life course shift along with wider ideals.

Also in the European context, but in spaces smaller and more intimate than a nursing home or rehabilitation center, Norwood analyzes how Dutch people negotiate end-of-life in relation to a distinctive architectural feature of home life (the prominent Dutch window), and in relation to a euthanasia policy that brings national policies on death and dying into this intimate domestic space. She demonstrates that the Dutch window and Dutch euthanasia policy both allow the Dutch public—with its emphasis on the collective—to enter the private space of death and dying. As such, even the end of life is marked by the sustenance of social engagement.

In the same way that spaces and places shape experiences across the life course, Danely's work on identity and the life course in Japan shows how actors also inhabit cultural understandings of time. Danely's chapter draws on phenomenological perspectives of selfhood and experience to examine individual development in the context of culturally linked notions of temporality and spirituality. Like Bateson and Martin, Danely draws on the idea of the life course as a narrative that incorporates experiences in ways that allow individuals to cope with change and insecurity. The Japanese case shows how multiple orientations towards time can exist simultaneously within a cultural context where the social existence of spirits of ancestors presupposes ongoing relationships of mutual care.

Section IV addresses the pervasive intimacy of families and generations. In diverse settings that include a Brazilian community (Diana De G. Brown, Chapter 8), Puerto Rican neighborhoods in Massachusetts in the United States (Marta B. Rodríguez-Galán, Chapter 9), and southern Sri Lankan villages (Michele Ruth Gamburd, Chapter 10), these authors show us how wider political economic change influences the obligations and opportunities of aging in families and communities.

Brown focuses on a working-class Azorean community in southern Brazil where older women in their sixties, seventies, and eighties undertake strenuous long-term caregiving responsibilities for ill spouses and parents.

Brown situates these women's experiences in the wider social context: notions of family and community values combine with the sparse government support for healthcare and caregiving, and leads older women to serve as caregivers. Brown examines these women's caregiving experiences and the satisfactions, visibility, and recognition they gain from them as active elders and women within their families, neighborhood, and through participation in a local Third Age group designed to provide health-promoting activities for people over sixty. Brown argues that at a life-stage when people may often be expected to be care-recipients, these older women's caregiving activities highlight their personhood and their empowerment as embedded within a thick set of kin relations and filial obligations.

Rodríguez-Galán focuses on the life-course of Puerto Rican grandmothers raising grandchildren in the United States. Asserting that the grandmothering role for low-income immigrant Latina grandmothers does not fit the normative U.S., non-Hispanic, white population's pattern for the grandmother role, Rodríguez-Galán examines these women's experiences and understandings in light of their life-course trajectories more broadly. As with other contributors in this volume, Rodríguez-Galán argues that wider context is critical to analysis. In this case, we see that the meanings of the grandmother's caregiver role for Puerto Rican grandmothers in Boston emerge from a confluence of state policies and assumptions; Puerto Rican cultural notions and their adaptations in a new environment; and the particular women's own life histories, social locations, and values.

Intergenerational relationships come up in all three of the family-focused chapters, and especially so in Gamburd's chapter, which focuses on practices and ideals related to property transfers and eldercare in Sri Lanka. Gamburd examines notions of duty and risk, as well as strategies that elders employ to minimize the possibility of neglect and to leverage attention and care. Using a novel methodology of eliciting commentary on realistic scenarios, and combining those with real stories from long-term fieldwork in the area, Gamburd is able to paint a picture of how families currently handle the progression of individuals through the life course. In doing so, she reveals some of the values that guide Sri Lankans when they make decisions about employment, care work, and the transfer of property. This specific case allows us to take away wider lessons for understanding intergenerational care and finances more generally.

Section V, Economies, brings aging and the life course into three distinct settings: eldercare in India, labor in the United States, and debt in Nigeria. For each case, ethnographic analysis reveals how economic life cannot be explained by principles that exist outside of social and political processes, cultural values and histories, and intergenerational relationships and commitments. This section brings to the fore questions of values and value transformations: how do people evaluate lives and life choices in a world where the economy presents new opportunities, needs, and challenges?

Sarah Lamb (Chapter 11) discusses debates in India about whether eldercare is best taken care of by families, individuals, the market, or the state. The rise of "old age homes" in India has elicited concern about what such institutions mean in terms of a range of cultural values, including the notion of intergenerational service as a repayment of debt from children to parents. With her deep ethnographic perspective on these issues, Lamb shows us what this transition to market-based eldercare means in the Indian social, political, and economic context. Lamb demonstrates that we must examine how transitions and transformations related to aging that appear in locations across the world take on unique forms and meanings in their particular contexts, and how a topic that one could read as simply economic (how to support an aging population in the face of dramatic demographic shifts) reveals our understandings of and hopes about what it is to be a person and how best to live.

Caitrin Lynch (Chapter 12) takes us into a needle factory near Boston, Massachusetts to examine the meanings of work for people who are working well above the conventional retirement age. This needle factory provides Lynch with the opportunity to examine how work can be a sanctuary for older adults who feel invisible in life outside of work. Lynch's analysis of workers' narratives shows that work provides older workers with a sense of membership and mattering that is qualitatively different from what work provided them at earlier points in their lives. In this chapter, a life-course lens on the meaning of work enables us to see how these experiences and sentiments are of a different order for older adults than for younger people. By considering the specific needs constituted by the life course, we can begin to rethink the notion that economic values are based primarily on wealth. Lynch's essay raises questions pertinent to the socioeconomic transitions we face as an increasing number of older adults need to and/or want to stay in the labor market.

Jane I. Guyer and Kabiru K. Salami (Chapter 13) take on "life courses of indebtedness" in rural Nigeria. Their rich long-term analysis reveals the benefits of a longitudinal study, and their essay is an important reminder to examine the life course from the perspective of youth and not just elders. Just as a person lives a life course, so too is there a "life course" of social and economic issues—in this case, of indebtedness. Focusing on changing understandings of indebtedness in Nigeria between 1968 and 2010, Guyer and Salami demonstrate the importance of analyzing how economic transactions look different across the life course: as people age they accrue responsibilities, capacities, and encumbrances that may not have been fully imagined at the time a commitment was undertaken. Guyer and Salami analyze how, over time, economic commitments are made and unmade and there are revisions of who owes what to whom. A life-course analysis of indebtedness allows us to see how relationships of affect and economy are intertwined with historical trajectories.

Jennifer Cole's Afterword serves as a powerful reflection on what has been accomplished and what lies ahead for the study of aging and the life course in anthropology. Cole contextualizes the contributions in this book in terms of the concept of "generations," and she urges us to attend to the similarities and differences in processes of intergenerational transformation that occur when youth move to adulthood on the one hand, and when older adults move towards old age on the other. Cole ends by posing challenges to vitalize the scholarship on "old age"—a call we have begun to map out in this book's focus on the dynamics of transitions and transformations.

Looking Ahead

A key aim of anthropology is to understand individuals and groups over time—their continuity and change, their efflorescence and demise. When this dynamic process is tied too closely to functional or developmental stages and ages, be they a sequence of psychological events or a normative pattern of social roles, the concept of the life course loses its ability to remain relevant in a world deconstructed and reconstructed by new technologies and modes of communication, economic globalization, and post-modernity. This book zeros in on people's responses to their personal and historical circumstances and treats the life course as operating with a sense of indeterminacy, creativity, and fluidity.[7] A life course more widely configured provides analytic purchase on a world where the intertwined dynamics of globalization and population aging are creating new forms of life, death, connection, and control.

Broadening the scope of aging studies within anthropology not only creates new points of convergence with other disciplines, but also allows us to advance our understanding of the transitions and transformations brought about by global and local changes in longevity and intergenerational relationships, and in the resulting emergence of changes in identities and life-course trajectories. Individuals and families, as well as governments and institutions, make sense of and respond to aging in ways that are simultaneously grounded in particular histories and understanding, but also constitute the ground on which new realities and ways of understanding are built.

Ultimately, we are arguing for analytic attention to both intimate and global trends—and each of the chapters in this book takes on multiple scales of analysis even as they are grounded in close ethnographic study. In this way, we echo Australian social theorist Brett Neilson, who writes that, "To think about the production of age in the contemporary world is thus to partake in a radical jumping of scales, from the most intimate spaces of the body to the large-scale spaces of capitalist accumulation and control" (2003: 175–176). Jennifer Cole, in her study of generational transitions and gender in a rapidly neoliberalizing Madagascar, has written about how people's daily efforts to make their lives meaningful also require attention to these different scales. She argues: "This conjuncture of the life course with broader economic and political change not only is produced by but also produces new cultural and historical formations. This is never a mechanical, unreflexive matter of one cohort replacing another as some theories of generational change have implied. Rather, it is a highly imaginative undertaking in which people's desire to be good and to be valued, their culturally shaped dilemmas, and their visions for the future meet the broader forces of history and culture in unpredictable, uneven ways" (Cole 2010: xii). Here Cole succinctly captures much of what motivates the contributions in this book. Creativity and culture, transitions and transformations on small-scale and large-scale: this is the context in which we need to rethink aging and the life course.

Life-course narratives pieced together from culturally situated experiences of transition and transformation provide new perspectives on the nature of self and society. Research informed by these perspectives will profoundly alter the ways anthropologists and others think about the category of old age, placing it within the everyday processes of power, nurturance, conflict, and innovation. Focusing on aging and the life course allows anthropologists to unpack the temporal dimensions of cultural practice, the ways people reflect on their pasts and imagine their futures. Globalization exposes these processes by introducing new possibilities and obstacles for cultural representation, adaptation, and communion. The demographic and lifespan changes of the twenty-first century make it evident that choices that define the aging world will be made by people of all ages and cultural backgrounds. This need not be a basis for inevitable conflict. Rather, by furthering our understanding of the linkages among and between generations, we have an opportunity to advance towards a deeper knowledge of our world and ourselves.

Notes

1. The shift in perspective from aging studies to life-course studies in anthropology can be seen not only in the growing number of publications on life-course topics,

but also in the emergence of new institutional frameworks for supporting scholars interested in this field (Sokolovsky 2009a). In 2008, for example, members of the Association for Anthropology and Gerontology (AAGE) established the Interest Group on Aging and the Life Course within the American Anthropological Association (AAA) in order to promote collaborative scholarship among anthropologists on research methods and conceptual approaches that could expand and enrich our understanding of the human life course. By the end of 2011, this interest group had attracted over 500 members within the AAA, and had begun taking steps towards establishment as a "section" in the AAA organization, a move that attests to the greater institutional and academic recognition of aging and the life course within the anthropology community. Many of the contributors to this volume participated in one of the first panel sessions organized by the AAA interest group, at the 2009 meetings in Philadelphia, and the enthusiastic response to the papers presented there convinced us of the value in assembling this book. This panel session was organized by Caitrin Lynch and Jason Danely and co-sponsored as an invited session by the General Anthropology Division and the Association of Senior Anthropologists (Interest Groups are not able to sponsor sessions). The panel was entitled "The 'Life Course' as an End of Anthropology (Though Not Life's End)" (December 3, 2009) and included an introduction by Jennifer Cole and discussion by Jay Sokolovsky. For more on the context of this session, see the November 2009 issue of *Anthropology News,* which is focused on "Aging and the Life Course."

2. Our approach is similar to what sociologists call the "Linked Lives" principle of the life course (Elder 1999). This principle of linked lives not only assumes that older individuals are influenced by their history and social interactions with others, but also that they have a certain degree of agency that allows them to influence the world around them. While life-course anthropologists would no doubt agree with this formulation, we also contend that greater attention must be given to how these linkages (and consequently ideas about age and generations) are culturally constructed across societies, as well as the meanings and values ascribed to such linkages. Recent works by social gerontologists seem to agree (see Dannefer 2009; Heinz, Huinink, and Weymann, eds. 2009, especially chapters 15–19 focusing on linked lives), and this trend may lead to greater productive convergence and dialogue between the disciplines in the future.

3. For a similar critique of social gerontology, see Baars, Dannefer, Phillipson, and Walker 2006; Biggs, Lowenstein, and Hendricks 2003; and Stuart-Hamilton 2011. These authors, in various ways, contribute to the "critical gerontology" movement that has called for greater reflection on the structuring assumptions of the discipline.

4. For an example of how global aging, as construed largely through demographic and economic data, is used to shock and alarm with a portrayal of a world in which vast numbers of dependent old people threaten world order as we know it, see Fishman 2010. While Fishman's take on global aging is not entirely doom and gloom, it does operate on the (not uncommon) assumption that global aging is a major problem for the world in the next century, pulling resources from the shrinking number of young people to benefit the old (mainly in Northern countries). Culture is not systematically incorporated in this analysis, and is instead substituted with personal anecdotes punctuated with titillating statistics. As a result, readers are not forced to rethink ethnocentric or ageist biases.

5. Kuper (2000: 61) notes how Boas's ideas about cultural anthropology were strongly influenced by the Berlin school of ethnology, including the anti-racist critiques of physiologist Rudolph Virchow. The extent to which Boas's work truly contributed to anti-racism has since been questioned by other scholars. However, as Herbert Lewis (2001) explains in his review of these critiques, most are without serious merit and do not account for the substantial evidence that Boas was indeed passionate about the fact that race did not determine culture and that anthropologists should strive to serve humanitarian causes that eliminate prejudice based on race and gender.

6. The Gerontological Society of America (GSA) was founded in 1945 and the National Institute on Aging (NIA) in 1974. In the same year as the NIA's founding, Glen Elder's book *Children of the Great Depression* (1999 [1974]) was published, marking an influential shift within sociological studies of aging towards a life-course model that has influenced other social scientists including anthropologists (Dannefer and Falletta 2007: 45).

7. See Johnson-Hanks 2002 for more on this perspective as a foundation for developing theories of the life course.

1. CHANGES IN THE LIFE COURSE
Strengths and Stages

Mary Catherine Bateson

THROUGH TECHNOLOGICAL AND MEDICAL ADVANCES, average life expectancies in industrialized societies are two to three decades longer than they were a century ago (Butler 2008: 4). We have extended the life course by the time period usually thought of as a generation, but I will argue that this has not meant an extension of old age, but rather the creation of a new stage of adulthood before old age—Adulthood II. Combined with the possibility of controlling fertility, this increase in life expectancy has had major effects on the lives of individuals, the way in which generations interact and overlap, and the age structure of populations. The resulting shift from a three-generation pyramid (numerous children, about half that many parents, and dwindling numbers of grandparents) has altered the ancient cycle of family and community life to a four-generation pattern (Bateson 2010: 13, 15, 19), in which the grandparent generation is much larger, healthier, and more active than in the past. It is now the great-grandparent generation that more nearly resembles the grandparents of yore. Children today may have multiple living grandparents, some of them continuing full time in their professions, and today's grandparents may be fostering their grandchildren or devoting themselves to the care of their own parents. Our expectations and attitudes, including those of today's seniors, have not, however, kept up with these changes.

In this chapter I will discuss the implications of these changes in the life course in relation to Erik H. Erikson's (1963 [1950]) model, in which the overlapping life stages of different generations are modeled as a cyclical system, referred to as the life cycle. In doing so, I am summarizing material presented in my book, *Composing a Further Life* (Bateson 2010), a qualitative study of creative adaptations to increased longevity, with an emphasis on patterns that can be discerned when individual lives are looked at as *composed*, within a larger social context, by multiple choices that together may achieve an *aesthetic* balance.

The 2010 study presents extensive quotations from open-ended interviews with a dozen individuals, most of whom were recorded for at least four hours over a period of several days, and who are identified by their real names. The men and women interviewed do not represent a formal sample either in the sociological or the psychological sense—they are more like the set of key informants an ethnographer might work with in a small community, individuals whose choices are distinctive and yet intelligible in the context of their culture. Describing them is somewhat like trying to capture the artistic style of an era—choosing a limited number of paintings of genuine interest and originality and looking at them as wholes, even while looking for similarities and trends. Adulthood II is new enough to demand exploration and improvisation, so the individuals I have worked with can be seen as pioneers.

Anthropological Studies of the Life Course

Anthropologists have approached the life course from a number of different angles since physiological growth and psychosocial development provide convenient points of comparison across cultures. Thus, there has been a long-term interest in the cultural highlighting of developmental transitions, especially puberty and marriage, and some ethnographic work has concentrated on single stages. In addition, the stages of life are often marked by partial segregation, offering fairly delimited populations for ethnographic study, such as an elementary school class or the population of a nursing home. Ethnographers, not necessarily interested in psychological development, have collected life history narratives, some of which have become classroom classics like *Nisa* (Shostak 1983) and *Crashing Thunder* (Blowsnake 1999 [1926]). However, until Franz Boas trained a generation of women as ethnographers, ethnography was done almost exclusively by adult men observing other adult men and focusing on areas where their leadership was obvious and little attention was paid to the stages of development in childhood.

At the same time, even while ethnographers paid less attention to women and children, they recognized the importance of elders and noted that men and women frequently increase their influence as they age and indeed retain authority over younger men. Patriarchy is, by its very etymology, not only about gender but also about age (see Wentzell, Shea, this volume). Older informants, male and female, looking back and reflecting on the years of their youth, have played key roles in reconstructing the traditions of societies disrupted by culture contact, and anthropologists and other newcomers, like children, have often found them more available than young people to answer their questions (Casagrande 1960). As a discipline, however, we have been slow in including all age groups and both genders in our study of humankind.

Erik Erikson and the Life Cycle: Childhood and Beyond

In my own case, I approached anthropology initially from linguistics and decided soon after getting my doctorate that I wanted to work with less abstract materials. I volunteered as a teaching assistant for Erikson in the mid-1960s and have worked with life history materials on and off ever since, focusing on systems of meaning and communication that seem to be illuminated by Erikson's descriptions.

Erikson's model of the life cycle (see Table 1.1, in which his model is in regular type and my additions are in boldface) is of particular interest to anthropologists because of its focus on the normal development of strengths and resilience, rather than pathology. He proposed a model of the human life cycle in which the earlier stages corresponded to Freud's theory of infantile sexuality (1962 [1916]), but in which the physical development of each stage presented a challenge (a "crisis") and was defined in relation to the epigenesis of a specific "basic strength" (or "virtue") on which later development depends. Each stage is associated with an approximate time period, an organ mode (such as incorporation/taking in), an emerging basic strength, and a potential core pathology. Thus, earliest infancy (Freud's oral stage) is a time of taking in (incorporating) milk and visual, auditory, and tactile stimuli. However, the complete dependency of the infant means that there will be times of discomfort or hunger with no way of relieving them except the hope that someone will come. This lays the foundation for hope and trust later in life, the lack of which leads to withdrawal. The next stage corresponds to Freud's anal stage as the infant learns not only to control his or her sphincters, but also to grasp and to focus attention, to hold on and to let go (retaining and eliminating), thus laying the foundation for will but vulnerable to shame and doubt.

Freud's phallic stage begins when the toddler is able to walk and run with some confidence, and is the stage of the Oedipal crisis that initiates struggles with guilt. The basic strength that Erikson described for this stage, which he called the play age, is purpose, and the pathology is inhibition. Our knowledge of this stage was amplified and extended by the work of Piaget. With play as "the work of childhood," this stage lays the foundation for competence in the conflict between industry and inferiority.

Much of the early discussion of psychoanalysis in anthropology was focused on the question of whether the Oedipus complex can be considered

TABLE 1.1 Adapted Ericksonian life stages.

STAGE: Organ modes and Psychosocial crises	BASIC STRENGTH (Core Pathology)
1. Infancy: Oral-incorporative Basic Trust vs. Basic Mistrust	Hope (Withdrawal)
2. Early Childhood: Anal retentive-eliminative Autonomy vs. Shame, doubt	Will (Compulsion)
3. Play Age: Infantile-genital-locomotor Initiative vs. Guilt	Purpose (Inhibition)
4. School Age: "Latency" Industry vs. Inferiority	Competence (Inertia)
5. Adolescence: Puberty Identity vs. Identity Confusion	Fidelity (Repudiation)
possible moratorium	
6. Young Adulthood: Genitality Intimacy vs. Isolation	Love (Exclusivity)
7. Adulthood I: Procreativity Generativity vs. Stagnation	Care (Rejectivity)
possible moratorium	
* **Adulthood II: (reprise of 5, 6, 7)** **Engagement vs. Withdrawal**	**Active Wisdom** **(Indifference)**
8. Old Age: **(reprise of 4, 3, 2, 1)** Integrity vs. Despair	**Receptive** Wisdom **Interdependence, Humility**

universal (Malinowski 2001 [1927]; Spiro 1983), but Erikson's description has a wider focus on the fact that this is the stage when the newly mobile and avidly curious infant is the most intrusive and most likely to "get into things," as we say, and get into trouble (1963 [1950]: 87–88). Another theme related to these stages that has been explored by anthropologists is the degree to which behavior is enforced either by shame (associated with the anal stage) at being caught, or by an internalized sense of badness—guilt (associated with the third or phallic stage) (Creighton 1990: 279–307; Erikson 1963 [1950]).

Erikson began his career as a child analyst, but this was followed by work with adolescents at the Austen Riggs Center in Western Massachusetts, and he eventually went on to work on later life and to write about the relationship between the psychological development and the historical role of such figures as Martin Luther and Mahatma Gandhi (1958, 1970). The identification of adolescence as a developmental stage accompanying puberty is associated with G. Stanley Hall (1969 [1921]) and the question of the universality of *sturm und drang* in adolescence became, through Margaret Mead's work on Samoa (2001 [1928]), pivotal in discussions of biological determinism. Erikson analyzed adolescence in terms of the struggle toward identity formation, and he later argued that this struggle was accentuated in the West by the development of individualism, which he explored in his psychohistorical study of Martin Luther, *Young Man Luther* (1958).

In defining the stages of adulthood, Erikson's treatment distinguished between the development of an intimate partnership in young adulthood, the years of adult engagement and generativity, and old age (maturity). His principle contributions were a) his extension of a developmental model through the entire life course, b) his emphasis on the strengths associated with resolving the psychosocial crises of each stage, and c) the connection he made not only between the child rearing patterns in different societies and the continuing cultures of those societies, but also their relationship with historical developments. His choice of the word "virtues" to describe these emerging strengths (the correct etymology of the word "virtue"), which seemed to some critics to be culture bound, and his use of familiar words like "love," "will," "care," and "wisdom," wherever possible, rather than academic neologisms, meant that his descriptions, always eloquent, were also evocative of experience.

At each stage, the developing child or adult is learning to function in his or her culture, but changes in the structure of the life cycle seem to demand the reexamination of learned systems of meaning and perhaps the creation of new ones. Such a reexamination occurred for women as they became able to control their own fertility and is presently occurring for both sexes with increased longevity and better health in late adulthood.

Intergenerational Patterns and Social Change

Erikson played a bridging role between psychoanalysis and anthropology through his associations with several anthropologists during the development of the culture and personality movement, most notably Alfred Kroeber, H. Scudder Mekeel, and Mead, but also Ruth Benedict and Gregory Bateson. However, his attention during visits to Native American peoples was focused primarily on child rearing patterns, which remained focal in the culture and personality movement. Erikson's discussions of later stages of the life cycle were not heavily influenced by the demographic variations he might have observed in the field, but instead remained close to the assumptions of his European and American experience. His later work on Gandhi in the Indian context did not alter the basic framework either, although lifespans were substantially shorter both on impoverished reservations and in colonial India. In fact, Erikson's approach to later stages of the life cycle fits traditional patterns fairly well because it is based on nineteenth- and early-twentieth-century demography. As he and his wife, Joan Erikson, grew older, however, they observed greater variation. They became interested, for example, in the work of L. Tornstam on "gerotranscendence" in terminal patients. Joan Erikson included this focus in her extended version of *The Life Cycle Completed*, which she published after Erikson's death (1997: 123–29); there Joan Erikson discussed the approach of death, presenting it as a ninth stage that follows old age.

Erikson and others have noted that an ethnographic description of the role of elders necessarily deals with the transmission of knowledge between generations, but the accumulation of knowledge and the integration of new ideas into a culture involves movement in more than one direction as older adults both teach and continue to learn and adapt to times of change. In Mead's study of the generation gap of the sixties, *Culture and Commitment* (1970), she developed a typology for different patterns of intergenerational transmission, contrasting societies in which cultural knowledge is passed primarily from old to young (postfigurative), between contemporaries (cofigurative), or—with rapid technological change such as exists in our own society—from the young to their elders (prefigurative). In the latter case, we can see that the young may adapt more rapidly to change; today we often learn new technologies (and sometimes new ethical norms) from our children and grandchildren. These distinctions are, however, a matter of degree, since learning is always moving both up and down the generations.

Anthropologists have described the role and contributions of older adults in preliterate societies primarily in terms of the category of "elders," individuals beyond their reproductive and child rearing years who play a crucial role in the preservation and transmission of knowledge and who have been both rare and treasured (Turnbull 1983). In industrialized societies today, the role of "elders" has altered as numbers have increased, literacy has made memory less important, and change has accelerated. The "elders" in ethnographic descriptions are often individuals in their early fifties, as they have been through history, already affected by various chronic conditions that affect mobility, strength, and mode of participation. Yet, a great number of the "seniors" of contemporary U.S. society (notwithstanding the invitation to join the AARP at age fifty!), are healthy enough to continue their careers or start new ones, marry and divorce, and return to school to learn new skills. But interestingly, these continuing capacities have not fully affected cultural assumptions, such as the "traditional retirement age," set over a hundred years ago, or the symbolism of living until the age of seventy (Psalm 90, verse 10), once rare, now commonplace, which meant that shorter lives (the great majority) have been regarded as truncated. Assumptions about later adulthood no longer fit the reality as the largest cohort in U.S. history, the Baby Boomers, enters a life stage that has changed radically.

Recognizing a New Life Stage: Adulthood II

The demographic and bio-medical shift in industrialized societies affects many aspects of society and of individual development to the point where it is necessary to consider a new life stage, post-reproductive but continuous with adulthood in other ways, inserted *before* old age. This new stage is shown in Table 1.1 in bold face without modifying Erikson's numbering system for the other stages. It seems most convenient to call this stage Adulthood II, a stage that begins when one or more of the major generative projects of adulthood comes to an end with the winding down of a career, or the departure of maturing sons and daughters, and itself ends when aging or other accidents of health begin to seriously affect participation. For a tennis champion or a dancer or a dot com entrepreneur, Adulthood I might end at forty. For a senator or an essayist, a career may continue until eighty or beyond, but often a change of emphasis suggests that a transition has taken place, as a senior senator may begin to be regarded as an elder statesman or the parents of adult children may redefine themselves as grandparents. Death, of course, can occur at any age, but just as death in childhood or infancy has become rarer, deaths in Adulthood I are less common and far more people reach Adulthood II. Many are unaware, however, of the many years that may lie ahead, or they think of them only in terms of their financial needs instead of dreaming dreams of what those years might bring.

There are a number of reasons for speaking of a new stage rather than subdividing existing stages, as Gail Sheehy (1995) and Daniel Levinson (1978) have done, or abandoning the stage model completely. I believe that the justification for recognizing a new stage is that it facilitates description, is socially useful, and echoes customs in many societies. From a descriptive point of view, Adulthood II seems justified because it fits the multiple dimensions of the Eriksonian model (it can be a time of crisis, but at the same time involves the development of strength—people not only behave differently, they take on new roles in ways that were rarely possible when even those who lived into their sixties were likely to have multiple chronic conditions that limited their participation). But the strongest descriptive argument for recognizing a new stage is perhaps the similarity between Adulthood II and Adolescence, which was also recognized fairly late. Both are times when bodily and social changes require a new understanding of identity with implications for all relationships and for the definition of how one participates and contributes in the world. The recognition of adolescence as a life stage has been important in the development of attitudes toward young people passing through this stage and in the formation of education policies. The recognition of Adulthood II as a new stage (rather than one that has been there for all human beings who outlived their reproductive years throughout history) is critical as healthy adults in the second half of life realize that stereotypes of aging, which they incorporated growing up in the mid-twentieth century, are not sufficient guides for making decisions about their years of continuing activity, years that are not yet "twilight years" but years of a new and significant kind of engagement.

Adulthood II is a stage that is emerging, or can be expected to emerge, in other industrialized societies, but like every other stage of life can be expected to show a different pattern in societies with different traditions. We should not fool ourselves, however, that this new stage has replaced old age as understood in the past, for large numbers of adults will eventually experience declining health and mobility, often lasting longer than for previous generations, and will have to come to terms with the approach of death. Old age has not disappeared or been conquered—it simply begins later for many people. My research deals with the choices individuals make in Adulthood II, finding themselves in better health than the (mostly negative) stereotypes of aging they grew up with would have predicted: "I'm seventy but I don't feel seventy," one hears, or "sixty is the new forty."

The Basic Strength of Adulthood II: Active Wisdom

If wisdom is derived from experience, these sixty- and seventy-year-olds have lived to ages that are commonly associated with wisdom, which Erikson's scheme assigns to old age. There are various scholarly approaches to defining wisdom (Hall 2007), and wisdom is generally associated with reflection, but many busy adults may not have found or made the time to reflect on experience and derive wisdom from it prior to the flexibility offered by this stage. The wisdom they bring to this life stage, or develop as they transition into it, may now be combined with health and energy to become what I have called *active wisdom*. This is in contrast with the more sedentary associations of wisdom in societies where chronic conditions such as arthritis took a greater toll on mobility. Old age is still with us, of course, but begins later. The grandparents of today's children are in Adulthood II, while our stereotypes of old age are more likely to fit their great-grandparents.

Variations on a Theme: A Non-Linear Approach

The changes in demography and health status play out rather differently in societies in which older adults are treated with formal respect, in contrast to the United States where aging is negatively regarded and strenuous efforts are made to appear younger. It also plays out differently depending on definitions of identity: if an individual is defined by his or her job, retirement may trigger identity diffusion, but if an individual is defined by membership in a family or clan, becoming the senior member may bring a variety of rewards. Similarly, different values are placed on work and relaxation, so that the cultivation of leisure may or may not be respected. In a society like the United States, where age does not necessarily bring authority, the "wisdom of age" may only be honored when combined with ongoing learning, and the aging may feel the need to prove their productivity and contribution. It is no accident that along with a growing recognition of the potential engagement of older adults in the U.S., pressure is growing toward "productive aging" (Morrow-Howell, Hinterlong, and Sherraden 2001).

The relationship between learning and change across the generations cannot be understood as linking only two generations. The contribution of grandparents to the survival of infants has been studied in a number of societies in terms of the "grandmother hypothesis" (see, for example, Tymicki 2009). This hypothesis, however, assumes a three-generation society, depending on the relationship between a new mother and her own infant on the one hand, and her infant's (primarily maternal) grandmother on the other. We do not know yet how the interchange will play out under the emerging conditions of a four-generation society, but we do know that often today the grandmother is caring for the great-grandmother—or leading such a busy life that she is not available as reliable backup for the new mother.

In a society in rapid change, the process of intergenerational transmission can be examined when, for instance, norms of childcare are modified or even reversed. For example, I was put to sleep on my back as an infant, but was taught to put my daughter to sleep on her tummy, yet (following research on sudden infant death syndrome [SIDS]) my daughter is now instructed to put her newborns to sleep on their backs (for the history of this shift, see Lipsitt 2003). My conversations with my daughter dealt with both models, not to mention shifts in modes of carrying infants copied from other cultures and norms of discipline. We are perhaps becoming *multifigurative,* with no primary defined direction of learning and teaching, but movement in multiple directions, with an increased possibility for conflict as multiple sources compete for authority. Bearing in mind that learning tends to flow in two directions, we will need to think through such complex resonances as a grandfather and grandson, both dealing with issues of identity at different ages, and each potentially learning from the other.

In applying the Eriksonian scheme, it is important to notice that, although Erikson associates each life stage with a particular psychosocial crisis and a particular basic strength developed through its resolution, he mentions that the issues of each stage are anticipated or recur in every other stage. The non-linearity of his approach is often ignored by readers who think in terms of a sequence of successful steps in maturation. This means, in effect, that grandparental authority includes the expectation that grandparents will still be learning and maturing. Thus, while the issue of identity comes to a head in adolescence, it arises at every stage, beginning with birth and the awareness of separation from the mother's body, and resolution can be extended or deferred by an institutionalized moratorium. Grandparents today may joke about deciding who they are going to be when they grow up. In looking at individuals moving toward Adulthood II, there is a striking similarity to the changes that accompany puberty: changing hormonal levels appear to cause personality changes; skin, hair, and body suddenly behave differently, and the individuals suddenly encounter a new set of reactions and expectations from others. Which is more disconcerting, to suddenly find oneself a sex object or to suddenly become invisible?

It appears that all three of the psychosocial crises that follow puberty arise again in Adulthood II: the crisis of Identity, the crisis of Intimacy, and the crisis of Generativity, although not necessarily in the same order. In brief, it becomes necessary to ask "Who am I?" ("Am I the same person I have spent my life becoming?") in response to these bodily changes and changes in the responses of others, just as it was in adolescence, above all in response to a change in career path or the end of an identity-defining career. It becomes necessary to review and adapt all love relationships if a marriage or partnership is to survive (late-life divorces are rapidly increasing) and if egalitarian and collegial relationships are to develop with adult children. It also becomes necessary to ask, "What do I contribute to or sustain, and who are the individuals or institutions I care for?" As these questions recur, the virtues of fidelity, love, and care are tested, sometimes strengthened and sometimes giving way to repudiation, exclusivity, and rejectivity, as shown in Table 1.1.

It is important to notice that there are alternative ways of adapting the life stages to increased longevity (see Danely, this volume). One fairly common adaptation in our society at present is to extend each stage, deferring marriage and then childbearing. Social time is fairly elastic, as we all discover: the time needed to complete a task increases as more time becomes available. Thus, it may be that just as adulthood comes earlier in many societies, conferred by puberty rather than post-graduate study, a stage equivalent to Adulthood II could be recognized in many if not all societies, even though life expectancies are shorter, especially where reflection is cultivated at earlier stages. However, the extension of the earlier stages still leaves many older adults in industrialized societies with a longer period defined socially as "old age" than they have good models for enjoying. For example, a man who has modeled his role as a father on his own father might not be able to model his role as grandfather on either his own grandfather or on his father's later years.

Continuity and Discontinuity

The current fashion in discussing longevity in the United States often relies on a rhetoric that may be derived from the immigrant past, the rhetoric of "reinvention" and new beginnings (for this as an American theme, see Lifton 1993). This rhetoric depends on an exaggeration of the degree of novelty in most inventions, since a typical "invention" is generally a recombination of possibilities already known. However, analyzing Adulthood II choices against the background of earlier life stages suggests that even choices that seem radically discontinuous have earlier roots and more nearly resemble translations or rearrangements. Retirement or an empty nest offers the opportunity to turn to a new pattern of activity that still stands in some sort of dialogue with earlier pursuits. Thus, a) an occasional avocation can be reshaped into a new career; b) one of many strands of activity may be selected for intensive development; c) practice may be replaced by teaching or consulting; d) knowledge may be applied to a different purpose; or e) a familiar goal may be pursued with a new degree of focus, flexibility, or comfort. In many cases, people's choices seem to reflect an aesthetic sense about the appropriate balance and shape of lives that I have referred to as "composing" (Bateson 1989). Thus, in my interviews, I find, for example, a woman who has created several foundations and is now acting as a consultant in the nonprofit world, and a priest who has been liberated from the management of a large complex parish now concentrating on preaching and the sacraments. Some professions offer continued engagement with lighter burdens and greater flexibility (see Lynch, this volume), often on a volunteer basis, while for many women the role of grandmother offers a kind of motherhood "lite," and many grandfathers, who may have felt they have missed something during their children's childhoods, are providing childcare for their grandchildren. (See Rodríguez-Galán, this volume, on grandmothering in Puerto Rican communities in Boston.)

Transitions to Adulthood II

Erikson commented on the existence of culturally defined *moratoria* (1963 [1950]: 262–63), particularly following puberty (represented in industrialized society, for instance, by attendance at a liberal arts college before starting a family or becoming economically self-sufficient), a period of not knowing what kind of adult life to commit to. Similarly, many people arrive at the end of Adulthood I without having thought through the next stage, having expected less energy and health (on the basis of stereotypes and observations earlier in life) than they are now likely to have. Here again, a period of travel or recreation, sometimes lasting several years, may provide a transition, as adults who realize that they no longer have to work search for the activities that will replace work. In effect, the beginning of Adulthood II initiates a new search for meaning (see, for instance, Krauss 2005) that may be found in introspection (as in formal or informal "life review"), in the activities often discussed as "giving back" or legacy, or in exploration of spirituality or the arts. A significant effort has been made to enlist persons in Adulthood II in the volunteer workforce, largely abandoned by women combining motherhood with paid work (Freedman 1999). There is also an ongoing effort to reframe working conditions and qualifications to permit extended employment. My personal conviction is that there is a potential for the emergence in Adulthood II of political advocacy for the future, along with broader ethical and spiritual concerns. We have the opportunity to observe a shift in consciousness in individuals, as well as the improvisations that occur when there is a shortage of available models.

Among the individuals I studied, various kinds of translation and selection occurred, but in each case there were continuities between past and present and some element of contribution that preserved a sense of being a valuable member of family or community, and in each case there seemed to be a process of discovering or defining meaning. Hank, a retired boatyard worker, adapted his skills from fashioning metal parts for big diesel engines to making delicate silver jewelry. "It's hard," he said, "for us to understand anyone wanting to just set in their place and do nothing" (Bateson 2010: 32).

Ruth, a retired social worker, managed to sum up many of these issues in the following comments:

One of the things, you know, that everybody says you must do as you get older and you're retired is think about volunteering, doing something that you love to do. Well, that's a terrific idea and it goes to exactly your point. What is it that I really love to do that may not be what I have done for the last five years or ten years, but I may have done twenty years ago? Whatever that was, reconnecting to that confidence that I felt, so I can really offer that and feel good about it. I don't want to volunteer to do something that I feel half-assed about. I want to do something that other people will feel is meaningful and that I feel is meaningful. And some of that, yes, is a process of rediscovering and reconnecting. I say, well, I really do like to read aloud, which I did when I was seven and I do now with my grandchildren when I see them. Maybe I can find an hour or two to do that, in a library, or recording for the blind, and I know I do that fairly well, that would give me pleasure, and it would be helpful. And it's a simple thing but figuring it out ... I think probably over time the simple things or little private things are going to be the most fun. The natural things. But then sometimes I lurch into the fantasy that it's got to be a big project, if it's not a big project, it's not worth doing. And if you think about it, it really doesn't have to be a big project. It can just be something I put my mind to doing and I do it on a regular basis and somebody else gets something useful from it. (Bateson 2010: 63)

Although my focus has been on Adulthood II, recognizing the reprise of earlier crises has suggested that there might be something to be said for the tradition of life rising to a peak and then declining. From an ethical point of view, that peak would seem to come for many individuals in Adulthood II, since several of the traits that were included in the concept of "gerotranscendence" and associated by researchers with late life or with individuals in the terminal stages of disease are present during Adulthood II. For instance, an increased tolerance of ambiguity, a movement away from absolute judgments, and a range of ethical concern that is both wider and more extended in time (Cohen 2005) emerge for many individuals in Adulthood II where they can be expressed in prosocial activism. This is how Jane, an actor who has turned to engaged philanthropy, designing and participating in programs to reduce teenage pregnancy, described this shift:

Well ... from about age 52 to 62, I began to change. I knew that I was becoming much more internal, much more introspective and spiritual, which I had never been in my life. And I felt a need to begin to alter the way we lived to be more vertical than horizontal. We were skimming along the surface. I wanted to start drilling down more and [my husband] couldn't because his locus of wellbeing came from outside, and mine was shifting to in here [touching her heart]. I wasn't sure how I would answer the question who am I, but I began to know how not to answer it. (Bateson 2010: 166)

Conclusion

For those who find a new form of engagement and a new way of looking at the world in Adulthood II, this is clearly a period of growth rather than decline. At the same time, the traditional image of a rising and descending curve, in which development goes into reverse, does suggest some of the ways in which the different strengths may come back into play at later stages. I believe that regarding old age as a second childhood is an oversimplification that is echoed in some influential societal attitudes (e.g., the belief that later life is a time to play), but that the strengths developed in the earliest developmental stages become critical as health declines. Thus, for example, the development of will, which Erikson associates with Freud's anal period, is reinvoked in individuals tenaciously clinging to familiar patterns and freedoms (such as driving or living alone), and the strength Erikson calls trust, developed in the first stage of infancy when the newborn is totally dependent, is essential when declining health makes it necessary to accept help from others with grace and to face the approach of death.

As anthropologists begin to study the emerging patterns of aging and changes in the life course, we should be alert to the ways in which older adults can be valued by society rather than seen as a problem, since the value placed on youth in American culture is by no means universal. In order to do so, it will be important to move from a deficiency model to one that emphasizes ongoing learning and development. Increased longevity may prove to be as significant in human evolution as the extension of human childhood. When aging is included as part of the creative process of composing a life, we may find that the later years are indeed years of grace and truth, adding to the harmony of the whole. Although the Eriksonian model requires adjustment to emerging demographic conditions, its enduring value is its emphasis on the ongoing development of strengths and resilience at every stage of life.

Acknowledgments

I wish to acknowledge a grant from the Alfred P. Sloan Foundation to the Institute for Intercultural Studies, which supported the travel for and transcriptions of interviews for my research, and the ongoing hospitality during the same period from the Center on Aging and Work at Boston College. My greatest debt however is to the older adults who contributed their time and insights to my understanding of their lives and of my own.

SECTION II

BODIES

2. NARRATING PAIN AND SEEKING CONTINUITY
A Life-Course Approach to Chronic Pain Management

Lindsey Martin

"I JUST WANNA GO BACK to my old life," Christina notes with an air of frustration in her voice. The usually tough-as-nails Betty says that pain "frightened the hell outta me." In this chapter, I analyze Christina's and Betty's illness narratives to examine connections among the life-course concept, pain management, and the use of integrative medicine. These narratives were recorded during a year-long (August 2008 to August 2009) ethnographic study of the Integrative Medicine Pain Clinic in suburban Detroit, Michigan, and they reveal how a disruption to the life course due to chronic and debilitating pain motivates patients like Christina and Betty to reinterpret their continuity and age-related identities. Through consideration of these women's experiences, I demonstrate how a clinic's life-course treatment approach can effectively address such disruptions by facilitating the creation of new narratives of the body and new identities.[1] This study shows us that because chronic pain patients experience and make sense of pain differently at various points of the life course, effective treatment may require both caregivers and patients to view chronic pain from a life-course perspective.

The Treatment Approach

Dr. William Bennett is a 41-year-old African American doctor who dreamed of opening his own pain management clinic to help patients who could not find relief through solely biomedical approaches. Opening its doors in the Detroit, Michigan suburb of Waterview in 2003, the Integrative Medicine Pain Clinic (IMPC) is a small one-story brick building located on a busy city thoroughfare. While the IMPC looks like an ordinary office building on its exterior, on the inside the IMPC breaks from convention by shedding the sterility associated with many medical establishments to create a home-like environment for their patients. Nature is emphasized in the clinic's décor as there are framed prints of flowers and plants, numerous silk plants and trees, and light green walls in the waiting area and treatment rooms. Jasmine, Dr. Bennett's wife and business partner, explains that they chose the colors for their calming effect, "When people are in pain they're already warm [from inflammation in their body] so you need to have them cool and calm, and ... green would be more of a cool and calming [color]."

Specializing in pain management, physical medicine, and rehabilitation, Dr. Bennett is also certified in medical acupuncture, and he gained a positive reputation in the community for treating "difficult" pain cases, meaning patients who do not respond well to biomedical treatments for pain. Anthropologist Arthur Kleinman and colleagues describe why pain is so hard to treat from a biomedical perspective: "Chronic pain has an anomalous status in biomedicine largely because it is so baffling to clinicians and academic physicians. The pain is seldom adequately accounted for by physiological lesions; its course and outcome do not conform to any known biochemical or mechanical process" (Kleinman et al. 1992: 4). Dr. Bennett believes that an integrative medicine (IM) approach to chronic pain management is "best," as he puts it, because it provides patients with more treatment options.

While the conceptualization and practice of IM are still debated (Caspi et al. 2003; Salkeld 2008), it is typically thought of as the simultaneous utilization of complementary and alternative medicine (CAM) (such as massage or acupuncture) and biomedical therapies (such as prescription medication) (Baer 2004; Bauer 2010; Caspi et al. 2003). Consistent with this integrated approach, Dr. Bennett's treatment plans often include natural plant-based pain injections as well as massage. Dr. Bennett, along with his dedicated staff that includes three massage therapists and two physical therapists, uses these IM treatment plans to address pain related to chronic illnesses, like fibromyalgia and arthritis, and accident-induced injury.

Pain has been recognized as a significant and critical contemporary health issue in the United States since the mid-2000s (Institute of Medicine 2011; National Center for Health Statistics 2006: 6). Anthropological studies indicate that chronic pain and patients' related health-seeking journeys are highly disruptive life-course experiences (B. Good 1994; M. Good, et al. 1992; Greenhalgh 2001; Jackson 2000, 2005; Kleinman 1988). Anthropologist Gay Becker's life-course disruption framework serves as an apt model to examine this condition and to understand the approach taken by the IMPC staff. According to Becker, "the course of life is structured by expectations about each phase of life, and meaning is assigned to specific life events and the roles that accompany them. When expectations about the course of life are not met, people experience inner chaos and disruption" (Becker 1997: 4). She writes that "order" or continuity provides us a sense of knowing what comes next in our lives (Becker 1997: 4–5). Becker argues that when chronic illnesses (for example, stroke) disrupt our individual bodies, our resulting lost sense of control over our lives shatters cultural beliefs about continuity. She frames health seeking in the United States as a life-course process where individuals, in an effort to achieve culturally valued continuity, search for treatment options to resolve the body's disruption. Yet, Becker argues that continuity, as it is understood culturally, can never be fully actualized; while we may try, the pervasiveness of individual life-course disruptions renders continuity forever elusive.

Recent studies on chronic illness indicate that not all individuals negatively interpret the effects of their health conditions upon the body, sense of self, and life (Bletzer 2007; Hinojosa et al. 2008; Reynolds and Prior 2003; see Wentzell, this volume, for how some Mexican men interpret their experiences of decreasing erectile function). However, when one's body has been limited physically by chronic illness, the process of moving towards life-course continuity can be fraught with difficulties (Becker 1997; Scheer and Luborsky 1991). Becker notes that often individuals must come to terms with how their bodies have forever changed and incorporate these experiences into who they have now become: "The body becomes an unknown terrain that must be relearned ... people must redraw relationships between self, body, environment, and daily life" (1997: 81–82). This redrawing process results in new understandings of continuity that may vary from idealized notions (Becker 1997: 82).

The IMPC's life-course treatment approach to IM chronic pain management takes a holistic perspective to patients' pain conditions by conceptualizing pain not just as a disruption to the patient's physical body, but as a disruption to the entire life course. This perspective is evident in the staff's efforts to identify the range of ways chronic pain is disruptive to patients' lives. For instance, the staff acknowledges that it may cause family tension or lead to unemployment or social isolation. On a daily basis the staff humanizes the patients in order to get to know them as real people who have real lives that they yearn to resume. The staff is sure to remember patients by first name and works to develop a close relationship with them by expressing an interest in a variety of aspects in their patients' lives. The staff relies on laughter and shares personal stories with patients to help make patients feel as though they are not merely another "disease" walking through the clinic's door.

In beginning to address their patients' life-course disruption, the staff legitimizes their pain by helping patients identify and learn about their conditions. This enables the patients to begin to make sense of what has happened in their lives and to understand the magnitude of the disruption. A co-created IM treatment plan is designed and enacted during the clinical encounter where a bond forms between the clinic practitioners and patients—a bond that helps patients come to terms with how chronic pain has forever changed their bodies and their life courses. Formal and informal conversations serve as a kind of "talk therapy" about the patient's pain, the treatment process, and other aspects of their life and pain stories. The IMPC enables patients to move towards continuity by creating a treatment schedule and offering numerous treatment options. A patient's continuity may also involve follow-up maintenance therapies at the clinic (for example, massage), and learning from IMPC staff skills necessary for self-care (such as healthy eating, home physical therapy exercises, stress reduction) in order to manage pain and its current and future effects on the life course.

I turn now to describe and analyze Christina's and Betty's stories. Christina's pain began at mid-life as she was juggling multiple life roles, while the intensity of Betty's pain disrupted her retirement and forced her to confront the possibility of losing her independence. Their cases reveal how the IMPC's life-course treatment approach helps to facilitate this process of re-interpretation by providing a supportive environment where these women could narrate their pain as they learned how to incorporate this disruption into their lives and how to manage their pain more effectively so they could move forward. Because these two women experienced disruption from the onset of chronic pain at very different life-course moments, the juxtaposition of their stories allows us to see how this process of reinterpreting continuity is affected by patients' life experiences.

Christina's Case: "I feel like I'm not me"

Before her life was disrupted by a car accident, Christina, a 49-year-old white woman, prided herself on holding a number of key roles in middle age that included being a wife, a mother to three children, a volunteer, and a fulltime student who worked two minimum-wage jobs. Christina now suffers from chronic debilitating pain that prevents her from engaging with these roles that deeply mattered to her. On her way home from one of her jobs on a rainy night, her busy life literally came to a screeching halt when a drunk driver hit her large truck with such force that windows shattered, the roof collapsed, and she was pushed out of her lane: "He hit me so hard—it was a three-lane highway. I was in the middle lane. When he hit me, I was facing the opposite way two lanes over." Christina has not felt "100 percent" since the accident and wonders if she will ever get back to being that way.

Christina's chronic pain, as well as numbness in her left arm, disrupted her life course in several significant ways. Suddenly Christina, who had worked since the age of fourteen, could no longer work because her two jobs required standing and physical strength to lift heavy items to be stocked on shelves. Christina also stopped attending school where she was studying to be a Medical Assistant. Her pain even affected how she maintained her home as she was not able to complete certain tasks such as cleaning floors: "There's so much that you're limited to do that you can't do. ... I feel like my hands are tied. I'm not me. I feel like I'm not me." Since the auto accident has prevented Christina from engaging in many of the life roles she held, at this time the "big highlight" of her day is leaving her home to see the staff at the IMPC.

Christina's pain also affects her family relationships because she relies much more than she used to on her sister-in-law and husband to assist her in everyday activities. Her pain also prevents her from lifting her young nephew: "My nephew just had a birthday. Can't pick him up 'cause he's thirty-five pounds. That doesn't seem like a lot of weight. To me, if it's thirty-five pounds or three thousand pounds it would be the same to me. I can't do it. It's very upsetting." Pain medication did not alleviate Christina's life-course disruption since she said the pills made her gain weight and feel like "a veggie."

Christina also has a number of stressors in her life that compound her pain: "Our middle son's in Iraq. He's in the Army. Does my husband go to work today or not? You know? It's horrible. I wouldn't recommend this life for anybody! It's like, okay, do I eat today or not? You know?" Prior to the accident, Christina kept a busy life managing the various roles that helped to mediate ongoing depression. With her post-accident relative idleness, she now has difficulties managing her depression, which causes additional stress in her life. Not only do Christina's chronic pain and its debilitating effects plague her on a daily basis, these disruptive stressors also challenge her goal of getting back to her "old life."

Christina came to the IMPC with high expectations for her care based on the recommendation of her family physician. The IMPC's approach had an immediate positive impression upon Christina who felt very welcome at the clinic; she cited the family-like atmosphere and described the staff as "caring people-persons." Christina was treated holistically in several ways. She notes how the clinic staff got to know her quickly by name. She said that by the second time she was there, the IMPC's medical assistant said to her,

"'Oh [Christina] you don't need to sign in. I know who you are.' Wow! I've been to my dentist's office for fifteen years and I don't think they know who I am." Christina also mentions the importance of the clinic staff asking how she felt, an experience she never had before at other doctor's offices: "They get to know who you are. '[Christina], how are you doin'?' Wow. There's just 'Wow.' That's all I can say because I've been to doctor's offices where I've never been asked how you feel."

Christina's pain is not focused in one particular part of her body but is widespread due to what she learned were trigger points (what Christina calls "knots") that formed in various areas of her body. The IMPC's website notes that these "knots" are "hardened area[s] of muscle tissue" that form in the body and cause pain.[2] She describes the pain sensation from these "knots" as: "Like fireworks.... Different spots, different colors. Like red being really 'owy' painful and blue not being so painful." Not only did Christina appreciate learning about trigger points at the IMPC, she liked that all aspects of her treatment were fully explained to her, an experience she never had with her other doctor:

> I used to have this doctor that all he wanted to do was write prescriptions. [I asked] "Well why am I feeling this way? Why is this happening?" [The other doctor said] "Oh just take this pill, you'll feel better." [Dr. Bennett] explains to you "Okay this is what's gonna happen. This is why you need to do this. This is why you need to do that." I know what I'm doing. And I know why. And I know what the risks are and I know what the good things, you know I know the bad and I know the good. This other doctor that I used to have many years ago never explained anything.

Christina also notes how she learned that all the treatments suggested to her—pain medication, heat, physical therapy stretches, trigger point injections, and massage—are meant to work in conjunction with one another.

The transition I observed between formal and informal conversation during Christina's first massage clinical encounter helped her form a bond with Roxy, her massage therapist. Roxy facilitated Christina's narration of her pain by asking about her accident and how she has felt since it occurred. Roxy also acknowledged the severity of Christina's disruption during the encounter by describing the accident as "a life-changing event and not for the better." In addition to facilitating Christina's narration, Roxy also gave Christina the opportunity to understand how her body was reacting to the massage. For example, Roxy explained that the audible crunching noise we heard as she massaged Christina was the result of Roxy breaking up trigger points in the muscle tissue. Not only did this clinical encounter help reduce Christina's physical pain by breaking up the trigger points, but it also provided a supportive atmosphere where Christina felt safe narrating her pain.

Reflections on Christina's Case

Christina became attached to the IMPC because the caring staff treated her as a whole person who is more than her pain condition and acknowledged that she is a person who has a life course that needs to be mended. One can infer that perhaps Christina found the IMPC a "big highlight" not only because the staff addressed her pain directly with treatment, but also because it gave her a socially acceptable way to deal with some of the depression that she had experienced throughout her whole life. At the time I spoke with Christina, she acknowledged that she still had a long road ahead of her, and considered herself to be "10 percent better." More important than the percentage, however, was the air of hope present in Christina's voice during her interviews. It was a hope that she will continue to manage her pain and start to piece together some semblance of the life she once knew.

Christina's hope is apparent in her commitment to the IMPC's treatment approach: she is willing to create a treatment schedule with the clinic and do physical therapy exercises at home. Christina is also willing to make financial sacrifices; her health insurance policy does not cover massage therapy, but the clinic offers the option of half-hour massages at a lower cost and Christina is willing to pay the out-of-pocket expense. Christina believes that massage will relieve her physical pain to "help me get better and get me back to work ... to who I was before the accident," and that she will "find a way to afford it." While massage therapy began to address the physical pain from Christina's trigger points, it also began to address some of the psychosocial issues that she was dealing with that most likely had increased her pain. The "talk therapy" that ensued during Christina's treatment provided her with an outlet to talk about the accident and air her frustrations about pain. We saw Roxy validate Christina's disruption when she acknowledged how Christina's auto accident was "a life-changing event and not for the better." However, paying for the massage therapy is no easy task for Christina. Her husband's job future is uncertain and to help her family survive financially, she had to work two minimum-wage jobs prior to her accident, both of which required physical strength. After her accident, Christina was robbed of the strength she needed to work, and she was also unable to work less physically demanding jobs due to the functional limitations her pain placed upon her.

The IMPC's belief in leading a healthy lifestyle also appears to have influenced Christina's reinterpretation of her continuity. Saying that she needs to take better care of herself, and conceding that she likes candy, smokes, and does not exercise regularly, she is nevertheless working to change her lifestyle (she mentioned her intention to eat healthier in order to lose the weight she gained after the accident). While their treatment approach is helping her cope with her disruption and incorporate the changes she must make in her life so she can better manage her pain, she still grapples with the desire to live her "old life." She mentions numerous times in interviews that she was deeply concerned about never reaching "100 percent" and concerned about how she could possibly live with that reality as a person at mid-life.

Betty's Case: "It's probably just arthritis"

Betty is an 89-year-old woman of Lebanese descent who has had many roles throughout her life: a devoted daughter to her mother whom she cared for at the end of her life, a wife, a mother to two children, a civilian employee with the U.S. military, and now a retiree. In August 2008, Betty suddenly experienced the onset of acute migraine-like head pain that became a debilitating chronic condition and was not resolved by several visits to doctors. Betty had been enjoying her active retirement that included enjoying her favorite food (Burger King Cheese Whoppers, she would always specify), exercising, and doing yard work: "I walk three to five miles a day and I just keep active. I mow my own lawn and do all my garden work and just keep busy." Betty, who did not take any medication except an occasional Motrin or Tylenol for headaches, suddenly had this active retirement sidelined for several months: "Now in fact I didn't wanna do anything because everything was just a chore to me. You know, if I walked it was painful. So consequently, I just sat. During the winter, I just sat. Picked up weight. Was terrible."

Although Betty often reflected on the happy times in her life, she also spoke to me about moments of great tension. Betty grew up poor, watching her own mother struggle to raise a family as a single parent without welfare during hard times. Betty married, but when her children were very young, her husband left her and she had to raise her children as a single parent while working two or three jobs to support her family. Betty describes her thirty-eight years of working in the contract and procurement field for the U.S. military as a civilian employee as a highlight of her life, allowing her to receive an education, travel the world, and become fluent in several languages.

Betty fully devoted herself to her career working for the U.S. military, but her career also brought with it enormous stress as she worked during major conflicts like the Vietnam War and Operation Desert Storm. Betty's history of working hard and making her "own way" in life has made her an assertive and independent older adult, but with her age she now faces infuriating stereotypes where she finds others treating her like she is "stupid" or "senile." Using colorful language, Betty challenges these stereotypes: "They don't get away with that with me.... Being in [the] service working with the military, sometimes my language ... I let it rip! Damn right. This is who I am, you know, take it or leave it."

Betty encountered similar age stereotypes among doctors who dismissed her pain as arthritis, and she attributes their dismissal directly to her age: "I say they don't show me any class.... I felt that, you know, when you're old ... the first thing they're gonna say 'Well, you know, it's just arthritis.'" Worried that her pain was the sign of a serious problem that would threaten her independence, Betty looked through her insurance provider booklet and found the IMPC, liked the fact the clinic was close to home, and decided to "Give it a shot." Betty is like other U.S. older adults whose chronic health conditions (for example, stroke, incontinence, Parkinson's disease) challenge their abilities to remain independent (Becker and Kaufman 1995; Mitteness and Barker 1995; Solimeo 2009).

The IMPC had an immediate positive impression upon Betty who liked that she was treated with a respect that was lacking at all the other doctors' offices. Betty's assertiveness is evident in her narration of her first meeting with Dr. Bennett:

> I walked in here [the IMPC] when I first found Dr. Bennett and the first thing I said to him—I had all my medical records with me—and I said to him "Well let's be honest. This is me and if you—I've been through hell and high water with this. Since August I've been in pain, and if you can help me, fine. If you can't, just don't waste my time. Don't waste your time. I could give two shits less!" And I said [to Dr. Bennett], "I'm sorry, this is me. Take it or leave it." ... He said "Oh you're gutsy!" ... he was very nice. I said what I appreciate 'bout—'bout this place is that no matter how old you are, you're treated with respect.... There's lots of respect here. To put up with me, my God!

Betty's experience at the IMPC was the opposite of her experience of being treated as a stereotypical old person. Rather, the IMPC provided the opportunity for Betty to narrate her story and air her frustrations, thus enabling her independent and "gutsy" personality to emerge in the clinical encounter.

The IMPC and Betty identified that it was the tension and stress she experienced throughout her whole life that was causing her pain. The IMPC used diagrams to explain to Betty how she developed trigger points that resulted from all this tension and stress. These painful trigger points were compressing her nerves, muscles, and veins in her head: "He [Dr. Bennett]—he said that it was muscles—muscle, nerves that were on top of each other. And he showed me the diagram and where—where the pain was, and what the pain—he described everything. How the pain reacts to the veins and the muscles in the head. The correlation between that." Betty now understood why she had pain that was so severe and intense that she wanted to "cut my head right off" and would "commit suicide" if she could not find relief. Now that Betty knows that tension causes the trigger points, she is working on relaxing more: "And I know that I have to ... relax. Because I've always had tension all my life so it's my fault too ... 'Cause I was always in the running. I'm always in a hurry."

Betty began a treatment protocol of physical therapy, massage, and trigger point injections to help alleviate her disruption and reduce tension. In the process of addressing Betty's disruption, the IMPC's holistic approach continued to affirm Betty's identity as an active older adult. During her massage clinical encounter, Elizabeth, her therapist, told Betty she did not have to hop off the massage table right away after the treatment so she could enjoy its relaxing effect on the body. However, Elizabeth then joked with Betty by acknowledging the reality that she would most likely be dressed and out the door quickly in order to resume her day. In line with the clinic's commitment to self-care, Elizabeth also suggested she take senior yoga classes to help with her tension. Elizabeth was also quick to mention a location where Betty could go and not encounter the "rocking chair crowd."

Reflections on Betty's Case

In coming to the IMPC, Betty found a needed sense of validation that she was not part of this "rocking chair crowd" and just another case of arthritis. In Betty's interactions with the IMPC staff it becomes evident that they did not view her as a stereotypical older adult like her other doctors did; her experiences with these other doctors most likely eroded Betty's sense of independence that is a key aspect of her identity. However, despite Betty feeling like she was getting order back to her life, she was forever left shaken by the experience that highlighted her fears of losing her independence. For Betty, remaining independent hinges on incorporating her disruption into her life by acknowledging that she must reduce her tension to avoid a recurrence of pain. Importantly, it was her relationship with the IMPC that moved her towards this reinterpretation of her continuity. The IMPC team acknowledged that Betty could regain quality of life, and it did so by avoiding the assumption that an older person would need to accept the onset of this pain problem and be forced to live with it.

Conclusions

Becker (1997) notes that once the body becomes disrupted by a chronic health condition, an individual can never go back, as Christina mentions, to one's "old life" because the physical body, one's life, and therefore continuity are forever altered. As we can see from Christina's and Betty's case studies, the clinic's life-course treatment approach to IM chronic pain management facilitated the narration of Christina's and Betty's pain so they could start to accept bodily disruption and incorporate it into their lives. Both these women learned from the IMPC staff how their bodies have changed since the onset of chronic pain, which helped them reinterpret their continuity and age-related identities.

However, as their cases illustrate, this process of reinterpretation works differently for the two patients. Reinterpretation is based on where the patient is in the life course when the disruption occurs (for Christina at mid-life and Betty in older adulthood) and is customized to the patient's life-course experiences that support their individual identities. For Christina, this process of reinterpreting continuity entailed the IMPC staff validating the magnitude of her disruptive experience upon the multiple roles (wife, mother, volunteer, student, and employee) she juggled as a woman at mid-life. For Betty, this process involved the staff acknowledging the tension she experienced throughout her long life. They worked with Betty to not only treat her trigger points but also to reduce her tension so chronic pain would not return and rob her of the independence that is a key aspect of her identity.

Importantly, not all patients find success with the IMPC's approach. Some IMPC patients with whom I worked were unable to move towards continuity either because they did not fully engage with the clinic's approach (for example, they were not open-minded about integrating all of the IMPC's available treatment options) or because they lacked the financial resources to do so, or because of a combination of both factors. The IMPC staff educates patients about their approach and offers financing options to make it accessible for everyone. However, the effects of the 2008 economic recession, particularly in the metropolitan Detroit area, appear to be an influential factor in the medical decision-making process.

Acknowledgments

This research was supported by a Blue Cross Blue Shield of Michigan Foundation Grant #1411.SAP. This work was supported in part by the Houston

VA HSR&D Center of Excellence (HFP90-020). The views expressed in this article are those of the author and do not necessarily represent the views of the Department of Veterans Affairs. I would like to thank Sherylyn Briller, Caitrin Lynch, and Jason Danely for their feedback on this manuscript. Thank you to all the research participants.

Notes

1. I use pseudonyms for the people and place to protect the confidentiality of the research location and participants. I conducted research at this clinic to examine how their particular integrative medicine approach to chronic pain management differs from the biomedical approaches discussed in the ethnographic literature. Methods included collecting illness narratives and life histories of patients; conducting semi-structured open-ended interviews with clinic staff; and documenting via direct observation and participation the clinic's daily activities and co-created IM clinical encounters between patients and staff.
2. To maintain confidentiality, the clinic's website will not be formally cited with its own URL.

3. VENTING ANGER FROM THE BODY DURING *GENGNIANQI*
Meanings of Midlife Transition among Chinese Women in Reform-Era Beijing

Jeanne L. Shea

CHINESE WOMEN IN BEIJING SPEAK about their experiences of midlife in ways both familiar and strange to an American ear. Most importantly, many Beijing women speak about the feelings of irritability and anger that often accompany what they call *gengnianqi* (pronounced gung-knee-en-chee), a Mandarin Chinese word usually translated into English as "menopause." Take, for example, the following vignette that I recorded during my fieldwork in China in 1994. This vignette exemplifies very well some of the ways in which Beijing women spoke back then, and continue to speak now, about their experiences of irritability during midlife and about the appropriate management of *gengnianqi*.

I am conducting an interview with Wang Xiulan, a 52-year-old Chinese woman who teaches at an elementary school close to her home in urban Beijing.[1] Known in her neighborhood as Teacher Wang, she and her husband have two children, a son who is working and a daughter still in high school. Sitting in Wang's living room, we are joined by 62-year-old Zhao Lichun, a retired community healthcare worker, and by Wang's teenage daughter who is doing homework at a desk off to the side. Wang indicates that she doesn't mind their presence, as "we're just chatting about everyday matters." I sit on the couch beside Wang, and Zhao sits in a chair to our right. It is summertime and very muggy in the cramped four-room single-story courtyard home, which is thickly layered with trappings of a decade and a half of market reforms—a large color television, a shiny stereo, and the daughter's English textbooks. As is customary year-round, we each have a steaming cup of tea. When I ask Wang about how her health has been since reaching middle age (in Chinese, *zhongnian*), she and Zhao begin to tell me about their experiences of *gengnianqi*.

Wang Xiulan: To tell you the truth, this *gengnianqi*, I have it a bit—really. Sometimes I can't control myself—can it be that this is *gengnianqi*? I myself also think that it must be *gengnianqi*. Based on my age, that is. I try my hardest to control myself, but there are still times when I can't control myself. Sometimes I feel irritated and under pressure, and then I yell and yell. Really! At the kids. And at my husband. Really. With my old man. I myself also feel that it's really awkward, and after I'm through yelling, I feel regretful about it, but it doesn't matter, I still can't control myself. If you tell me to control myself, well, I just can't. All of a sudden, *weng* [onomatopoeia for buzzing sound of bees]! It rises up! And then I yell at people for a bit, and then that's the end of it. [She laughs.] But everyone is very understanding. But at my work unit, I can control myself. Whether it's with my coworkers or whoever, I've never yelled at anyone at work.

Jeanne: Oh, so at work, you can control yourself.

Wang Xiulan: Yes, isn't it true that the closer you are with someone, the more you yell at them? I feel like it's this way. At home, I often end up yelling at my kids. Sometimes I yell at my husband. I haven't ever argued with anyone else, really! And I'm not angry at them with my whole heart—really, my family is very good to me.

Zhao Lichun [to Jeanne]: Yes, their family is a really harmonious family.

Zhao Lichun [turning to Wang's teenage daughter who lifts her head to listen]: Your mother is having *gengnianqi*. Don't pay any attention to her yelling. You also know, you need to exercise mutual understanding and forgiveness. The family can say, "Your mother is having *gengnianqi*. Never you mind. Just forget about it. Leave it alone." Then the more tolerant and understanding the family is, the less she will lose her temper. You've got to say to yourself, "My mom is *gengnianqi*." Don't pay any attention to her. Understand and forgive her.

Wang Xiulan nods. Her daughter also nods and then returns to her homework.

Zhao Lichun [turning to face Wang]: The whole family can say, "She's *gengnianqi*. Don't pay any attention to her." So then everyone can forgive you. My *gengnianqi* was also like this. Everybody knew I was in *gengnianqi*, and they all looked after me. They said, "She's *gengnianqi*, never mind her." Anyway, at first, I just got worse and worse—but you shouldn't be like that—the more you lose your temper, the worse it gets. Then later, when I started acting irritated, my kid started asking her father to ask me, "Isn't your *gengnianqi* over yet?" After that, I tried my hardest to control myself. And then when I was about to lose my temper, I just wouldn't let myself. When I was about to lose my temper, then I would quickly get away from whatever it was that was bothering me. Then in a moment, it would pass.

Wang Xiulan [to Zhao Lichun]: Right. It is best to control yourself a little.

Zhao Lichun: So I'd advise you to get through with this *gengnianqi* quickly like I did. You've got to take it seriously in your spirits and in your thoughts. Then take the right amount of control over it. If you control yourself, then it'll pass very quickly. But if you let it flare, then it'll just keep getting worse and worse as time goes on. With me, after only half a year, I was all better.

Wang Xiulan: Oh, well, hmm, my *gengnianqi* started last year at Spring Festival. Well, look at that! It's been quite some time already!

Zhao Lichun: That's for sure!

While the importance of irritability and anger to contemporary Chinese women's notions of *gengnianqi* and midlife aging has been briefly mentioned in previous scholarly publications (e.g., Adler et al. 2000; Ge and Shen 1994), published works to date have failed to provide an in-depth exploration of the narrative uses of *gengnianqi* in the everyday social contexts inhabited by Chinese women. Striving to assist in filling that gap, I draw upon fieldnotes from participant observation that I conducted in Beijing between the mid-1990s and 2008, transcripts from dozens of interviews like the one with Wang and Zhao, and data from a survey that I administered in 1994 to hundreds of women between forty and sixty-five years of age in two communities in Beijing (see Shea 2006).

In analyzing my data, I bring together several complementary analytical frameworks, including cultural phenomenology (Csordas 1994), narrative analysis (Mattingly and Garro 2000), and a poststructuralist model of female midlife (Dickson 1991; Kaufert 1982; Leng 1997). By paying close attention to what individuals say about their own everyday experiences, cultural phenomenology and narrative analysis are instrumental in illustrating differing cultural meanings, logics, and plot lines, as well as the idiosyncrasies of personal agency, individual experience, social circumstances, and historical contingencies that go beyond cultural generalities. Poststructuralist analysis of female midlife is useful for going beyond both universalistic pathologizing biomedical models of menopause (e.g., Notelovitz and Tonnessen 1994) and popular Western feminist narratives that posit nearly symptom-free natural aging for women in Asian cultures (e.g., Berger 1999).[2]

Drawing upon Haraway's (1991: 181) cyborg theory and its attempt to suggest "a way out of the maze of dualisms in which we have explained our bodies and our tools to ourselves," poststructuralist analyses break down and blur the boundaries between a host of categories of Western modernity. Best known for blurring the lines between human and machine, cyborg-inspired analyses have gone far beyond this initial starting point to unsettle numerous dichotomies commonly found in Western debates about female midlife and in much biomedical and early feminist discourse. Such analyses create "new hybrid" (Franklin 2006: 170) frameworks that disturb such Western analytical binaries as natural and biomedical, organic and artificial, natural and cultural, biological and cultural, natural and social, scientific and popular, physical and nonphysical, natural essence and social construction, and oppressed versus resisting (Haraway 1991: 149–50, 159, 163, 176–78; Leng 1997: 266–67; Lock 1998a: 35; Van Wolputte 2004: 251, 263). In tandem with embodiment theory (Csordas 1994), poststructuralist analyses draw attention to the frequent arbitrariness of the point at which such bipolar categories are divided, their mutual contingency upon each other, and their mutually constitutive and sometimes mutually transformative interactions. Noting a youth-centered tendency in much cyborg-inspired analyses to date, recent calls have noted the need to "gray the cyborg" (Joyce and Mamo 2006: 100) by focusing attention on the varied perspectives and agencies of "heterogeneously situated aging men and women who are often the object of scientific knowledge and practice" (115–16). This chapter contributes to this endeavor.

The present analysis is the first to combine these three approaches in an exploration of Chinese women's ways of speaking about *gengnianqi*. In the pages that follow, I argue that just as it is inaccurate to depict women's experiences of midlife aging in China as mere reflections of biomedical theories of pathology, so too is it inaccurate to portray those experiences as solely a feminist antithesis in which the natural exuberance of midlife shines through. Instead, Chinese women's narratives about *gengnianqi* are better understood as cyborg phenomena that diverge from both Western biomedical depictions of medicalized menopause and popular Western feminist visions of easy natural aging in Asia. Chinese women's *gengnianqi* narratives are cyborg-like in that their stories defy ready categorization in terms of common Western analytical dichotomies such as natural/cultural, natural/biomedical, science/society, organic/artificial, mind/body, positive/negative, self/other, controlled/free, agent/object, East/West, and resister/oppressed. Instead, women's talk about *gengnianqi* entertains a variety of both natural and social causes and treats midlife anger as arising from both organic bodily and artificial social processes. (See Martin, this volume, for a discussion of the integration of multiple causes and approaches into treatment of chronic pain in the United States.) While very culturally distinctive, *gengnianqi* discourse is not entirely home-grown, but, rather, comprises creative local interpretations of a term originating in linguistic flows from Europe. Not presenting the entirely rosy picture for which Orientalizing strains of Western feminism yearn, *gengnianqi* talk entails a complex mixture of positive and negative feelings about getting older and, moreover, deals centrally with women's responses to the historical waves of social transformation that have overtaken modern China. Finally, I show how women's talk about *gengnianqi* involves forms of resistance that are more ambivalent than heroic, simultaneously serving and trivializing midlife women's interests, and generating hybrid tales of being at once liberated and controlled.

Gengnianqi as an Emergent Cyborg Phenomenon

I refer to Beijing women's talk about *gengnianqi* as a cyborg phenomenon because it is neither a direct expression of socially unmediated natural women's individual experience (see Haraway 1991), nor a mere reflection of Western biomedical discourse, nor a demonstration of classic feminist deconstruction of that discourse, nor a simple expression of dominant Chinese traditions. Instead, women's talk about *gengnianqi* represents an experimental hybrid, a cobbling together of various pieces of purportedly scientific technical ideas with personal flesh and blood experiences in order to try to interpret or explain what is happening or has happened to them or to people they know. Beyond exegesis, women's *gengnianqi* talk is also an active way of shaping the social import of their past and present lives and the concrete thrust of their current and future lives. That is, it is both a means of social understanding and a channel for personal agency.

The term *gengnianqi* entered China during the early to mid-twentieth century via a Japanese translation (*konenki*) of the German term *klimackterium*, of which the English "climacteric" (meaning menopause or "the change of life") is a cognate (Lock 1998b: 62; Scheid 2007: 58). Comprised of the characters for increase, years, and period (the same characters as *konenki*), *gengnianqi* can be literally translated as "the time period during which one gets on in years."[3] Chinese health professionals, not to mention ordinary people, were initially slow to adopt the term, and it was not until the mid-1960s that "*gengnianqi*" became included in traditional Chinese medicine treatment manuals (Scheid 2007: 58). In my conversations with educated women in Beijing in the 1990s, many pointed to early in the reform era (dating from 1978 on) as the first time they remembered the term being used in public discourse. These women were unsure of the exact year, but recalled it having been sometime in the late 1970s or early 1980s when Deng Yingchao, widow of the late Premier Zhou Enlai, had published an article on her difficult experience with *gengnianqi*. Calling for this "fifth stage in a woman's life" to be valued in Chinese labor law, just like earlier life stages are, Deng's 1984 article in *China Woman* magazine (Deng

1984) challenged the neglect that women's later life had thus far received in China. Ever since, the term has been gaining in public recognition, usage, and import.

Among laypersons in Beijing, *gengnianqi* is not equivalent in its connotational field to either of its ancestors, and it is quite distinct from contemporary Western biomedical notions of the climacteric or menopause. While Chinese medical professionals often translate *gengnianqi* into English as "menopause," the end of menstruation is frequently not a consideration in ordinary Beijing women's operating definitions of *gengnianqi*. For example, in my 1994 survey (N=399), more women associated *gengnianqi* with aging in general or irritability than with menopause per se. Specifically, 84.4 percent saw it as "a transitional phase during which one makes entry into old age," and 74.6 percent agreed that it was "a reason why middle-aged and old people lose their tempers." While the cessation of menstruation is an integral part of "menopause" for American women, only 65.8 percent of my Beijing sample associated *gengnianqi* with "the time period during which women cease to menstruate." When asked whether they themselves were in *gengnianqi*, one in five of the peri- or post-menopausal women (in an epidemiological sense) said that they were not sure if they were currently in *gengnianqi*, and 5 percent said that they would never have *gengnianqi*. Almost 10 percent of the overall sample (including pre-menopausal women) said that they had never heard of *gengnianqi* or that it is a myth, and almost a quarter said that they were unsure whether or not they were in, or would ever be in, *gengnianqi*.[4]

In the case of Teacher Wang in the opening vignette, although she did note in passing the rough correlation in time between the end of menstruation and *gengnianqi*, her remarks about *gengnianqi* were much more focused on a connection with broader processes of growing older in familial, social, and historical context.[5] Furthermore, in striking contrast to much contemporary biomedical discourse about female midlife, during the entire interview, including the discussion about irritability and *gengnianqi*, neither Wang nor Zhao ever mentioned anything about estrogen or hormones, but instead focused on family interactions. Many other women who spoke with me about *gengnianqi* did not connect it even with the end of menstruation, let alone hormones. Some women also mentioned cases of older men becoming irritable and prone to angry outbursts at home during *gengnianqi*. Although today with the influence of global pharmaceutical marketing in urban centers, more women in Beijing are aware of Western discourse on hormones and a small minority take or have taken hormone replacement therapy, hormones still do not form a central concern for most women.

Whereas hot flashes are a focal point of Western biomedical representations of female midlife, they are not a focus of most Chinese women's talk about *gengnianqi*. Although Wang seems to relate at least some of her midlife irritability to hot flashes (see "*weng*, it rises up" in the opening vignette), this was often not the case. While many midlife Chinese women talked about themselves or others becoming irritable in midlife, the vast majority did not report hot flashes. Furthermore, even among those women who did have both hot flashes and irritability in midlife, the phenomenology of the experience tended to be distinct from the North American experience of marked embarrassment recorded by Emily Martin (1997, 2001) and others. That is, the Chinese women in my survey sample who had experienced hot flashes at midlife typically did not feel embarrassment in connection with them, although many reported concurrent irritability. For example, at the time of the survey, Wang had been having hot flashes every day over the past couple weeks. However, she reported that at no time in those two weeks or any time before that did she feel embarrassed during a hot flash; when they "rose up," she had only felt physical discomfort and irritability. She also did not associate feeling nervous, uneasy, or depressed with hot flashes.

At the same time, *gengnianqi* does not fit the popular Western feminist stereotype of easy aging for women in Asia. My interviews and participant observation in Beijing show that in speaking about *gengnianqi*, women are talking about dimensions of midlife suffering, not about the Western dream of aging without physical or emotional discomfort. My survey data further show that while hot flashes are rare among midlife Chinese women in Beijing, other unpleasant physical and emotional symptoms like irritability and backache are fairly common (Shea 2006). Furthermore, the stereotype inaccurately lumps together all Asian women's experiences of midlife. Although the Chinese term *gengnianqi* came by way of the Japanese term *konenki*, both concepts and experiences of midlife show important differences across the two cultures, which is not surprising given the numerous cultural and historical differences between China and Japan. Margaret Lock has argued that Japanese women see the midlife *konenki* transition as first and foremost linked with quietly bearing the burdens of bodily aches and pains such as shoulder stiffness, backaches, headaches, and aching joints (Lock 1993: 35, 209, 213–15, 219, 232, 265; 1998b: 63). Irritability and anger are not central features of the Japanese conception of *konenki* and are seldom reported by midlife Japanese women (Lock 1993: 219–20, 223, 234, 238, 333–35).

Women's Agency, Hybridity, and Social Usages of *Gengnianqi*

Gengnianqi is a very much emergent and messy semantic domain subject to a great deal of social variation in meaning and usage. There is no clear cultural consensus among women in Beijing about what *gengnianqi* is, what it means, what it does, or what should be done about it. Instead, there are a plethora of explanatory models (Kleinman 1986), which allude to a variety of naturalistic and social causes for perceived changes during the midlife transition, one of which is feeling irritable. These explanatory models vary in their usage from individual to individual and sometimes within one individual across conversational contexts.

Interviews with women like Wang and Zhao show the kind of creative local agency that Chinese women exercise in taking up the concept of *gengnianqi* into their narratives. Many women freely admit their creativity by saying that they are not really sure what *gengnianqi* means or how to define it. For example, later in the interview quoted earlier, Wang asks herself why she has been losing her temper a lot over the past year or so, "I think, could it be *gengnianqi* that is creating this disturbance? Or is it because my periods have ended? Is it because of that? I'm not sure. But I think that it is *gengnianqi* that has been causing it." Soon after she added, "My *gengnianqi* has been '*geng*-ing' for more than a year. My goodness! What is this *gengnianqi* anyway? ... I really can't say. In my heart I know, but I can't put it into words."

Interlinked with this uncertainty and improvisation, *gengnianqi* discourse is a cyborg phenomenon in terms of the hybridity of Chinese women's attributions concerning the etiology of the irritability they associate with *gengnianqi*. A few of the women I interviewed mentioned that they had heard that it might be related to hormones, but except for a few physicians in the sample, most women who mentioned it said that they were not sure if that was true. Other women said that they had heard that *gengnianqi* is due to stale blood left in the womb after the end of menstruation, but they were not sure if that was just hearsay. Sometimes those same women ventured that they had also heard that it is due to the process of midlife aging for men and women that results in a build-up of hot *qi* (life essence or vital energy) that rises up in the body and must be released or dissipated to prevent illness in later life.

Coexisting with these different naturalistic explanations were social explanations in which women linked current irritability and bodily discomfort with past and/or present social difficulties. In invoking *gengnianqi*, Chinese women often use it as a veiled idiom of complaint (Kleinman 1986) about the injuries and insults inflicted upon them currently and/or over the course of their lives by their husbands, children, mothers-in-law, work units, community powerbrokers, and even by their former, too zealous or too obedient, selves. Along these lines, later in the same discussion from the opening vignette, Wang and Zhao raise their own concerns about how they are treated by their families:

Wang Xiulan: Sometimes my daughter jokes with me, "Mom, you are *Lao Gengr*." [Pauses to make sure that the interviewer understands the Beijing slang.] Old *Geng* ... the *geng* of *gengnianqi*. Old *Geng*. Anyway, then she says to me, "Hey, Ma, here. Here's some of your *Gengnian An* for you to eat" [referring to a local patent medication with purported tranquilizing effects[6]], and she hands me some of those pills. But I won't take it. I say, "I won't take it! It's you that should take it!" And I just yell and yell and yell. [She laughs.]

[The daughter, eyes on her homework, presses her lips together to fight back a grin.]

Zhao Lichun: That's right. I also had times when I got irritated, and they would say, "Oh, you're hungry—that's why," and I'd lose my temper with them. Now really, what's wrong with saying that you're hungry? But I felt like they had wronged me. The more they wouldn't do things my way, the more I'd lose my temper. Like I'd say, "Put that soup bowl here," and he'd put it there. And I'd say, "Why did you put that soup bowl there? You should put it away!" Right? ... [That] really rubbed me the wrong way. And then my kid would say, "Quick, quick, Ma is hungry! Give her something to eat! Then she'll be okay." Oh, my goodness, now did they not insult me by saying that? And I'd say, "My goal was to get you to put your soup bowl back where it belonged! When did I say anything about being hungry?" So they made it all the worse by doing that. If they had just let me have my way a little bit and not make so much trouble for me, then it wouldn't have been so bad. Right?

Wang Xiulan: That's right!

Wang speaks here of her indignation when her daughter calls her "Old *Gengr*," and she challenges her daughter's assertion by yelling that it is the daughter who needs medication, not her. Then Zhao describes her feelings of resentment when her attempts to get her family members to put things back where they belong is met with chiding from her own daughter and husband who claim that hunger-induced irritability must be driving her to pester them. In effect, both Wang and Zhao use their narratives to pose the moral question of whether they are justified in feeling that their family members are not treating them with enough deference. At the same time, such incidents are treated by Beijing families as trivial, allowing women to safely ask profound questions about their status within the household, while being excused as "just *gengnianqi*," rather than being seen as personally responsible and thus accountable for disrupting family harmony.

Women also used social explanations of irritability during *gengnianqi* to make attributions to bad historical fortune and former physical, educational, and material deprivation. Chinese women talked about having been born too early to really take advantage of the market reforms and opening up of China, and thus too old now to get a better education, career, or salary, or to take full advantage of the bounty of food and clothing now available for consumption. This often resulted in a feeling of regret of having been "born too soon." For example, Teacher Wang said, "Sometimes I think, when I was young and the children were little, everything was so much hard work and we were so poor.... I say, look at now, living conditions are much better, and my children are big, so I should really take the opportunity to enjoy the good fortune. But I'm old. Even when I want to eat, I can't eat that much anymore. Even if I'd like to wear some nice clothes, I can't really wear much of anything. Sometimes I feel pretty regretful."

The theme of feeling regretful due to having had to make too many sacrifices in the past was common. Many Chinese women whom I interviewed spoke ruefully of having had to sacrifice themselves, their education, their health, their well-being, and their ambitions. Some women complained that aches and pains and health problems were surfacing now because, decades ago, their mothers-in-law had not allowed them postpartum to "do the month" properly (thirty days of complete rest and tonic foods). The women born prior to the early 1940s remembered being forced to make sacrifices in serving their family under Confucianism prior to 1949, such as not being allowed to go to school so that they devote themselves to domestic tasks and/or to avoid being assaulted by soldiers during the Japanese occupation of China (1931–45). Many of these older women also recalled having suffered from malnutrition and edema during the famine following the Great Leap Forward (1958–61), and women across the age span remembered having a very limited diet prior to the 1978 market reforms. The oldest women spoke of how they had to serve their mothers-in-law in the "feudal" past, but now in the new market economy had to serve their daughters-in-law and cook, clean, and babysit because their daughters-in-law now work full-time. (There are specific effects of women's paid work on intergenerational relationships in other cultural contexts too; see Lamb and Gamburd, this volume.). A few of the oldest women who were considered intellectuals had been persecuted during the anti-Rightist campaign in the late 1950s and/or the Cultural Revolution (1966–76). Women across the age range also talked of how they had to ignore their own well-being and that of their family during the Maoist era (1949–78) in order to serve the people and the party (see also Shen 1990). Many of the youngest women (born in the early 1950s) talked with great regret at being "sacrificial objects of the Cultural Revolution." This is because when formal schooling was interrupted nationwide during the most chaotic years of Maoist radicalism (1966–69), this cohort (called *lao san jie* in Chinese) was left short of a middle school education. People just a few years older than the *lao san jie* were much more likely to have completed at least a middle school education and could thus get better jobs. People just a few years younger were allowed to resume school en masse in the 1970s, whereas the *lao san jie* was generally expected to go straight to work without the benefit of making up the schooling they had missed. Ironically, contemporary narratives of social suffering in Maoist times may be traced in part to the Chinese communist inculcation during pre-and post-revolutionary times of popular ritual complaint in the form of "speaking bitterness" sessions directed at connecting personal suffering with past and present social injustices associated with "feudal" traditions.

Many Chinese women see such injuries and insults as building up in the body over time like "steam in a pressure cooker"[7] and needing to be released in a measured way during *gengnianqi* in order to avoid lasting physical or mental health problems. *Gengnianqi* is seen as a critical point at which the pressure must be relieved in order to be healthy in old age. While not all women I encountered had issues with built-up anger during *gengnianqi,* those who did assumed that they had been previously prevented from adequately regulating (*tiaojie*) themselves physically or emotionally. The risks of permanent negative changes to one's physical or mental health or temperament were associated with either letting one's anger lash out at others with no limits on space, time, or intensity, or with not being allowed enough space and time by themselves and/or family members to come to terms with the past and to take special care of themselves in an effort to lessen the impact of past suffering on the aging body. Chinese women like Zhao stressed that you need to manage *gengnianqi* right, and part of managing it right was that just as you cannot lose total control over yourself and shout accusations at people at work, neither can you just keep everything bottled up inside. Instead, "you need to take the right amount of control over it" and find safe ways to release the pent-up anger and hurt, some of which may be through yelling at family members who will forgive you, and more of which should be through self-regulation by insisting on time for oneself, sometimes decompressing by spending time alone and sometimes doing fun and healthy things with other people, such as chatting with same age female friends or going to the park to do *qigong* or *taiqi* exercises or folk dancing. Women like Wang and Zhao stress the need for a balance between women's self-control and women's self-care, coupled with understanding and tolerance on the part of family members.

Thus far, I have treated *gengnianqi* discourse as a helpful form of resistance in which women rethink past and present in terms of protesting injuries and insults and insist on some time and space to vent, decompress, demand more deference, and take care of themselves. Such resistance is to women's benefit by giving them some reprieve to deal with the wounds of the past and present and re-regulate themselves to reach a new balance with better health and well-being. However, *gengnianqi* discourse does not

FIGURE 3.1 Chinese women doing tai chi sword exercises in a Beijing park, 2007. Photo by Jeanne Shea.

always serve women's best interests even when the stories are coming from women themselves. In Wang and Zhao's case, for example, they described some of their outbursts as quite reasonable (such as Wang's anger at being called Old *Gengr* and Zhao's outrage at being told she must just be hungry), but implied that others pushed the boundaries of reason. For example, Zhao mentions as not completely reasonable a time when she demanded that her husband immediately eat an orange that he had left on the table, despite the fact that he had a stomachache:

> *Zhao Lichun*: One time my husband had a peeled orange on the coffee table. And I said, "Quick, eat that up." But he said, "But my stomach hurts." Then I said, "Come on, quick, eat it!" But he just repeated, "But my stomach hurts." And then I'd lose my temper, and the more I'd lose my temper, the worse it got. You know, he should've just gone along with me a little.
>
> *Wang Xiulan*: That's true!

Zhao's statement that her husband should have gone along with her "a little" belies her mixed feelings about this incident. On one hand, Zhao felt justified in trying to prevent her husband from leaving a mess and wasting good food, but, on the other hand, she indicated that she had gone too far in trying to make him eat the offending piece of fruit despite his stomachache.

Even though we can see some of the familial joking about *gengnianqi* as a diffuser of tension, helping family members to tolerate an irascible matron, at the same time, it can be seen as a way of downplaying the seriousness of older women's complaints—"oh, it's only *gengnianqi*." So, similar to the limits of PMS rage as resistance in the United States (Martin 2001: 138), the very safety of this idiom of complaint is tied to the limits of its social power. As long as they are kept within the bounds of home, a short time frame, blamed on the nebulous "medical" signifier *gengnianqi*, and not taken too seriously, then midlife Chinese women's angry complaints are tolerated. Stories from my fieldsites that told about other Chinese women who went too far, however, indicate that beyond the home, at work, or carried out too intensely or over many years, midlife Chinese women making angry complaints and demands risk being labeled mentally ill, getting laid off from work, and/or being ostracized as bad wives/mothers/mothers-in-law/citizens. So, in *gengnianqi* discourse, we find a cyborg-like resistance (Van Wolputte 2004: 263) in which women are perched ambivalently between advocating for themselves in opposition to social demands and agreeing with the demands of society while struggling to control themselves.

Conclusion

Chinese women's discourse on *gengnianqi*, midlife suffering, and irritability differs in important ways from Western models of female midlife that stem from both conventional biomedicine and popular strains of Western feminism. Rather than viewing Chinese women's expressed experiences of midlife as either mere extensions of global biomedicine or pristine reserves of women's natural experience, I have argued that Chinese women's talk about *gengnianqi* is better seen as a cyborg phenomenon: Beijing women hold a wide variety of understandings of the term *gengnianqi*, some derived from biomedicine but more arising from creative interpretations emerging from lay Chinese society. Rather than projecting the rosy picture stemming from popular Western Orientalism, Beijing women express a great deal of ambivalence concerning their personal bodily experiences of midlife aging. They also present mixed feelings about their treatment at the hands of family and society and about the social changes that have marked their life course thus far. They further express a large degree of uncertainty about the sources of any suffering that they have experienced. Portraying themselves as neither vessels of inherent pathology nor chalices of pure contentment, they depict their experiences of midlife as deriving from a wide range of natural and cultural sources, ranging from a buildup of hot *qi*, to being prevented by an evil mother-in-law from resting up postpartum, to having been persecuted during the Cultural Revolution. In their talk of irritability, anger, lashing out, and attempts at the "right amount" of self-control during *gengnianqi*, Beijing women display neither clear triumph over, nor total resignation to, their lot, but, rather, an uneasy synthesis of the two. Neither hegemonic dupes nor anti-hegemonic heroines, Beijing women are currently wrestling with more modern egocentric and traditional sociocentric views of the roles and meanings of older women and their lives. Further research is needed to assess how widespread and long-lasting the association between *gengnianqi* and midlife anger is in Chinese populations, and whether and how meanings and dynamics of *gengnianqi* and midlife irritability have similar qualities amenable to "graying the cyborg" in different locales.

Acknowledgments

This research was supported by the National Science Foundation Graduate Fellowship, the Committee on Scholarly Communication with China Graduate Fellowship, the National Institute of Mental Health Predoctoral Award, the Cora DuBois Dissertation Fellowship, the University of Vermont (UVM) Dean's Fund Award for Faculty Research, the UVM Asian Studies Faculty Research Award, the Freeman Foundation, the Parimitas Foundation, and the Lintilhac Foundation.

Notes

1. All names of research subjects are pseudonyms.
2. This portrayal of midlife Asian women as relatively free of patriarchal domination is ironic given that in other Western contexts Asian women are pitied as the helpless victims of a more severe form of male oppression than that which Western women contend (Bulbeck 2001). Furthermore, it is common for scholarly sources to contrast the relatively low incidence of symptoms in Japanese as compared with North American midlife women (e.g., Davis 1996), but they do so with far greater analytical nuance.
3. The characters for *gengnianqi* and *konenki* are: 更年期.
4. Almost a quarter of the women said that they were unsure whether they would ever experience *gengnianqi* because they felt that to experience *gengnianqi* by definition entailed a period of heightened irritability, irrationality, acting out, extreme discomfort, and/or physical vulnerability.
5. Wang's last period was in October of 1992. She said her *gengnianqi* started in the early months of 1993.
6. *Gengnian An* is a patent medicine from Chinese medicine. Its main ingredient is oryzanol or ferulic acid, an anti-oxidant. It is purported to have tranquilizing effects, in part because the "*An*" in its name (meaning peaceful) is also in the Chinese word for Valium, *anding yao*. Most women found it ineffective.
7. This recalls the saying that through many years of being a daughter-in-law, one is pressure-cooked (*ao*) into the form of a mother-in-law (i.e., irritable and bossy).

4. "I DON'T WANT TO BE LIKE MY FATHER"
Masculinity, Modernity, and
Intergenerational Relationships in Mexico

Emily Wentzell

I INTERVIEWED OSVALDO IN AN urban Mexican hospital, as part of a research project examining how men's experiences of decreasing erectile function affected their ways of being men. Like many men I spoke with, Osvaldo, a 64-year-old retired mechanic, described his own experience of being a man in relationship to the experiences of others. He compared his own behavior to that of "the Mexican man" in the abstract, as well as to that of his father and son. For example, Osvaldo answered my questions about what it is to be a "good" man by telling me that "the Mexican man" was in fact quite bad, exhibiting macho behaviors like womanizing, drinking too much, and being violent. Also like many other interviewees, Osvaldo both critiqued machismo and identified it as a key theme in his life. He described seeking to temper his own macho tendencies in an attempt to "be different" than his own father, a professional soldier who Osvaldo said had been cold and physically abusive to Osvaldo's mother before eventually abandoning their family. However, Osvaldo worried that despite his attempts to model a different kind of masculinity, his son was taking after Osvaldo's father. In this chapter, I analyze men's discussions of the need for Mexican masculinity to change over time, on both the individual and societal levels, in order to show how these narratives of change influence how men like Osvaldo think about and enact manliness.

Osvaldo described a lifelong struggle to balance the male privilege that he enjoyed against the excesses of machismo that his father had modeled. He said that when he was a boy, "I thought, 'I'll be different, but I won't let my wife take advantage of me either.' We make agreements." He, like other men I spoke with, saw machismo as a trait that men could exhibit to varying degrees, and in more or less socially damaging ways. When describing his relationship with his own wife, Osvaldo constantly compared his actions to his father's, commenting that his were more progressive and less macho. For example, he said that although he had been unfaithful, his actions were not "macho" because he did not perform them in a sexist way. He explained, "It's machista to grab the woman, that's it. I tried to satisfy them." Similarly, he ranked his own violent encounters with his wife as less severe than those he witnessed as a child. He said, "My father is one of those [a macho]. He beat my mother. I only slapped my wife, maybe two times, with an open hand. My father used to put my mother over his knees and spank her with a belt!" Thus, Osvaldo saw his own difference from his father's machismo not as a wholesale rejection of violence, infidelity, or men's ability to control women, but a deliberate tempering of these traits. Osvaldo justified his actions by framing them as improvements on his father's behaviors that demonstrated an intergenerational shift away from extreme machismo.

Seeking to continue this shift within his family, Osvaldo said he had deliberately taught his two sons to treat women well. His sons were now married, and Osvaldo expressed dismay that one of them seemed to be taking after his grandfather. While he called one son a "good" husband and father, he was upset that the other "treats his wife badly." Despite his efforts to "educate them differently," he said that "the oldest hits his wife, I don't like it, but I don't interfere. It makes me angry, I tell him not to hit her. Don't you think that she feels it? She's not an object!" He lamented that his attempts to teach his son to avoid marital violence had been unsuccessful, hypothesizing that his son might be predisposed to beat his wife because "he has my father's genes."

Osvaldo's story illustrates key themes that were common among the men I interviewed. They almost universally said that machismo was both a very real Mexican trait and a serious social problem. Even men who seemed to exhibit macho behavior in their own lives said that Mexican men as a group were—and needed to continue—becoming less macho over time so that their nation could advance. Many mentioned Mexico's need to "modernize," describing more egalitarian gender roles as a key element of an appropriately modern nation. By discussing intergenerational differences, especially the need for sons to "be different" from fathers, men articulated their beliefs about the nature of Mexican masculinity and the life course. As demonstrated by Osvaldo's justification of "only" minor marital violence as an improvement on his father's macho actions, men often used linear narratives of positive change over generations to make sense of far messier lived realities.

Research Population and Analytic Approach

This chapter is based on a 2007–8 ethnographic study of men's experiences of aging, illness, and changing sexual function in a government-funded hospital in the central Mexican city of Cuernavaca. The aim of this research was to shed light on how age- and illness-related changes in sexual function shaped men's ideas about, and practices of, masculinity. I interviewed 250 mostly working-class male urology patients, who ranged in age from eighteen to ninety-four. Most interviewees were between fifty and sixty, seeking treatment for urologic problems related to age or chronic illness. Many participants said they experienced these interviews as cathartic, welcoming the chance to talk about their health and the sensitive issue of changing sexual function in a supportive environment. The format of on-site interviews, rather than the more traditional anthropological method of participant observation, was necessary for ensuring the confidentiality that the hospital required I maintain for all research participants, as well as for putting participants at ease about discussing intimate issues. While the interview method has the limitation of providing data on only reported, rather than observed, behavior, using this method made my research on this sensitive topic possible. Further, while interview participants may be likely to give voice to cultural scripts in ways that over-emphasize the importance of certain themes to their lived experience, the tensions they articulate between their own behavior and that dictated by such scripts is a fruitful ground for analysis.

I have written elsewhere about participants' ideas about the relationship of masculinity to the medical diagnosis "erectile dysfunction" and erectile function aids like Viagra (Wentzell 2011; Wentzell and Inhorn 2011; also see Martin's discussion of the relationship between medical intervention and notions of the life course, in this volume). Here, I will focus on men's broader statements about changes in masculinity over their lives and their relationships to changing ideas about gender over Mexico's history. However, it is important to note that participants' recent experiences of erectile function change and/or ill health likely clarified or altered their ideas about their own and men's ideal lives, relationships, and sexuality. I will discuss men's characterizations of changing relationships between sex and manliness over the individual life course, and recent cultural calls for Mexican men to become different, that were influenced by participants' embodied experiences of aging and change. Thus, while study participants made sweeping statements about the course their nation should take, and the changes "Mexican men" had experienced and should undergo, these understandings were fundamentally shaped by their recent perception of change in their own lives and bodies.

Participants' concerns relating to masculinity, sexuality, and health guided our open-ended discussions. Like Osvaldo, many participants broached the topic of machismo in order to critique Mexican manhood, grounding these critiques in narratives of national, intergenerational, and individual change. Many men presented Mexican masculinity as a shared problematic trait that was nevertheless changing as the nation became more modern, as sons acted differently than fathers, and (for the older participants) as they themselves became less macho over their life courses. As Osvaldo's description of his difference from his father shows, men's definitions of macho versus good masculinity and differences between older and younger men were relational rather than static. Similarly, while I will gloss certain ideas about masculinity as belonging to "younger" or "older" men, this refers to men's characterizations of themselves as "acting" old or young, rather than their numeric age. Further, while I present the most common attitudes that study participants attributed to older or younger men, there was great lived diversity within these groups. Finally, as in Osvaldo's case, men's struggles to be "different than their fathers" were not limited to those who identified as "younger," since some participants who now viewed themselves as older men reported that they had always tried to act in non-macho ways.

This analysis follows an anthropological tradition of studying how generational differences and father-son tensions in Mexico mirror broader processes of social change and friction (Gutmann 1996; Hirsch and Nathanson 2001; Lewis 1963 [1961]; Salguero Velásquez 2007). Analyzing men's intergenerational tensions can be fruitful because they reflect both ongoing debates about how gender roles shape Mexican national identity, and ongoing cultural concerns that Mexican men are predisposed to behave badly. (For a similar discussion, see Robbins in this volume, who explores the relationships between individual life course narratives and notions of the state in Poland.) Social scientists have demonstrated that throughout Mexico's history, politicians and cultural commentators have argued that individual forms of masculinity and femininity reflect on the nation as a whole (Bliss 2001; Kelly 2008). Today, these discussions center on the need to discard "traditional" gender roles to achieve national "modernization" (Carillo 2007).

The concept of machismo, a patriarchal style of masculinity characterized by womanizing and emotional withdrawal, has been central to these debates. This understanding of Mexican manliness is actually quite recent; in the 1950s, poet Octavio Paz asserted that Mexican men were inherently emotionally remote and sexually aggressive because they were the product of coercive unions between conquistadors and indigenous women (Paz 1985 [1961]). Thus, machismo itself is understood as the legacy of a particularly troubled familial relationship. While Paz's work was a literary interpretation of Mexican history and culture, his characterization of machismo has been immensely influential in Mexican culture. This notion of machismo has become a central, if widely contested, way that Mexicans define men's innate tendencies (McKee Irwin 2003). Here, I take an anthropological approach to this concept, discussing how men use machismo to understand their own actions and families. While my interviewees often understood masculinity as a cultural or biological essence, I understand it as a category of actions consisting of "what men say and do *to be men*" (Gutmann 1996: 17, italics in original).

To understand aspects of selfhood like gender and age as context-dependent social practices, rather than biological essences, anthropologists seek to understand how interactions between multiple arenas of life shape people's ways of being men, women, and people of a certain age. Nancy Scheper-Hughes and Margaret Lock (1987) have proposed a "three-body" model for understanding how such interactions shape the contexts and content of people's lives and physical bodies. Scheper-Hughes and Lock argue that in order to escape from reductive and inaccurate understandings of mind and body or nature and nurture as separate, it is important to understand how bodies and embodiment (the experience of having a particular body in a particular context) are shaped by multiple levels of society. They suggest combining three perspectives to understand embodiment: 1) attention to the "body-self," or people's lived and felt experiences of having a body; 2) attention to the "social body," or the way broader structural forces shape human interaction on the societal level; and 3) the "body politic," or the ways that social and political control shape human interaction (Scheper-Hughes and Lock 1987). Here, I use this three-body model to understand how study participants' understandings of change over time on the personal, intergenerational, and national levels shaped their own embodied experiences of manliness and filial relationships. In the following sections, I discuss study participants' understandings of change over time in relationship to each of these three bodies. First, a section on the body politic examines men's simultaneous critiques and embodiments of machismo and their views of this form of masculinity as a hindrance to national progress. Second, a section on the individual body/self presents older men's narratives of change over time in their embodiment of manhood and manly sexuality, which reflected broader ideas of change over time on the national level. Third, a section on the social body discusses both older and younger men's expectations for intergenerational change, which many hope will lead to different forms of masculinity in Mexico.

Masculinity in the Body Politic: Machismo and National Modernization

I never brought up the term "machismo" in interviews, instead asking about participants' life experiences to see how they acted "like men" in their daily lives. However, most participants saw their own actions as interconnected with broader debates about masculinity in Mexico, frequently explaining their own behavior in relationship to that of the abstract "Mexican man." Regardless of their own behavior, most participants characterized this "Mexican man" as intrinsically, and problematically, macho. Yet men had different ideas about the source of this machismo. Some, like a 58-year-old driver who told me that Mexican men are taught that "the woman needs to be behind," attributed macho infidelity to Mexican culture. This driver added that men must learn that "the wife isn't a thing—she's a person, she's a comrade." In this characterization, machismo is a cultural teaching that people have the power to critique and reject.

Many men followed Octavio Paz's logic of machismo as a cultural inheritance. A 24-year-old physical education teacher saw machismo as a historical response to men's ongoing fears of losing control of relationships with women. He said, "A lot of machismo exists.... They're afraid that if they let their guard down, they'll become whipped. That's the macho's closed way of thinking, from pre-Hispanic times." Others frequently understood machismo as a biological trait of "the Mexican man," an idea linked to the common notion that Mexicans are a unique race created by indigenous and Spanish mixing. Participants frequently said that the "hot" Mexican constitution predisposed men to womanize, drink, and have a bad temper. A 56-year-old veterinarian told me that, "Here in Mexico, [infidelity is] something normal. They say the Mexican is passionate."

Whether they cast machismo as learned or innate, many participants believed men could avoid behaviors like infidelity if they struggled against their biology and/or socialization, especially if fathers were to teach sons differently. For example, a thirty-year-old government office worker initially told me that Mexican men were not predisposed to be faithful, saying, "Lamentably, the Mexican man doesn't have that characteristic." However, he then paused and reconsidered, adding, "Not all are like that. Also, their parents play a role—if the father is a machista, with lots of women, the kids pay attention." When discussing the need for Mexico to "modernize," men often raised the possibility of moving away from "traditional" gender roles, like machismo, to enhance equality between men and women. The notion of more egalitarian gender roles as crucial to modernity comes from a variety of sources, ranging from the Mexican and global feminist movements to local self-help groups to the increasing global media valorization of romantic love based on emotional intimacy (Alvarez 2010; Amuchástegui Herrera 2008; Wardlow and Hirsch 2006). My interviewees overwhelmingly saw this change as crucial to Mexico's "modern" future, and feared that macho behaviors, even those that they themselves felt powerless to cease, would delay national advancement.

This notion that the nation is on a path from less to more modern, and that people help or hinder this process by acting in modern or traditional ways, is widespread in Mexican culture. Sociologist Hector Carillo argues that this notion deeply shapes people's understandings of manliness and sexuality, as people make value judgments about sexual and gender practices based on their places along a traditional/modern continuum (2002). Self-consciously acting in "modern" or "traditional" ways, especially in terms of sexuality, femininity, and masculinity, has long been a way to assert social superiority in Mexican culture (Amuchástegui Herrera 1996; McKee Irwin, McCaughan, and Nasser 2003). Perhaps because of their urban, working-class demographics, study participants overwhelmingly linked their past "bad" manly behaviors to "tradition." Many critiqued the "traditional" marital relationships that they had lived out, calling for "modern" love-based partnerships. They were describing what social scientists call "companionate marriage," a form of marriage aimed at producing individually satisfying emotional closeness through practices like conversation, shared hobbies, and mutually-satisfying sex, rather than— or alongside— the economic production and social reproduction that were ideal main outcomes of traditional forms of marriage (Wardlow and Hirsch 2006). In Mexico, as in many other world regions, companionate marriage has become the ideal and is seen as a "modern" form of interaction (Carillo 2007; Hirsch 2003). While people's romantic lives often fell short of these ideals, and were also shaped by competing discourses like that of inevitable machismo, most study participants identified this sort of marriage as an important part of "Mexico today."

Whatever their marriages looked like, the majority of study participants identified "responsibility" for one's family as key to being a good husband. Regardless of age, the vast majority agreed that providing financially was a key way men show responsibility. A 28-year-old graduate student said that he had been taught that the man provides, "fiscal solvency ... earning the money, it gives you a type of power ... you can help your partner more." The related capacity to work hard defined good masculinity for many participants, who said their strong work ethic enabled them to be good husbands and fathers even in the face of adversity. (See Lynch, in this volume, for further discussion of the role that work plays in selfhood across the life course.) For instance, after explaining that his age and health problems forced him to partially retire from his job, a 69-year-old construction worker said that he continued without pay for the sheer joy of it: "Work is beautiful—I feel happy working. I do small jobs in the house, [such as] painting or gardening."

Despite this shared emphasis on hard work, financial provision, and responsibility, men of different generations tended to have different understandings of exactly what supporting one's family entailed in regards to specific roles and responsibilities. For example, a 76-year-old retired construction worker compared caring responsibly for one's family to raising livestock, saying that one must, "care for the woman, care for the children—you have to raise the little chickens." Timoteo, a 51-year-old librarian told me, "Here in Mexico, it's seen as bad if a man does the housework—they call him whipped. So, one doesn't participate much in sharing housework." However, thinking further, he added that, "men are going to have to change their attitude," since women were now working outside the home. Frequently, men who described strictly gendered divisions of labor in their own households noted that the next generation would have to do things differently. Younger men often strove to enact this "modern" system of shared labor. A twenty-year-old medical student said that it shows a "lack of masculinity" to fail to help one's wife in the home. He said that while Mexico used to have a "macho tradition," "I don't say that it has to be that way. The woman fortunately has the same rights as the man. She can work. Both should work to reach their goals together." Thus, despite study participants' common belief that Mexican men are, somewhat innately, machos, they often believed that changes were required in order for their nation to advance. Overall, participants drew from widespread and generation-specific cultural understandings about the nature of Mexican manhood, the nation's needs, and the meanings of marital practices ranging from housework to sex, to variously explain and critique their and others' ways of being men.

Change over Time in Older Participants' Masculine Body/Selves

Older study participants who talked about the need for men to "be different" often described changes over time in their own ways of being men. Looking back at their lives, they tended to fit their complex and often messy histories of affairs, fights, joy, and love into linear narratives of shifts over time from "traditional" to more "modern" manly practices that mirrored their hopes for the nation more broadly. They described a life path they believed to be so common for men of their generation that one participant glossed it as "the Mexican classic," in which men shifted from a "macho" youth to what one man called an "ex-machista" older age (Wentzell and Salmerón 2009).

Many men said that "good" masculinity for older men involved focusing on family and home rather than on friends and lovers. While older men still expected to work hard and provide for their families financially, they believed this work should become domestically oriented. They felt duty-bound to provide emotional support and family leadership—like being a "role model" of socially positive personhood for grandchildren—which they had not previously seen as key to being a good man. Many believed that their personal change fit with broader social shifts on the national level away from "traditional" machismo.

Prompted by both bodily aging that hindered penetrative sex, and social encouragement to act age-appropriately, many interviewees who saw themselves as "older" reported curtailing the extramarital sex that had been key to their youthful masculinities. Many participants saw persistent performance of youthful sexuality as inappropriate since they now inhabited "weakening" bodies. They described frequent sex as a pleasurable practice that had once largely defined them as men, but that now no longer really mattered. (Shea, in this volume, discusses how age-related bodily changes may result in social change in China.) For example, a 75-year-old retired factory worker told me, "Erectile dysfunction isn't important. When I was young, it would have been, but not now."

In keeping with this shift, and the recent cultural idealization of companionate marriage, many older participants reported that their marriage had undergone a romantic renaissance. Many older participants married primarily to assert adulthood rather than for love, selecting wives based on compatibility but also their potential as productive spouses. While most reported always seeing tender marital relations as ideal, men often reported making youthful "mistakes" in this area, remaining emotionally distant from their wives during youths focused on work, friends, and mistresses. Older male and female participants only rarely expected male marital fidelity. Instead, they valued discretion and uninterrupted financial support of one's family during a man's dalliances. Later in life, as they became less physically able to have sex in the context of increasing social valorization of companionate marriage, many older men said they had forged more emotionally intimate relationships with their wives and families. They often described this shift as personal growth. A 68-year-old appliance repairman who became faithful when older said that in youth, "You don't think about anything. With age, you start to think more." Thus, study participants strove to enact age- and socially-appropriate masculinities differently over time, in ways that reflected broader cultural changes in ideals of "good" manhood.

Generational Change in the Social Body

Older participants frequently said they were proud of their own histories, but social shifts toward gender equity meant that their youthful behavior was no longer suitable for citizens of a "modernizing" nation. They often said that younger men would need to "be different." Such statements did specific social work, excusing speakers' youthful indiscretions while enabling them to claim "modern" values. Further, while almost all study participants called for change in abstract Mexican men's ways of being men, men enacted such change very differently. Some older men had always been faithful to wives they loved, while others said they would never be faithful. Conversely, while most younger men tried to act "modern" in certain ways, many were unfaithful or did not share housework, and some, like Osvaldo's son, were quite "traditional." However, the majority of self-identified "younger" men consciously acted in opposition to "traditional" Mexican manhood. (For a discussion of ways that economic transactions shape intergenerational relationships, see chapters in this volume by Gamburd and by Guyer and Salami.)

Younger men often described childhoods marred by their fathers' violence or womanizing. Many younger participants said their parents' relationships had been problematically unequal, and they were angry about their fathers' mistreatment of their mothers. As adults, they often attempted to intervene in these situations; one set of siblings bought their mother her own condo, saying she had "suffered enough" at their father's hands. More frequently, sons uneasily monitored the actions of fathers who now treated their mothers well, but who had not always done so. These sons frequently critiqued the "Mexican classic" pattern of manly life-course change as antiquated and antithetical to their ideal of companionate marriage. While older men frequently said that they had always tried to treat their wives "well," some only began to see emotional closeness as important to a good marriage later in life. Younger men often critiqued such patterns of marital change, arguing that spouses should always be loving, kind, and faithful.

Younger men frequently said they wanted to avoid putting their own wives through the pain that they had seen their mothers experience, especially in terms of neglect or domestic violence. One participant explained, "It fell to me to see my dad hit my mom. I never hit my wife, or my children. Those punches come to nothing, they're actually the problem." Many younger study participants used their parents' marriages as models for what not to do, seeking instead to build more companionate and egalitarian relationships they saw as befitting a "modern" man. Frequently, younger men said that to be a "good" man, they would "be different than my father!"

For instance, a thirty-year-old office worker said that his parents had married young, and his father was a "macho Mexican" who ordered his family around. He told me that in his own life, he wanted to avoid a situation where, "You're the macho, you give the orders" because "as a society, we've opened our eyes a little." Similarly, a thirty-year-old electronics installer said that it is important for both partners to "be mature, to grow together. A husband and wife should share everything. If we both work, we should share the housework and child care, share economic responsibility." He thus voiced an ideal of gendered change over time in which husbands and wives should grow together through shared labor and communication, which is quite different from that of the "Mexican classic." He developed this perspective from "life experience," including his parents' separation and his father's maltreatment of his mother. However, he believed that his point of view was sadly uncommon "because of machismo, which is ugly and bad." In my research and in studies of Mexican men in their twenties and thirties, participants self-consciously decided to think differently than their parents about relationships and gender roles (Jiménez Guzman 2003; Ramirez 2009; Salguero Velásquez 2007).

All the younger participants in my study had married, or hoped to marry, women who they loved, and they saw maintaining romantic passion as crucial to keeping their marriage happy. This led younger study participants to seek marital sex lives that were very different from older participants', both in terms of fidelity and marital sexual practice. Compared to older participants, a much higher percentage of younger participants reported fidelity to their wives. When I asked Luis, a 35-year-old carpenter, to describe important attributes of a good husband or father, he instantly replied, "Fidelity. It's important because I've lived through, or rather, I was the child of, dysfunctional parents who separated because of infidelity. I've lived a hard life—fidelity helps a family to be happy." He said that few people believe that he is faithful, since "the Mexican man is naturally unfaithful. But I look at my kids ... you see kids shut in the house, no one to look after them, because of infidelity.... I want to be a good role model for my kids." Further, those younger men who did cheat tended to explain their actions not as older men usually did—as an expression of their innate Mexican manliness—but instead saw affairs as emotional escapes necessitated by failures of marital intimacy. While men of all ages understood their own behaviors in light of the cultural belief that they were predisposed to machismo, younger men were far more likely to reject macho practices, while older men were generally content to age out of them.

Conclusion: Changing Masculinities Relate to Men's Intergenerational Relationships

Prior research on Mexican masculinities has shown that very different performances of manliness seem appropriate to men at different phases of life (Escobar Latapí 2003; de Keijzer and Rodriguez 2007). Here, I revealed some of the key relationships through which men understand and embody these changes: relationships with the notion of a modernizing nation, their own aging bodies, and with their fathers and sons. Participants' use of narratives of change over time on these levels demonstrates that change in masculinity is a fundamentally relational process. While many participants described similar understandings of their and abstract Mexican men's masculinities, they may experience their relationships with their nation, bodies, and families through very different sexual and marital experiences. They also changed their own ways of being men, or sought to change "Mexican men" more broadly, with the help of or in opposition to those close to them. Finally, participants aligned themselves in different ways with popular understandings of certain manly practices as "traditional" or "modern."

While this chapter focused on relationships between older and younger men, and ideas about national change, men also call for change in their peers' ways of being men. For example, Luis the carpenter told me that not only he, but all men of his generation, needed to strive to be very different kinds of husbands and fathers than their own role models. He illustrated this by relating a conversation that he had with a male co-worker. This co-worker told Luis that he and his siblings had been beaten by his father, and expressed on-going anger at his father over the abuse. However, this co-worker said that he had begun to beat his own children and felt powerless to stop. Luis told his co-worker, "You're doing the same as your dad, but you can change."

Thus, while men's emotional and sexual relationships with women are key sites for demonstrating machismo or more "modern" manhood, their relationships with other men were also crucial arenas in which they defined and enacted their masculinities. Here, I have shown how men understand change over time in intergenerational relationships to relate to their nation's hoped-for shift from a bastion of machismo to a more "modern" society. While gender scholars have long argued that masculinity is a relational practice, this research highlights the centrality of intergenerational interactions to the performance of gender. These relationships make a range of different forms of masculinity thinkable, possible, and appropriate as time passes and circumstances change.

Acknowledgments

This research was funded by the Wenner-Gren Foundation, Fulbright IIE, and the American Association of University Women. I thank the research participants for sharing their experiences with me, and the urology department staff for their assistance and support. I am also grateful to Caitrin Lynch and Jason Danely for their comments on earlier versions of this chapter.

SPATIALITY AND TEMPORALITY

5. SHIFTING MORAL IDEALS OF AGING IN POLAND
Suffering, Self-Actualization, and the Nation

Jessica C. Robbins

DURING THE EIGHTEEN MONTHS FROM 2008–2010 in which I conducted ethnographic fieldwork among older people in Poland, I had a crash course in Polish history. Many older Poles understand their own life experiences as intimately connected to national history, frequently weaving together personal stories and national narratives. A particularly striking example of reading the personal through the national was offered by Zbigniew, an older man who was then a patient at a rehabilitation center run by Catholic nuns in Wrocław, one of my primary research sites.[1] A retired engineer and recent widower, Zbigniew had come to the institution to recover after an operation left him unable to take care of himself. When we first started talking, he was very shy, saying that he would happily talk with me, but that he did not have anything interesting to say. As I often did when people were reticent, I asked if he could begin by telling me a bit about his biography—for instance, where he was born. He answered that he was born near Kraków before the war. Almost an hour later, during which time I had asked only encouraging follow-up questions, he ended his story with some of the most personal details of the previous hour: his wife passed away four months ago from cancer and he was grieving. Yet except for framing his story with his birth and his wife's death, he spoke more about the history of Poland in the twentieth century, including the extraordinary difficulty of the wartime years and the oppression he and his family felt during socialist times,[2] than about the details of his own life. After this hour-long story, I still did not know the profession of his children, why he had moved from Kraków to Wrocław, and other seemingly basic personal details.[3]

There is more that could be added here—for instance, because I am a young American woman, perhaps older Poles felt the need to teach me about Polish history more than they did when telling stories to fellow Poles. It is also possible that Zbigniew's grief was too painful for him to bear, leading him to avoid the details of his life in favor of more impersonal topics, but this does not seem likely, given both his openness and his intertwining of political history and personal lives. Or perhaps this was his way of keeping me at a distance in the process of building rapport, since we were just getting to know each other. However, given the consistency with which I heard such stories from others whom I came to know very well over a period of many months, I see Zbigniew's story as part of a larger pattern of meaningful and intimate connections that older Poles make between their personal lives and Polish national history. Close analysis of this ethnographic data elucidates the contemporary complex moral transformations of aging persons and the Polish nation-state.

In this chapter, I analyze two aspects of this intertwining of the personal and the national. First, I focus on the most common trope—that of shared individual and national suffering—to show that these connections are crucial to older Poles' attempts to create moral lives in the displaced context of institutional life. Second, I focus on links between personal lives and Poland's recent membership in the European Union (EU) to show the moral anxieties and possibilities that are part of this national transformation. I conclude by arguing that postsocialist ideals of aging shift in complex ways that are related to time and space, social relations, and national transformations, and I suggest that older Poles' experiences of aging shift along with these ideals.

This research draws on eighteen months of ethnographic research in Wrocław and Poznań, two cities in western Poland, in a variety of institutions for older Poles. I analyze data from my two primary research sites in Wrocław: the *Zakład Opiekuńczo-Leczniczy o profilu rehabilitacyjnym* (the above-mentioned rehabilitation center), and the *Uniwersytet Trzeciego Wieku* (University of the Third Age, hereafter UTW), a continuing-education institution for retirees.[4]

Narrating Loss, Creating Relatedness: Aging and Illness Away from Home

Zbigniew uses conventions of storytelling that are widespread among older Poles, who commonly describe their experiences of aging and illness by drawing upon a national historical narrative of suffering, victimization, and constraint that reaches back to the eighteenth century. These narrative practices comprise a way for older Poles to establish themselves as good and moral persons, from which basis they attempt to strengthen existing kin relations and build new ones. Crucial to this process is the spatiotemporal context of social relations.

Place is crucial to aging in Poland. Generally, Polish people do not want to live in a retirement home, a nursing home, or any institution, instead preferring to grow old in their own homes or in the homes of their children or other kin. Institutional living is stigmatized because it is seen as evidence of problematic families that do not care enough about their older relatives.[5] Although in conversations I have had with older Poles during my fieldwork, many people acknowledged that such institutions are sometimes necessary—for instance when homes are not adapted for the physical needs of sick elders, or when family members have too much work to take care of elders—this does not mean that people want to live in such institutions. Instead, many Poles believe that good and proper aging should take place at home, with or close to family members.

When older Poles do move to institutions, they often experience their new lives as deeply isolating and unsatisfactory. Yet this is not always so, for some older Poles can transform this existing moral logic by creating new homes for themselves while living in institutions. However, not everyone can create new homes with equal success. The structure of temporality—more specifically, a sense of permanence—is what allows some people to create new homes, while a lack of permanence prevents others from ever feeling "*u siebie*" ("at home") while living in an institution. In this way we can see that kin relations are processual and constructed through practices, places, and pasts (Carsten 2007; Franklin and McKinnon 2001a; see also Danely's discussion, this volume, of similar dynamics in Japanese beliefs and practices around aging, death, and the life course).

The following vignettes are all from people I met at the Wrocław rehabilitation center. The eighty-bed center is populated by people (mostly women over the age of sixty)[6] who have had major medical events, such as strokes or major surgeries that have left them dependent on the care of others. Although this institution is intended for a temporary few-months-long period, in reality, many people remain there for over a year as their physical conditions fail to improve, or while waiting for openings in institutions intended for long-term care. A few beds are set aside for people to remain there permanently.

Alicja: Uncertainty and Isolation

One afternoon when I visited Alicja in her room at the rehabilitation center, she told me how happy she was to see me because her granddaughter had just left and now she was alone (even though her two roommates were also in the room). Formerly a farmer, Alicja is seventy-two but looks much older, and she moved to this institution following a stroke that left her in a wheelchair, rendering her legs and entire left side useless. Already a patient at the rehab center for a few months at the time that I met her, Alicja stayed there for well over a year while waiting for a place in a long-term care institution. During this time, she did not know when she would be leaving or where exactly she would be going. For Alicja, her suffering is at once bodily, social, and political (cf. Scheper-Hughes and Lock 1987). The bodily dimension is immediately visible, as she often strokes and pulls on her gnarled and clenched left fist, trying unsuccessfully to overcome her paralysis. The social and political dimensions become apparent in her laments about absent kin and the declining Polish nation.

Though I frequently saw Alicja's granddaughter and son there, and Alicja often mentioned the help they provided in the form of financial assistance and material goods (e.g., by bringing her fruit, coffee, personal care products), she often complained to her roommates, staff, and me about being abandoned by her family. "I am such an orphan," she said. At her request, several times I helped Alicja use the rehab center's pay phone to call her granddaughter to ask when her next visit would be and to ask her to bring specific items. I often felt that these teary complaints, laments, and favors were part of attempts to bring me—or anyone who would genuinely listen—into her world, to make her suffering recognized and known.

Alicja often connected this suffering to that of the Polish nation, in one breath commenting on the difficulty of that day's physical therapy session, and in the next on the sad state of today's Poland, where the grocery stores are full of "dirty" foreign produce and farmers have no one to whom to sell their crops. She once gave me an apple that her granddaughter had brought her, entreating me to eat it because "Polish apples are the best." At Alicja's lament on the prevalence of foreign produce in stores, her roommate and roommate's daughter joined the conversation, saying foreign produce is good because that is why non-native products such as bananas are now available but obviously, "people want Polish potatoes, Polish carrots, Polish dairy products, because they are better." Alicja conceded this point, as they together reaffirmed the excellent taste of Polish apples.

More than simple nostalgia for her youth, Alicja sees such foreign influence as evidence of a national historical narrative of dependence and lack of freedom that began with the division of the country during the partitions in the eighteenth century. Echoed in stories other patients told of national suffering, Alicja is an extreme example of how older Poles relate their own physical suffering to historical and contemporary national travails. This standard narrative is often framed in religious terms, in which Poland becomes a Christ figure and suffering is therefore redemptive.[7]

For Alicja, placing her experiences within a temporal scale that is both broader and deeper than her own life is an attempt to connect to her fellow

Poles, both ancestral and contemporary (see Danely, this volume). Deeply upset by both her bodily changes and her move to institutional care, and lacking certainty about her future, Alicja seeks refuge in telling stories about the historical Polish nation. Yet the structures of her daily life, in which there is no place for her kin, confound these efforts and leave her deeply sad and isolated.

Marta: Creating a Sense of Home

Despite the widespread longing for home, some people at this rehabilitation institution have overcome the physical, emotional, and structural barriers to creating a home. Marta is a 67-year-old woman who lives at the institution permanently and is one of only two people I met who said that she feels *u siebie* (at home) in this institution.

Marta moved to this institution because her multiple sclerosis made her unable to walk, severely limited the use of her arms, and rendered her incontinent. She has a large family who visits her frequently, including her young grandchildren, who all bring her food, coffee, and personal care products. One of her brothers, a hairdresser, cuts the hair of many residents. Marta thrills to the gossip of the institution, always informing me who had passed away, whose condition had worsened, or whose daughter just returned from vacation in Spain. She closely follows the news on Radio Maryja, the very conservative nationalist Catholic radio station, and shares what she learns there with other patients, often trying to engage them and me in political discussions. She boasts that she makes coffee for her roommates, other patients, and me as proof that she is at home and still able to be hospitable, a quality that is greatly valued in Poland. Marta has made one close friend at the center; she waits for her friend so they can attend chapel together, and she knows the details of her friend's medical conditions and life history. Unlike that of other patients, the table in Marta's room is decorated with trinkets, candles, and seasonal items, which to her are another sign of being *u siebie*. At holidays, Marta visits her old home, where her son's family now lives, but she is always relieved to return to the peace, quiet, and stability of the institution. She told me repeatedly that she prefers to live at the rehab institution, where her bodily needs are adequately met and, crucially, where her everyday life matches with her moral ideals.

Although Marta has been in the institution for roughly the same amount of time as Alicja, she has successfully created a home for herself because she has a sense of security about the future, which has allowed her to create new social relations. Part of Alicja's suffering stems from her self-understanding as living outside her ideals of a moral life, primarily marked by the absence of kin. Alicja's uncertainty about her future prevents her from forming connections with others in the institution, which might otherwise ameliorate her anguish at being away from home. Marta, however, takes comfort in her secure future and new friendships, and finds it easier to accept her changed bodily conditions. The temporal scale of Marta's illness itself—the slow debilitation of multiple sclerosis, rather than the sudden violent disability of Alicja's major stroke—seems to affect her ability to create a satisfactory moral world for herself in institutional care, despite the broader cultural imperatives against such a life. This emphasis on permanence reveals the fundamental role of temporality in how personhood and social relations can be created, transformed, or unmade in later life (Carsten 2007; Danely, this volume; Kaufman 1986; Lamb 1997).[8] Dominant logics of good and proper aging in Poland can be transformed through building new social relations based on shared memories and understandings of the nation.

Euro-orphans and Euro-seniors: Anxiety, Possibility, and the European Union

Understandings of the Polish nation have been affected by Poland's membership in the EU, a topic that was often an entry into discussions on history, politics, and social life. Older Poles often expressed ambivalence, rather than strong positive or negative feelings, about Poland's EU membership, thereby revealing the complex ways that patriotism and history, kin relations and morality, and personhood and sociality are intertwined in their lives. In this section, I first use a case study of a research participant who attends the University of the Third Age (UTW) in Wrocław to demonstrate the complex meanings of EU membership for national identity. Then I use data from other research participants associated with the same UTW to describe the transformation of moral ideals of aging as they relate to Poland's EU membership and to broader postsocialist transformations.

Cecylia: Emigration, Ambivalence, and "Euro-orphans"

Since Poland joined the EU in 2004, there has been a large work-based emigration to Western Europe; estimates of how many Poles have left range from five hundred thousand to two million. Since 2008, some émigrés have returned home because wages abroad are too low relative to the cost of living and because they miss their families. For many Poles, family ties are the most important kind of social relations. Friendships matter too, but especially for older Poles, relationships that count as family matter in a qualitatively different way.[9] It is through kin relations that persons are formed and come to understand themselves (Carsten 2000), and through which a sense of national identity can be created, maintained, or weakened. When Poles go abroad for work, kin relations can become weaker, damaged, or broken, thereby threatening a family's sense of Polishness. As the previous section demonstrates, national identity is crucial to older Poles' understandings of themselves as moral persons.

Cecylia is a widowed 67-year-old woman I met through the UTW. Outgoing, talkative, and opinionated, Cecylia shared many details of her life with me; our meetings often lasted over four hours and at times bordered on lectures. She thinks that Poland should be part of the EU, indignantly claiming that "Poland has been part of Europe for thousands of years." In other words, she sees it as a historical fact that Poland belongs to Europe, which she conceptually equates with the EU. She emphasizes her own family's history of nobility and tradition of higher education in defining her Polish—and therefore European—identity. For her, the EU represents an external validation of Poland's proper geographical and moral location, although at the same time it heralds a loss of Polish identity for future generations because of increased possibilities for working abroad.[10] "I am happy that my grandchildren can choose their own college [and] that they can choose for themselves where they want to live. But I would like them to feel that *here* [Poland] is their country, their homeland, their roots, you know? That they would feel that they are Polish, and that they would try to make things work well in Poland." For Cecylia, preserving Polish language, currency, and Catholic religion are particularly important for maintaining Polish identity alongside EU membership.

Cecylia's daughter lived and worked in Germany for several years as a physical therapist, but has since returned home to Wrocław because she missed her family. Unable to find work as a physical therapist, her daughter now works in accounting for a large supermarket chain. She dislikes her job and complains that she cannot earn enough to have a life that is "middle-class." Cecylia is thrilled that her daughter has returned, not understanding how one could live so far away from one's family. Abroad, she said, one can meet acquaintances (*znajomi*) and colleagues (*koledzy*), but not true friends (*przyjaciele*) or family (*rodzina*). She asked, "If something were to go wrong, on whom could one count?" Being away from family and from Poland creates deep instability and uncertainty for Cecylia.

Implicit in Cecylia's comments is the idea that building close relationships takes time, an impossibility in light of her daughter's short stay in Germany. Yet more than time is required, as another story shows. Cecylia's cousin moved to Canada with her husband and small children, leaving Poland on the eve of martial law in 1981. She tells Cecylia that she still longs for Poland, crying into her pillow at night as she dreams of her true home. For Cecylia, this is further evidence that Poles should not move abroad because there they lack true friendships and kin relations. Yet her cousin has family in Canada: though her husband has passed away, her children and now grandchildren live there. This is why she will not move back, despite tears on her pillowcase for almost thirty years. Cecylia's cousin's sadness, her daughter's return to Poland, and Cecylia's own anxiety all privilege physical closeness to consanguinal, rather than affinal, kin relations and ancestral connections, both of which suggest a strong desire for continuity with the past. Such emphasis on the past echoes Alicja's and others' narratives focused on ancestral connections.

Cecylia's concern about progeny living and working abroad, common among older Poles, has another side: she and others are often very proud of these same relatives. Older Poles boasted to me about their children's and grandchildren's lives abroad as evidence of success. The public arena also reflects this ambivalence about life abroad, as evident in conversations and newspaper articles about "*Eurosieroty*" ("Euro-orphans")[11] and the television series "*Londyńczycy*" ("Londoners").[12] Cecylia's and other Poles' pride and anxieties reveal values towards certain types of kinship ties and reflect ambivalence about a new set of life conditions connected to Poland's EU membership.

The University of the Third Age and @ctive Senior

Though emigration is often a point of tension for older Poles, for some people Poland's EU membership signals a possibility to create a new moral ideal of aging. Through gerontology lectures and published materials, the UTW encourages attendees to make aging a positive, active, and creative time when one can learn new subject materials and skills and form new friendships. Participants consciously adopt the self-fulfillment logic espoused by the UTW, thereby fashioning a new form of personhood based on the goal of self-actualization. Though this goal is individual, the process through which this self-fulfillment occurs is fundamentally social. Common to many Polish cities, the Wrocław UTW offers lecture series, seminars, classes, and workshops on a variety of topics (e.g., physics, languages, computers, dance, sailing, etc.). People who attend the UTW are generally younger, healthier, more highly educated, and overwhelmingly upbeat when compared to the population at the rehabilitation center.[13] They describe their current lives as active, busy, and fulfilling, often saying that they are just as busy as when they were working. In particular, women describe the UTW as creating opportunities for them "to do something for themselves" ("*robić coś dla siebie*") for the first time in their lives, now that they do not have to work, take care of elderly parents, or raise their own young children (though many do have grandchild-rearing responsibilities). This understanding of aging and the person stems largely from ideological work done by university and community leaders that is directly connected to EU membership.[14]

One such leader is the former director of the UTW, Walentyna Wnuk, a retired professor of andragogy (the science of teaching adults) and a current adviser to the mayor on seniors' affairs. She is trained as a "cultural organizer" (*"kulturalny animator"*) and sees herself as skilled in helping people achieve their potential. She is active in EFOS (European Federation of Older Students at Universities), an international coalition of Universities of the Third Age. This group's goals, as described on their English-language brochure, are to "activate elderly people, integrate them in the learning society and stimulate the intercultural dialogue as a transfer medium. In this way we will contribute to an active citizenship of the elderly people." This professor used similar vocabulary when describing her work, such as organized trips for students of the UTW to meet with their representative in the European Parliament in Brussels and Strasbourg. These trips were transformative, she said, because they changed the minds of people who were against Poland's EU membership. Older Poles need to learn to be "open," she said, in direct contrast to the socialist past, when society, and presumably persons, were "closed." Through educational programming and social organizing, this professor aims to create a new model of aging and a new type of person—a "Euro-senior" (*"Eurosenior"*)—who is appropriate to the current world order.

The second such community leader is a businessman, Marek Ferenc, who works at a center that provides support and resources for non-governmental organizations and who ran a pilot program in 2008 called "*@ktywny Senior*" ("@ctive Senior"). He developed this idea partially based on his own observations of differences between North American and Polish experiences of aging. The *@ktywny Senior* program was his first such attempt to change older people's experiences and understandings of aging. In conjunction with a local medical clinic, he recruited people in one neighborhood by offering free ongoing medical screenings to retirees on the condition that they attend this program consisting of classes on healthy aging, communication, and computer skills (the emphasis on computers is evident in the "@" in the program's name). The primary goal was to create "activity" ("*aktywność*") through teaching such concepts and practices as a "responsible lifestyle," "the negative consequences of an irresponsible lifestyle," and "social integration." Responsibility is needed, he said, because older Poles expect medical care to come from doctors and pills rather than from preventive care. Social integration is necessary, he said, because after 1989 many older people were forced to retire early and therefore were excluded from the computerization of society that occurred in the 1990s. Older people feel "unnecessary," he said, so it is necessary to help them become part of society. At the end of the program, participants were encouraged to come up with slogans to represent experiences and ideals of aging. Most striking is the slogan "seniors are people too" (*"seniorzy też ludzie"*), referencing the discrimination and dehumanization that many older Poles feel (see also Lynch, this volume, for similar feelings among some U.S. older adults).

Both Ferenc and Wnuk are working towards transforming both older persons, making them more "active" and "open," and the role of older people in Polish society, making them less "isolated" and more "integrated." Their attempts to align themselves with the EU and its values are reflected in these community leaders' use of the same words to describe changes in Poland following EU membership. The participants in both *@ktywny Senior* and the UTW also use similar transformative language to describe changes in their lives based on their experiences in these programs, suggesting that this ideological work is at least partially successful.

Such language echoes ideals of postsocialist self-transformation that other scholars of postsocialism have identified and analyzed (cf. Dunn 2004; Fehérváry 2002). Inherent in these transformative attempts are new moral ideals based on self-knowledge and self-responsibility that consciously break with the socialist past and aim for the future (and the "West"). Often assuming a binary model of personhood that is either collectivist or individualist, and connected with false ideas of "transition" from socialism to capitalism, these new ideals do represent continuity, at least inasmuch as these individualist ideals are accomplished through social relations. As Cecilia's understanding of personal, national, and European identities suggests, such transformations in persons are complex processes of memories of the past and hopes for the future that illustrate the individual, social, and political aspects of the life course.

Conclusion

Attempts by community leaders, UTW attendees, and permanent residents of the rehabilitation center to transform experiences and ideals of aging center on the moral aspects of these ideals. Such variety of efforts suggests that there is no agreed-upon moral ideal of aging in Poland. Despite this state of flux, there are certain common elements that shape such moral ideals: place of residence and expectations for the future, proximity of kin and the strength of ties of relatedness, and material and ideological effects of national transformations all intertwine in experiences of aging. Ever-present in this tangle of persons, places, and ideas are memories of personal and national pasts that impinge upon present experiences and ideals of aging. These spatiotemporal, social, political, and historical factors join together in both the complex suffering of illness and institutional living, and the earnest efforts at self-actualization, that characterize many older Poles' lives.

Acknowledgments

This research was supported by grants and fellowships from the Wenner-Gren Foundation (Dissertation Fieldwork Grant #7736); the National Science Foundation (DDIG #0819259); and, at the University of Michigan, the Center for European Studies, the Center for Russian and East European Studies, the Department of Anthropology, and the Rackham Graduate School. Thank you to this volume's editors, Jason Danely and Caitrin Lynch, and the anonymous reviewers for critical guidance on this manuscript. This research was made possible by the overwhelming kindness of many individuals and institutions in Poland, whose names, for confidentiality purposes, I cannot include here.

Notes

1. All names are pseudonyms, except for those of public figures. All conversations were in Polish and all translations in the chapter are mine. Unless otherwise noted, all examples and citations come from my fieldnotes and recalled experiences. I use the term "older" throughout this chapter and my research, rather than focusing on particular age groups, for two reasons. First, this reflects conventional Polish usage, in which people say "*starszy,*" or "older," rather than "*stary,*" or "old," which is perceived as rude. Second, old age appears as rather undifferentiated in the public sphere in Poland; that is, people from age fifty to one hundred are included within the term "older."
2. His brother fought for the *Armia Krajowa* (Home Army) during World War II, and like other former Home Army members, faced severe discrimination by the postwar Polish government.
3. I only had one opportunity to talk at length with Zbigniew because he was discharged soon after we met.
4. I conducted ethnographic research in Wrocław and Poznań from September 2008 through April 2010. I interviewed approximately 100 Poles (mostly over age sixty) in both cities, and conducted participant-observation at several institutions in each city. In Wrocław, my primary sites of research were a *Zakład Opiekuńczo-Leczniczy o profilu rehabilitacyjnym* (rehabilitation center) run by Catholic nuns, a *Dom Pomocy*

Społecznej dla osób przewlekłych somatycznie chorych (Social Aid Home for persons with chronic physical illnesses) run by the state, and the *Uniwersytet Trzeciego Wieku* (University of the Third Age). In Poznań, my primary sites of research were the *Środowiskowy Dom Samopomocy dla osób z chorobą Alzheimera* (Local self-help home for persons with Alzheimer's disease) and the *Uniwersytet Trzeciego Wieku*. In both cities, I also interviewed individuals who I met through these institutions (e.g., director of a home hospice program, local aging activists, and directors of senior centers and non-governmental organizations). I conducted multiple interviews with approximately twenty individuals, which, supplemented with informal conversations and observations, allowed me to construct life histories. The entire body of data that I collected includes fieldnotes, voice recordings, photographs (e.g., institutional and domestic interiors, institutional and public events, photo displays), documents (e.g., archive of journals and publications from the University of the Third Age in Wrocław, memoirs, institutional publicity materials, newspaper clippings), and objects (e.g., gifts, arts-and-crafts projects).

5. See Birdwell-Pheasant and Lawrence-Zúñiga 1999 and Norwood (this volume) for discussions of aging and place in Europe. See Cohen 1998 and Lamb (this volume), for discussions of aging and place in India, and Gamburd (this volume) for a discussion of the stigma of institutional living in Sri Lanka.

6. On average there are two to three times more women than men at the rehabilitation center. When I asked administrators, doctors, and patients about this difference, I received several explanations: men do not live as long; men die of their health problems rather than needing rehab; men are weaker and cannot endure the hardships of rehab. None of these explanations is sufficient to address these differences, but the comments themselves reveal assumptions about gendered experiences of aging in Poland.

7. See Porter-Szücs 2011 for an extensive historical analysis of the links between Catholicism and the Polish nation.

8. By personhood, I mean the morally significant and socioculturally created expectations and experiences of what it is to be a person.

9. My research shows that there is a gender difference as well, with older men having many fewer friends—sometimes even none—than older women do.

10. Legal work without a visa became possible for Poles in some EU countries after 2004 (see http://www.migrationinformation.org/Profiles/display.cfm?ID=800 for a list of those countries).

11. "Euro-orphans" refers to the phenomenon of one parent leaving Poland to work abroad, while the other parent and any children stay in Poland. When the parent who has emigrated does not return and does not send remittances home, there are hosts of economic, social, and familial problems, according to popular press.

12. This popular television show tells the stories of young Poles who moved to London for better economic opportunities, though they mostly work in low-skill, low-paying positions (e.g., bartenders, construction workers). Older Poles often criticize this show because they think the characters are misrepresentative of the recent emigration, which included many highly educated people, and because the characters engage in shameful behavior (e.g., drinking to excess, cheating on partners, stealing).

13. See Brown, this volume, and Greenberg and Muehlebach 2007, for discussions of the "Third Age" in Brazil and Western Europe respectively.

14. The UTW in Wrocław has existed since 1976. I was generously given all UTW publications since its founding and am conducting a textual analysis to determine the exact role of EU membership in this ideology. Although I suspect that this goal of self-actualization appeared in concert with post-1989 neoliberal trends in Poland and Eastern Europe, and that EU membership in 2004 crystallized the framing of these ideals, I am also studying the UTW's pre-1989 activities in order to understand other disciplinary, ideological, and historical connections than pre/post-1989. Thanks to Elżbieta Matynia for her discussion of the UTW, new forms of personhood, and neoliberalism.

6. A WINDOW INTO DUTCH LIFE AND DEATH
Euthanasia and End-of-Life in the Public-Private Space of Home

Frances Norwood

THIS CHAPTER EXPLORES TRANSITIONS RELATED to space and place as people use, manipulate, embrace, and push against physical and societal constraints, norms, and policies at the end of Dutch life. With the proliferation of life-saving technologies and medical interventions, hospitals and nursing homes around the world have come to dominate as primary end-of-life settings (Brodwin 2000; Gleckman 2009; Kaufman 2005; Lock, Young, and Cambrosio 2000). In the Netherlands, however, home has retained a foothold at the end of life with approximately one quarter of all deaths each year occurring in the home with the aid of an extensive system of home health care and regular house calls by general practitioners (Centraal Bureau voor de Statistiek 2004; Norwood 2009).[1]

Home marks a significant place in life and at the end of life in various cultural contexts (Birdwell-Pheasant and Lawrence Zúñiga 1999; de Certeau, Giyard, and Mayol 1998; Rapoport 1969; Ronald and Alexy 2011; Rowles and Chaudhury 2005; Rybczynski 1986). In the Netherlands, home is where public and private converge, mediated by the very particular way Dutch people often use their windows and by end-of-life care that enters the home in the form of euthanasia policy and discussions. Dutch homes are unusual in that front windows are prominent and frequently left unobstructed, giving the passersby a view into the homes and lives of many Dutch families across the country (Cieraad 1999; Rybczynski 1986; Vera 1989). In addition, home is where the majority of euthanasia cases occur in the country with the longest-standing legal practice of euthanasia (physician terminating a life at that person's explicit request for reasons of lasting and unbearable suffering) and assisted suicide (physician providing a person the means to terminate that person's own life for reasons of lasting and unbearable suffering). This chapter is about how and where individuals may adhere to or break free from constraints imposed by illness, aging, and culture. It is about how Dutch people negotiate end of life in relation to two of the major ways that culture enters the home—through the prominent Dutch window and via euthanasia policy. Using data gathered during a fifteen-month ethnographic study of death and dying in the home and nursing home between 1999 and 2001, I explore the intersections of public and private life at the end of life as they converge in the typical Dutch home.[2]

To better understand how a window and a policy impact Dutch life, I borrow Michel de Certeau's concept of "spatial practices." De Certeau argues that spatial practices are something that you do not necessarily see. They are "networks of these moving, intersecting writings [which] compose a manifold story that has neither author nor spectator, shaped out of fragments of trajectories and alterations of spaces" (de Certeau 1984: 93). Spatial practices are those practices in relation to built environments that are both determining (disciplinary space that structures how space is used) and allow for human agency, creativity, and resistance—transformative practices that in spite of the structure continue to elude discipline (de Certeau 1984: 98). De Certeau equates spatial practices with a speech act and suggests that walking is to the structuring city as a speech act is to language. He writes:

> If it is true that a spatial order organizes an ensemble of possibilities (e.g., by a place in which one can move) and interdictions (e.g., by a wall that prevents one from going further), then the walker actualizes some of these possibilities. In that way, he makes them exist as well as emerge. But he also moves them about and he invents others, since the crossing, drifting away, or improvisation of walking privilege, transform or abandon spatial elements. Thus Charlie Chaplin multiplies the possibilities of his cane: he does other things with the same thing and he goes beyond the limits that the determinants of the object set on its utilization. In the same way, the walker transforms each spatial signifier into something else. And if on the one hand he actualizes only a few of the possibilities fixed by the constructed order (he goes only here and not there), on the other he increases the number of possibilities (for example, by creating shortcuts and detours) and prohibitions (for example, he forbids himself to take paths generally considered accessible or even obligatory). He thus makes a selection. (de Certeau 1984: 98)

For the Dutch person who comes home to die, she too is structured by the spaces in which she finds herself—a declining body, a home transformed by illness. But just like de Certeau's walker, she makes creative choices within the constraints of a dying body and a dying space, transforming the number of possibilities by "creating shortcuts and detours." Using ethnographic vignettes from my research, I want to highlight some of the more typical transitions and transformations that take place in relation to spatial practices at the end of Dutch life.

FIGURE 6.1 Photo by Nicole Marshall, printed with permission.

Through the Window: The Public-Private Space of Home

A prominent feature in any city or town in the Netherlands is the broad and open windows of many homes that offer a largely unobstructed view from the street into the front rooms of the house. The window may be framed by lace, adorned with art, or sometimes ornamented with a semi-opaque strip across the bottom part of the window to partially block visual access to the interior. At night when the home is lit up from within, the curtains are left open to clearly display glimpses of Dutch home life to anyone who passes by. Through the meticulously clean window, the public is allowed to enter the Dutch home, creating what researchers call a "semi-public space" within the front interior of the typical Dutch house (Vera 1989: 225).

Privacy has not always been associated with the concept of home in Europe. Medieval homes were often live-work spaces left open to the public on the ground floor. It was not until the seventeenth century that private space came to be a central feature of the Dutch home (Rybczynski 1986: 15–49). While the front of the home remained open to the public, at least visually, through the large Dutch windows that dominated the seventeenth-century façade, the hearth at the back of home, the ground floor garden, and the upstairs floors marked the newly privatized space—space that is often described in Dutch terms as "*gezellig*" or warm and cozy. Historian Geert Mak writes, "The dual nature of this domesticity was to characterize the city for centuries to come: on the one hand the cordial openness of the merchant who meets his customers in the front house and will close neither shutters nor curtains at night, on the other, the contained, private life of the inner hearth, that curious atmosphere which the Dutch delineate with the word *gezelligheid*, the snugness which is soft on the inside and hard on the outside" (2000: 29).

The exact onset of this open window culture, and why it has continued into present day, is less than clear. Some suggest it may be based on a collective ideal that has been linked to the Dutch Reformation of the sixteenth and seventeenth centuries (Horst 2001; Schama 1987; Vera 1989). Sociologist Hernan Vera found indications that open window culture may well have originated with the Reformation and the influx of strict views around predestination linked with Protestant Calvinism. By leaving one's windows with an unobstructed view into the home, Dutch people could display to their neighbors their chosen place in the community. Vera also found reference to open window culture following World War II, cited as a "collective and protracted reaction" to the forced covering of windows during the war (1989: 219–20). Social historian Han van der Horst suggests that the practice of keeping one's home life on display may well be a modern-day cultural response to social pressures to act in ways that do not communicate excess or overt individuality. The phrase often heard today is *"doe maar ge-woon, dan doe je al gek genoeg,"* which is translated to mean, "be normal, that is crazy enough" (Horst 2001: 214). It is a phrase invoked when describing what is "typically Dutch" and it serves as a reminder that there is an aspect to Dutch culture that emphasizes conformity to the group standard epitomized by this long-standing tradition of an open window culture.

Regardless of the exact origins, at least two consequences have evolved as a result of these curtainless spatial practices. First, there is a space within the typical Dutch home that can be characterized as semi-public. The public does not stop at the façade of the home, the front hall, or the entryway, as it does in most European homes. Instead, the eyes of the Dutch public enter unannounced through the Dutch window to view their neighbor's possessions and the flow of home life.

Once you enter these homes and live in these open front rooms you quickly come to notice a second important consequence of the Dutch window—private life as public performance. Just as in Erving Goffman's example of the man who prepares his social face when approaching the front door of a house, I too came to manage my own expression as I approached a Dutch home and as I lived within the semi-public space at the front of the house (1959: 8–16). Living and working in Dutch homes, I initially had the eerie sensation of knowing my activities were visually on display. Over time, however, I came to feel comforted and connected somehow, knowing that I could be seen and could myself view the street scene outside my window. In the Dutch home, the window mediates the flow of culture from society to family, offering gradations of public and private. Swedish anthropologist Ulf Hannerz writes:

> [Dutch windows] offer the sensation of great openness: culture flows through these windows, as it were, from private to public spaces and vice versa. It may be a conspicuous claim that "I have something to trade," made by a scantily dressed young woman in a window framed by red neon lights; or, simply and piously, that "we have nothing to hide," in the instance of the elderly couple glimpsed through the next window, with their backs turned, lace curtains not drawn. Through the window the market displays its goods, and forms of life other than one's own can be inspected, at least surreptitiously, in passing. And this is a two-way flow, for windows also allow you to keep an eye on the street scene. (2000: 176)

Clearly, "Dutch private" is not exactly private. Instead it is porous, allowing for gradations of semi-public space that impacts how people use their homes, even within the home. There is an aspect of a collective ideal that permeates even Dutch private life, impacting many of the transformations that occur in the home near the end of life. The following is a look at how public and private meet as people age and grow ill in the space of home.

Aging in the Public-Private Space of Home

In a country that is based on a collective ideal, it is perhaps not surprising that the Dutch home is permeated by gradations of both public and private. When people become seriously ill in the Netherlands, but not so ill that they must relocate to a nursing home, it is typical for them to stay on the ground floor in a bed or hospital bed situated in the den or sitting room overlooking—for those who can afford this coveted space—the back garden. Rarely did I ever see seriously ill family members sequestered in the privacy of an upstairs bedroom. Instead, ill family members slept on the ground floor, keeping them central within intimate family space and just beyond the reach of the semi-public front rooms of the home. The follow-

FIGURE 6.2
Photo by Nicole Marshall, printed with permission.

ing vignette introduces public and semi-public spatial practices around the Dutch window, demonstrating how some Dutch people use open window culture as a spatial practice related to aging and living with chronic illness in the home.

> ***Through the Dutch Window.*** *One morning on a house call with Kees, a home-care nursing assistant, we visited one of my favorite Dutch families. This family, not exactly typical of many I visited, highlighted in exaggerated form several key aspects of family life in relation to the Dutch window. My first indication that this might not be the typical Dutch home and family came on our bike ride up to the house. Kees tells me as we pull up and park our bicycles that this is one of his "zwaar [literally, heavy] addresses." I contemplate what that might mean as we walk up and I see a woman, probably in her fifties, smoking a cigarette outside the front door. She lets us in. Mr. and Mrs. van der Vries, the man and woman of the house and the reason for our visit, are seated with family and friends around their dining room table, which is situated facing the large front window of their home. Mr. van der Vries, in his nineties, is no longer able to move around on his own, but likes to participate in the activities of the home. He has been getting pressure sores where his wheelchair supports his legs and Kees is here to change his leg bandages and dress his open wounds. Mrs. van der Vries is still mobile but has been getting some swelling in her legs.*
>
> *We walk up to the dining room table, where Mr. and Mrs. van der Vries and several of their friends are seated with a direct sightline of the street. The window, I note at the time, is almost like an interactive television, with moving people and images that the room's participants watch. Every now and then the window-television talks back as someone in the room points out a neighbor and they exchange waves just a few yards from each other, mediated only by the glass of the window. A radio is blaring and Mrs. van der Vries is swaying to the music as she catches up on the latest gossip with her friends. Mrs. van der Vries asks where I am from as Kees gets to work on Mr. van der Vries' biggest wound. Mr. van der Vries says "ow, ow, ow" as Kees removes the bandages and I hear the woman who let us in call someone a "trut [a bitch]." I introduce myself as a researcher from the U.S. and Mr. van der Vries says, "Ah, you are from America," and "that's good because Americans helped liberate Holland after The War." Another woman enters from the street and again I am introduced as the American. Mr. van der Vries is turning ninety-two tomorrow and they are planning his birthday party. I help Kees measure the size of the pressure sore (it's gotten bigger). Kees then bandages Mr. van der Vries' leg and checks the swelling on Mrs. van der Vries' legs before we prepare to go. The radio is blaring and as we leave Mrs. van der Vries raises a hand to wave to a passerby on the other side of the window.*

The van der Vries vignette is an exaggerated example of how Dutch people use their windows. Their window behavior was out of the ordinary, not because they were using the window as a means to view and comment on their neighbors, but because they made it *obvious* what they were doing.

By arranging their chairs and the dining room table to face the street, they violated the unspoken rule of the Dutch window: to look but not engage (Vera 1989: 223–4). Most elderly people I visited would have their chairs positioned so they were not facing the street, but cattycorner to the window (sideways but facing slightly into the room), thus appearing to visitors and passersby as if they were just going about their own business. Rooms in nursing homes (spaces I came to think of as arranged to re-create the idealized space of home) were typically decorated with furniture from home and almost always included one or two upholstered chairs situated cattycorner to the large picture window that often overlooked a canal or pond. When elderly residents were not in bed, this sitting space was often where the doctor and I would find them. But just as the Dutch window allows those outside the home to unobtrusively observe within, those outside quickly learn that they too are being watched. I remember one house call, for example, in which the woman we visited pointed out that she had put her teeth in when she saw us come up the walk, indicating to me that our approach to the house had not gone unobserved.

Looking at window culture as a spatial practice suggests that across the life course the Dutch public is poised to enter the home in various ways. Window culture communicates a collective ideal, where Dutch participants both put their "private" home life on display for others to witness, and in turn hold their neighbors surreptitiously accountable for their own displays in the public and semi-public space of street and front home. Dutch people may also transform this structuring element of Dutch life by adapting or resisting window culture. For some, this means choosing not to participate in open window culture, letting private be private, for others, like the van der Vrieses, this means using window culture for their own altered purposes.

For persons who are elderly and aging in the Netherlands, window culture offers a type of public contact at a time when they may be less able to participate in biking, *boodschappen* (errands), and other hobbies and activities outside of the home. While loneliness remains a factor, especially for those who become isolated in nursing homes or from family and friends (Horst 2001: 230), "public" enters the Dutch home not just through the window, but also through a vast system of social welfare and healthcare policies. Thuiszorg, the national Dutch Homecare Agency, offers nursing and personal care in the home up to four times a day on a sliding scale fee or free of charge to those who cannot afford it. Homecare services available through Thuiszorg include assistance with medications, meals, wound care, incontinence, self care, home modifications, and housekeeping. Overnight respite, where a personal care attendant stays overnight to give the family a chance to sleep, is also available. In addition to nursing and personal care attendants, general practitioners have a long-standing tradition of house calls. According to my research, on average seven out of twenty-eight patient visits by Dutch general practitioners each day are house calls to the home or nursing home (Norwood 2009: 131). The Dutch public enters the home to such an extent in the Netherlands that one of the most frequent complaints I heard from families was of too many "strangers" in the home, referring to the number of visits by home health employees near the end of life.

Another key way the Dutch public enters the home is via euthanasia policy. The Dutch government legalized euthanasia and assisted suicide by court decision in 1984 and by law in 2002. Since 1984, Dutch citizens have had access to assistance in dying and the majority of people (87 percent) who choose euthanasia receive it in the home or nursing home (Onwuteaka-Philpsen et al. 2007: 99; Griffiths, Weyers, and Adams 2008:167).[3] The following section describes what happens when the Dutch public enters the home in the form of spatial practices around requests for euthanasia.

FIGURE 6.3
Photo by Thil
Lapikas-van
Schothorst,
printed with
permission.

Euthanasia and Dutch Privacy at the End of Life

For someone with a serious illness or a terminal prognosis, it is not uncommon for euthanasia to be considered as an end-of-life option, but only rarely does it occur as a life-ending act. In 2001, the final year of my study, nearly 25 percent of persons who died initiated euthanasia discussions, yet only one in ten who initiated discussions died by euthanasia or assisted suicide. Compared to the number of people who die each year in the Netherlands, the percentage of euthanasia deaths is low. In 2001, approximately 2.8 percent of all deaths (3,931 persons) could be attributed to euthanasia or assisted suicide and in 2005 that number dropped to 1.8 percent (or 2,455 persons) (Onwuteaka-Philipsen et al. 2007: 100).

What has evolved from end-of-life policies in the Netherlands is a practice that is largely based in talk—a discussion that rarely ends in a euthanasia death. "Euthanasia talk" is frequently invoked at the end of Dutch life, filling in the spaces left by the lost or diminishing ability people have at the end of life to participate in social life outside of the home. The Dutch home at the end of life is already full with the presence of the Dutch public with home-care employees and home visits by general practitioners. But once euthanasia talk is invoked, the Dutch public presence in the home increases—with frequent home visits and discussions orchestrated by the general practitioner with patients and their families around a person's request for euthanasia (Norwood 2009: 30).

Euthanasia occurring largely as a talk-based practice is not unusual in a country that emphasizes a collective ideal. The Dutch have a practice that they often use for collective decision making, called *overleg. Overleggen* means "to consider, consult, or confer" (Hannay and Schrama 1996: 609), but the literal translation of the word does not adequately describe the nuance and the prevalence of this practice in Dutch life. From the office to social groups, *overleg* is a commonly used practice for consensus building and decision making (Norwood 2009: 42). When euthanasia talk is initiated, the role of the physician increases markedly as physicians use euthanasia talk to establish whether a patient's

FIGURE 6.4 Photo by Frances Norwood.

request meets the requirements for due care.[4] But in addition to its most obvious purpose—planning for an assisted death—patients, families, and physicians also use euthanasia talk to negotiate Dutch ways of living in the midst of dying. At the point where most medical interventions stop, euthanasia talk endures, maintaining and extending social connections and social roles even at the end of life. The following vignette shows how the Dutch public enters the home at the end of life in the form of euthanasia talk.

Euthanasia Talk. *I met Mrs. de Jong at the beginning of my study. She was an 82-year-old widow living at home alone with the help of Thuiszorg and her daughter and granddaughter who visited frequently. The year before we met, Mrs. de Jong had fallen and was taken to the hospital where doctors diagnosed her with cancer of the lower intestines and liver and an aneurysm (a blockage in her aorta that was growing and as it grew pushed on her esophagus making it increasingly difficult to swallow). Her general practitioner, Dr. Westerman, explained to me that her cancer was inoperable at this point and her aneurysm could burst at any time, which would probably result in a fairly peaceful death. Until then she would be treated for increasing pain and discomfort from the pressure on her esophagus and as a result of her cancer. When I met her in September 2000, she was in some pain, had not been able to eat or drink for several weeks, and was losing weight. At that time she asked for euthanasia from Dr. Westerman, explaining to us that "there isn't anything to be happy about anymore" and that she "can't do anything for people anymore."[5] Her life had become no longer meaningful to her and she worried about being a burden on her daughter. She was in pain and she was tired. For three weeks, Dr. Westerman, Mrs. de Jong, and her adult daughter talked about her euthanasia request. Mrs. de Jong put her request in writing, making a formal euthanasia declaration that, like all the other requests I saw, was also signed by family members, in this case, her daughter. She had to raise the request several times before her doctor proceeded to schedule an appointment for a second opinion. The second doctor agreed to the request and a date for her euthanasia death was scheduled, but like most euthanasia requests the euthanasia death did not happen. On the day of her scheduled death, Mrs. de Jong's daughter asked her mother to cancel it, explaining that she was not ready to lose her mother. Mrs. de Jong agreed.*

I visited Mrs. de Jong and her daughter over the course of the year following her canceled euthanasia request. She was able to eat again, but it was difficult, and she often complained of pain (for which she received morphine), benauwdheid (a word for both emotional anxiety and a physical tightness of the chest, for which she received Prozac), and of being just plain tired (for which there was no cure). Dr. Westerman and I visited one day to find Mrs. de Jong sitting in the upholstered chair in the front window of the house; the sliding doors to her makeshift bedroom overlooking the back garden where we normally visited her were closed. I had never seen Mrs. de Jong sitting up before, but Dr. Westerman told me afterwards that she did that when she wasn't tired. There she was with her small frame perched in the chair, her light, wispy gray hair and sagging jowls. She smiled an absolutely radiant smile as she and Dr. Westerman flirted back and forth over niceties. Dr. Westerman, an older gentleman with a playful manner, had a great way with many of his patients and Mrs. de Jong was no exception. "How are you feeling," Dr. Westerman asks. "I have terrible benauwdheid," *she says, and "have been very tired." Dr. Westerman wants her to show him how she uses her new inhaler, which is sitting next to her pack of Camel cigarettes on the table at her side. She obediently demonstrates for him how she uses the inhaler and Dr. Westerman shows her how to take deeper breaths with it. He mentions the cigarettes and that they are not good for her; she says, "Yes, I know you have to say that." She says she just plays with the cigarette and doesn't really inhale. Dr. Westerman says, "Show me," and she picks one up and lights it like an old-time smoker, taking one draw, then another. Dr. Westerman says, "You're inhaling." "Really?" she asks. The doctor listens to her lungs with his stethoscope, then pops a* snoepje *(candy) into his mouth from the jar by her chair and offers one to me. So, you had a question for Mrs. de Jong, he says, turning to me. "Yes," I say, "I was wondering if you are okay with your decision not to go through with euthanasia?" "Ja," she says, "I do regret not going through with it, especially at night when I am miserable and wish I were dead. But when my granddaughter and my family visit, it is different." "Then," she says, "I am happy with my decision."*

The practice of euthanasia runs deep at the end of Dutch life and much of what it is I cannot begin to touch on in this short chapter.[6] Focusing on euthanasia talk as a spatial practice, however, I can at least say two things. First, the Dutch have deeply embedded cultural practices for home death, which even in the private spaces in the back of the home are firmly permeated by the public domain. Dutch people for the most part do not die alone. Prior to the end of life, Dutch people live with their home life on display to the larger community. As people get sick and approach end of life, however, they often shift from the semi-public rooms in the front of the home to the rooms at the back of the home, but they almost always stay on the main floor of the home in the center of communal family space. Of all the homes I visited, in only one did I find someone sleeping on the top floor of the home, sequestered in a bedroom away from the daily flow of family life. When euthanasia is invoked, the Dutch public enters the home in the form of the general practitioner, who orchestrates family meetings and repeated doctor-patient discussions around the request for euthanasia. This means that even when planning for an early departure from life, the Dutch have created a practice that emphasizes and maintains social connections and social supports.

Through euthanasia talk and euthanasia deaths, Dutch people have produced a spatial practice, just like de Certeau's "walker," that alters and transforms end of life. For the one in ten each year who request euthanasia and do, in fact, die by euthanasia in the Netherlands, individuals have found a way to use public euthanasia policy and practices to alter the timing and course of death. Medical sociologist Clive Seale suggests that euthanasia is a social response from dying persons who wish to have the biological death of the body more closely coincide with the death of the social being (Seale 1998: 7–8). But the fact that most people experience euthanasia as talk suggests that there is more to euthanasia than simply a realignment of the timing of death for the social and physical bodies.

For Mrs. de Jong, like many who engaged in euthanasia talk, her ultimate decision was to live with the understanding that euthanasia remained an option. For her, the choice to remain living was rooted in her connection to family—her daughter and granddaughter. Yet, through her standing request, she had something she needed—an emotional insurance policy of sorts, an "out" in case the suffering became too great or her daughter's stance against her request changed.

The consequence of how euthanasia talk has emerged is powerful. In spatial practice, euthanasia talk, even when it does not end in euthanasia death, offers dying persons an alternate route through end of life. For the dying person, euthanasia talk offers a way to emotionally manage fear, uncertainty, and isolation caused by the often-chaotic course of an end-of-life illness. It gives all participants (patients, families, and physicians) an active role at a time when roles are often at best unclear and at worst diminishing. Euthanasia talk offers an ideal image of death that can be used by families to manage the difficult realities of daily decline and loss and to reaffirm family and societal connections. Ultimately, euthanasia talk has emerged as a practice that affirms and maintains social bonds, keeping people connected to Dutch life even as they die at home. From the window to euthanasia policy, the Dutch public enters the home and with these tools, Dutch people alter, transform, and push against biological and social forms of life and death.

This transformation of end-of-life through euthanasia policy serves as a modern-day response to the intrusion of culture. The act of euthanasia is, in essence, where Dutch society has been able to take illness back from culture to restore some semblance of a "natural" ideal. Working against the preponderance of medical interventions and technologies typical of end of life around the world (Brodwin 2000; Kaufman 2005), Dutch people have been able to reclaim end of life from sterile hospitals and intrusive medical interventions. Euthanasia policy in the Netherlands has allowed the Dutch to replace the image of an isolating, highly medicalized trajectory with an ideal image where family members are assembled bedside in the home and the loved one slips painlessly into death with the help of the physician. The fact that euthanasia deaths rarely occur in reality does not seem to matter. But while this image may be based on a "natural" ideal where machines and interventions do not dominate the end of life, the act of euthanasia clearly is not natural. It is more than simply unplugging machines and withdrawing interventions; it is replacing one cultural intervention with another.

In the Dutch home, illness, aging, policy, and culture strike a delicate balance between public and private. Constraints of chronic illness and disease dictate a transition of individuals from semi-public space in the front of the home to more private space in the back of the home. But for those who die at home in the Netherlands, it is rare for someone to truly die alone. Even at the end of Dutch life, sociality to some degree is maintained and there exist choices even among the constraints imposed by the end of life.

Acknowledgments

Funding for this research was provided by the University of California-San Francisco, University of California-Berkeley, the Netherland-America Foundation, and the American Association of Netherlandic Studies.

Notes

1. In 2003, approximately one third of all persons who died in the Netherlands that year died in the hospital; more than one-quarter died at home and one-fifth died in either a residential/nursing, elder care, or acute care nursing facility (*verzorgingshuis, bejaardenhuis*, or *verpleeghuis*). The remaining died in other locations (CBS 2004). In contrast, in 2001, 57 percent of Americans died in hospitals, 20 percent died at home, and 17 percent died in nursing homes (Brumley 2002).

2. This chapter is the result of a fifteen-month study of euthanasia and home death in the Netherlands between 1999 and 2001 that included observation and field-based interviews with 15 physicians (13 general practitioners and 2 nursing home physicians) and 650 of their general population patients based in Amsterdam and in a cluster of small towns outside of Amsterdam. Observations with physicians occurred in the physician's office and on house calls to the home and nursing home, including acute-care facilities (*verpleeghuizen*), nursing homes (*verzorgingshuizen*), elder-care facilities (*bejaardenhuizen*), and independent living situations (*aanleuningwoning*). Intensive case study research was conducted with ten general practitioners and twenty-five of their end-of-life patients (fourteen with euthanasia requests and eleven without). Case studies included multiple observations, interviews (audiotaped and not taped) with patients, family members, close friends, physicians, and home care employees over the course of the study. In addition, observation was conducted with Amsterdam *Thuiszorg*, the national Dutch home care organization, and interviews were conducted with more than thirty-five experts in Dutch culture and end-of-life care. For more on the original study, see Norwood 2009.

3. In 2005, general practitioners carried out 87 percent of all euthanasia deaths in the Netherlands (Onwuteaka-Philpsen et al. 2007: 99; Griffiths, Weyers, and Adams 2008: 167). General practitioners work in the home, nursing home (*verzorgingshuis*), elder-care facility (*bejaardenhuis*), and independent living situations (*aanleuningwoning*). They do not typically work in acute-care facilities (*verpleeghuizen*).

4. According to the 2002 *Termination of Life on Request and Assisted Suicide (Review Procedures) Act* (Article 293, 294, 40), euthanasia and assisted suicide must always be performed by a physician who (a) holds the conviction that the request by the patient was voluntary and well-considered; (b) holds the conviction that the patient's suffering was lasting and unbearable; (c) has informed the patient about the situation he was in and about his prospects; (d) the patient holds the conviction that there was no other reasonable solution for the situation he was in; (e) has consulted at least one other, independent physician who has seen the patient and has given his written opinion on the requirements of due care, referred to in parts a–d; and (f) has terminated a life or assisted in a suicide with due care.

5. Maintaining a meaningful role in life is a key aspect that dominates what patients talk about at the end of life. For a discussion of how older adults find meaning and a sense of "mattering" through doing things for others, see also Lynch in this volume.

6. For more on euthanasia and how it is practiced in the Netherlands, see Norwood 2009.

7. TEMPORALITY, SPIRITUALITY, AND THE LIFE COURSE IN AN AGING JAPAN

Jason Danely

> Time will say nothing but I told you so,
> Time only knows the price we have to pay;
> If I could tell you I would let you know.
> —W.H. Auden, "Villanelle"

MOST DAYS, THE MAIN ENTRANCE to the Takara Senior Welfare Center is half-hidden behind a line of clean white vans parked beneath a large, concrete staircase. The vans provide transportation each day for a majority of the twenty to thirty older adults, many in their nineties and older, who attend the Adult Day Service Center located on the building's first floor. Day centers like Takara are common throughout Kyoto City, providing a much needed respite service for children or other relatives caring for older adults and for elders living alone or with limited mobility. Nonetheless, staff at all three of the day centers I visited during my fieldwork research in Kyoto from 2005 to 2007 complained of understaffing and a dependence on regular volunteers to truly meet the need in their community.

Staff at the Takara Day Center expressed interest in the research I had been conducting on aging and spirituality in Japan, and welcomed me as a regular volunteer at the center, adding that a few of the patrons have traveled abroad or speak a little English and might find it interesting to talk with me. When at the center, I did what I could to assist the staff and other volunteers: drying hair and feet, trimming toenails, and shaving the men as they came out of the bath. I helped distribute cups of warm or cool tea and aided patrons who needed help with finding reading materials and using the toilet. Unlike the staff, I found a lot of time to simply sit and chat with patrons. Takara is a municipally managed institution with no religious affiliation (in fact the center's rules explicitly forbid religious activities or promotion). Yet traces of patrons' spiritual life could be found in the content of reminiscences that characterized our conversations, as well as in more subtle markers, such as the small brocaded protective talismans many had attached to their canes. On one visit to Takara, I struck up a conversation with Amano-san, a woman whom I would always see reading the newspaper rather than socializing with others. When I asked Amano-san what she was reading, she looked up from the page and responded:

Amano: Times have changed. My time is over. 100 years old!

Jason: You'll be 100 this year?

Amano: 97. After 3 years I'll be 100. One year is 365 days, so that is about 1000 days, right?

Jason: Yes.

Amano: Are there people who live a long time in America?

Jason: Well, yes, but not the same as in Japan.

Amano: How old do I look?

Jason: [genuinely] In your 80s?

Amano: I'm 97 years old. I'll be 100 in 3 years. [pause] One year is 365 days, so about 1000 days.

Jason: Does the time go by quickly?

Amano: [pause] How old do I look?

Jason: In your 80s?

Amano: [smiling] More!

Jason: 90?

Amano: More!

Jason: [now teasing] 91?

Amano: I am 97! After 3 years, I'll be 100. There's a friend of mine who is 107 years old. Still healthy! [pause] Do they have people who live a long time in America?

For Amano-san, and for many of the very old with whom I spoke at day centers, this kind of repetition lends a characteristic rhythm to everyday conversations, stitching together remarks on time and the self in wavelike patterns reminiscent of W.H. Auden's poem "Villanelle."[1] Like "Villanelle," the conversation expresses something about the mysterious experience of time as both linear (years, days, ages) and cyclical (indicated by repeated phrases). As Amano-san and I recycled over and over again through the fact that she was ninety-seven years old, new information or new expressions about that fact emerged, recreating the moment and drawing attention to them. In spite of the fragility of her short-term memory, or perhaps because of it, old age seemed to be experienced as a repeated moment, but new in each repetition. For most of the very old I spoke with at Takara and other centers, it was the pleasant memories and playful boasts that circulated most often, repeated again and again as if for the first time, and I never tired of hearing them however much they were repeated.

My conversation with Amano-san opens up a wider field of questions regarding time, experience, and the life course: What captivated Amano-san so much with her *age* at this point in her life course, when so many women her junior shy away from or joke about such matters? Was she indicating something in the spiraling pattern of her words about the milestones and aspirations that mark the Japanese sense of the life course? And why was it important to her that I *recognize* this—that I recognize *her*, as age and appearance—as she drew me into the conversation with her repeated query: "How old do I look?"

In order to understand the temporal world of older Japanese people like Amano-san, who feel their "time is over" but who nonetheless aspire towards living a long life, it is important to consider the cultural context that informs their perspectives on time and the entirety of the life course (Hazan 1984; Myerhoff 1984; Randall and Kenyon 2004; Seltzer and Hendricks 1986; Tsuji 2005). In his foundational article on culture and temporality, American anthropologist Irving Hallowell argued that not only is time experienced differently across societies, but also that temporal orientations are culturally constituted through the richly symbolic narratives that can be located in spirituality and myth (1937: 667–670). Following Hallowell, I argue that in Japan, the phenomenology of the life course emerges from social interactions involving mutual recognition with unseen spirits and invisible worlds that structure memories, aspirations, and emotions. Life courses, after all, are not necessarily limited to discrete individual selves, but might span across generations and include actors living and deceased, human and superhuman. It is this kind of thinking that I explore in this chapter, and which I believe has a particular impact on how anthropologists view the process of aging and the way it is situated within the life course.

During my fieldwork, I noticed that for many older Japanese adults, the individual life-course events, recollected from the perspective of later life, were embedded within larger life-cycle narratives that often included the spirits of the dead. These narratives became places to inhabit in later years, identities that were shored up by a faith in the world beyond and the benevolent watchfulness of the spirits of the dead (*hotoke*). Most people found it difficult to distinguish among the *hotoke*, the ancestors, and the gods; they are all intimately connected to the lives of people in this world (*kono yo*) as well as to nature (*daishizen*). In this way, I came to see the Japanese life course as operating by what essayist Edward Hoagland calls "continuity through conductivity," a kind of reanimation of life through "the electricity of empathy" (2009: 38), grounded in the seamless unity of nature (including the spirits of the dead, in the Japanese case).

I am attracted to Hoagland's phrasing because it presents an alternative vision to orthodox Buddhist conceptions of rebirth (cyclical time), as well as to the notion of absolute and infinite continuity of the ancestors (linear time). Rather, in Japan, ancestors are contingent entities, dependent on the charge of life that is perpetuated through practices of mutual recognition, such as giving (and receiving) offerings of food, water, and flowers at graves and altars. Anthropologist James Green argues that such remembrance and recognition creates spaces of imagined community, "past, present, and future—that we inhabit, if only in the mind" (2008: 157). Green continues, "Taken as a whole, memory is really a species of storytelling, one that is artful, strategic, and oriented toward both past and future" (2008: 157). Transformations of memory that occur through practices of memorial lead to transformations of recognition, and of places to inhabit, if only in imagination, as one grows older (see Taylor 2008).

Receiving and Returning a Life Course

Keeping time in old age is a moral activity, marking and recognizing past achievements and future aspirations in stories that are constantly being told, recorded, and compared (McAdams 2005). One community center I frequented in Kyoto had a communal notebook that all visitors were free to write in, but Morioka-san, a man who had been attending the center since it was opened in 1995, was one of the very few who had made any entries, including one in which he detailed the meanings of each auspicious year of old age according to Japanese custom.[2] Although his wife is too frail to attend the center, 89-year-old Morioka-san still goes there almost every day, often watching the busy goings-on of the others from a chair placed on the periphery. After seeing his note, I decided to ask him about his attitudes toward aging, asking him what he found most important (*ikigai*) at this point in his life. Immediately he replied, "Taking good care of my wife." After a short pause he added, "I also want to live to 100," and producing a pen and a notebook from his breast pocket he wrote the words "*Tenju wo mattou suru*," with a steady calligraphic precision, vertically down the page.

When talking with older adults about the life course in Japan, I often heard the phrase "*Tenju wo mattou suru*," or "living out one's natural life." This was a typical response to several of my inquiries about how long a person wanted to live, or what they considered to be an adequately long life. Aesthetic symbols celebrating a long life, such as the crane or the tortoise, proliferate in the artwork, poetry, and even garden landscaping of Kyoto, which had been the main seat of power in Japan for most of the last thirteen hundred years. The well-known congratulatory cry "Banzai!" literally means "[May you live] ten thousand years!"[3] (as in, "Long live the King!"), and is sometimes directly linked to centenarian celebrations in popular media, such as in the NHK Television ten-minute documentary series *Hyakusai, Banzai!* (*One Hundred Years Old, Banzai!*), which profiles inspiring stories of Japanese centenarians. But to live a *long* life, which, statistically speaking, the average Japanese person doubtlessly excels at, is not the same as "living out one's *natural* life," a phrase that seems to pronounce the individual life course as a small part of a larger cosmic destiny, its aims and meanings ultimately transcendent.[4]

Japanese adults like Morioka-san not only aspire to "live out a natural life" (sometimes referred to as "the life that has been given by the ancestors"), but also to eventually return this life to the social system through the generative life cycle that would make them ancestors as well. These aspirations are part of a larger moral script that transforms feelings of loss and dependence accompanying moral self-evaluations about becoming a "burden" (*meiwaku*) on others or "living too long" in old age. Morioka-san's desire to take care of his aging wife is just as much a part of his desire to live a natural life as other forms of cultivating interdependence and generativity. As sites of recognition, Japanese life-course narratives imply caring and being cared for, interdependence, and the need for trusted others who restore one's sense of identity in time (Norimoto 1962: 56–57; Traphagan 2004: 179–181; Woodward 1991: 87–88). This aspiration towards interdependence is particularly important for the growing number of older Japanese adults contemplating uncertain family support, coping with the pain of grief, and finding ways to assign hope to their experience.

The phrase "natural life" was occasionally prefaced by "god-given," (*kami-sama kara no*). Here again, there is a sense that one's life is ultimately not one's own, a sentiment typically associated with reference to one's ancestors in commonplace comments like "If it were not for my ancestors, I would not have been born." The gods and ancestors are part of the living individual's story, marking the boundaries of the "natural" by their own supernatural presence and allowing the living to experience themselves in the context of a more expansive and spiritual sense of time. In "storying" (Randall and Kenyon 2004) their lives through continued interdependent relationships with others, such as gods and spirits, older Japanese adults embody what Japanese psychologists Yamada Yoko and Kato Yoshinobu[5] have called "*ryōkō*" ("parallel going"), or "the parallel coexistence of contradictory principles, concepts, phenomena, and so on" that allows for "the coexistence of multiple time perspectives and various forms of time consciousness" (2006: 157). Integrating simultaneous multiple time perspectives into one's "natural" life course story allows for the co-presence of contradictory forms of being: continuity and discontinuity, engagement and disengagement, receiving and returning, grief and hope, despair and integrity (Lambek 1996). In this sense, Yamada and Kato's work on the cultural psychology of the Japanese life cycle highlights the ways that future-oriented memorials, such as those performed by older adults for the household dead, are "moral practices" (Lambek 1996: 258) that shape identity.

If *ryōkō* links the temporal domains of this life and the next, how does death figure into this story of the life course? Older adults sometimes used the phrase "*Tenju wo mattou suru*" when discussing thoughts of death and suicide. "I've often thought about suicide," one woman in her early eighties admitted to me, "But I just can't do it. I have to *live out my natural life*." A man in his early seventies told me, "I don't worry about when I'm going to die. I just have to *live out my natural life*." Another woman who had voiced concerns about frailty and dependence in old age told me in more or less the same fashion, "I'm old. I don't want to live too long, but I have to *live out my natural life*."

In the *Genius Japanese-English Dictionary*, one of the English translations of the phrase "*Tenju wo mattou suru*" is "to die of old age," but neither the word "death" nor any of its various euphemisms appear in the phrase itself (and this translation would be clearly inappropriate in the examples above). This translation, however, highlights an interesting contrast in talking about life and death: in English, when the energies from an object such as a battery or a light bulb have dissipated, the object is typically referred to as "dead"; whereas in Japanese, one would say that it is "life" (*jumyō*), with the connotation that it is a life *fulfilled* (in death). These linguistic hints signal differences between Japanese and Western conceptions of the interdependence of life and death, differences that have implications for how we interpret comments about living out a natural life. Death, as a transition between one's life as it is lived and one's life as it will be remembered by others, presents a different kind of moral script in which managing capacities for mutuality becomes prominent. "*Tenju wo mattou suru*" is a prototypical script that produces part of one type of life-course narrative, where the moral enactment of the script (living a long life, or living to one hundred) exists with the seemingly contradictory insecurity of one's place within it (in deference to nature, one's cosmic destiny, and the ancestors).

Living a "god-given natural life" reminds me of a banner I once saw prominently displayed during a Buddhist retreat I attended in Kyoto: "Now, life is living you." The sentiment that this somewhat cryptic banner is meant to convey is the Buddhist idea of "interdependent arising" (*engi*), or the realization that one's identity is a result of exchanges with others across the life course. According to Religious Studies scholar Norimoto Iino (1962), the prominent Japanese Zen Buddhist philosopher Dōgen Zenji understood this kind of interdependence in terms of temporality. Norimoto writes, "All things depend upon one another. This Indian thought of interdependence is interpreted by Dōgen in the sense that *being is time*. The bamboo is time; the tiger time; enlightenment time; man time. The past, the present, and the future are three occasions of all-encompassing time. Each passing moment is precious. It should be appreciated as a great gift to be spent well" (1962: 54–55).[6]

When an older Japanese person tells me that he or she is living out a "natural, destined life," I cannot help but think that this is an expression of this will towards interdependence, the desire to be recognized as part of something transcendent, to *be time* in Dōgen's sense of the term, where past, present, and future are contained in one another, just as reminiscences of the past and "possible selves" (Markus and Herzog 1991; Markus and Nurius 1986) are all contained in the "lived sense of indeterminacy" (Han 2011: 21) of the present.

In Japan then, life, in the spiritual sense of the generative life cycle, is seen as something that circulates like a "great gift," its value tied both to timing and its function as an object of interdependence (Langford 2009; Leavitt 1995; Mauss 1990). In the process, possible selves are distributed over relationships with others, framed by the social institutions, and woven together in "experiential knots" (Johnson-Hanks 2002: 872). The institution of ancestor memorial introduces new points of exchange (of traditions, dispositions, bodies, souls) that might be considered what anthropologist Jennifer Johnson-Hanks calls "vital conjunctures" through which the self can be experienced or imagined as "structured possibilities" that motivate action (2002: 872). Aspirations, such as living to one hundred or living without becoming a burden to others, exist in the context of imagined futures of joining the ancestors as well as recognition of one's own life as that which is granted by the ancestors. One's identity in the life course is situated and structured by the generative life cycle, which is further situated and structured within the natural cosmic cycle (see Bateson, this volume on the non-linear nature of development in the life cycle).

Japanese Cultural Psychology and the Life Course

Yamada Yoko's Generative Life Cycle Model (GLCM) (2003; Yamada and Kato 2006) is one of the more intriguing attempts to adapt Erik Erikson's model of the life course (and particularly the idea of adult generativity) to the Japanese cultural context. In GLCM, vital energy of the self is distributed throughout a social system "nested within a series of interconnected, concentric life cycles" forming a spiral (Yamada 2003: 24) that recalls Hoagland's idea of continuity through conductivity. Included in GLCM is the idea of a life course as situated within "a long succession of related lives" or "a larger cycle of life from generation to generation" (Yamada 2003: 109).[7]

Yamada's work echoes Hallowell's in the sense that it strikes at one of the most fundamental elements of any life course: *time*. In an article co-written with Kato Yoshinobu, Yamada writes that, "In the spiral model of GLCM, time has a reversible nature," giving more significance to movements of "repetition and recycling" (2006: 149). Yamada and Kato describe this reversible, repetitive, and recycling notion of Japanese time in life-course narratives as *ryōkō*. They argue that this orientation (which they contend is culturally elaborated but not unique to Japan) gives actors a greater ability to imagine continuity, generativity, and security than unilinear models that end in death (Yamada and Kato 2006: 156).

Finally, Yamada's GLCM provides implications for considering the belief in ancestors and other spirits of the dead (*hotoke*) as important objects of life-cycle narratives. Yamada claims, for example, that for Japanese people, "interaction with their ancestors allows them to feel that they occupy a certain position in a long succession of related lives" (2003: 109). The concept of *ryōkō* is seen here as well, since it enables us to simultaneously hold the idea of the circulation of the soul, as well as that of the spirits' progression to the other world.

Memory, Spirituality, and Other Worlds of the Life Course

In Japan, the primary focus of religious or spiritual practice is the veneration and memorialization of the household ancestors and the *hotoke*, or the family dead, at graves and domestic altars (Smith 1974). It has been argued that age generally brings a greater concern for the spirits of the dead, creating identification through empathy (Traphagan 2004; Young and Ikeuchi 1997). Certainly part of the reason older adults have a stronger identification than younger people with the spirits of the dead is that older adults are more likely to have personally known the deceased persons when they were still alive. The *hotoke* are their siblings, parents, spouses, and even non-kin who are associated with memories of intimate attachments. Younger people I spoke with who had lost close relatives such as parents or siblings also expressed much more interest in the *hotoke* than their peers. However, unlike older adults, bereaved younger adults' experiences were highly specific to a particular deceased individual and involved thoughts and feelings that did not lead to much self-reflection on personal mortality. There was, in other words, little experiential or social context in which to place these grief experiences into a life-course narrative. For older adults, by contrast, memorializing the ancestors means both imagining one's future self (joining the ancestors) as well as returning to the point of one's origin in the realm of the spirits (referred to generically as *ano yo*, or, "the other world").

Ano yo is imagined as a sort of repository of spirit, the place where the soul travels after death and the place where it arises from at birth. Although I heard several people remark on this concept of "the other world" (*ano yo*) in the context of return, one encounter I had with my neighbor, Miura-san, summed it up best. At a community meeting of older adults held in an old elementary school, Miura-san approached me saying:

> After we graduate, we don't come back [to the elementary school building], but really after junior high school, we cut off our ties with our school. Then we get to be over seventy and we are given this opportunity to come back here [for the community meetings]. Then I think, "I myself was once young!" and we remember all those old things. There's no way of avoiding getting old [pointing to her cane]. Getting old is *harsh*. But there is the other world! Every day you look in the mirror and your appearance changes little by little, and you think about going to the next world. You don't think about it when you're young, but as you get older, you start thinking about it.

To Miura-san, the life course progresses from youth to old age, the former characterized by moving through different physical and social environments, and the latter by reminiscing about former selves (going from old age to youth). By introducing *ano yo*, she is also imagining a future where a new possible self will be found. She can no more avoid the "next world" as she can avoid growing up and growing older in this one. She imagines the "next world" as free from the harsh reality of old age, but stops short of calling it a return to youth. Reminiscence, in this instance, is an example of future-oriented memorial, wherein past experiences are recycled by storying them into the future. Childhood is only comprehensible from the perspective of old age, and old age from the perspective of the spirits. Similarly, there are several examples in Japanese folklore where the gods are old men who can transform into young children. Folklorist Yamaori Tetsuo argues that these stories reveal an ancient conceptual link between the simultaneity of the ends of the life course and the revelation of the spiritual (1997). This spiritual link is most clear when we consider the nature of Japanese ritual memorials.

FIGURE 7.1 A woman offers incense and ceremonial plants at the pagoda-shaped gravestone where her family's ashes are buried in eastern Kyoto. Photo by Jason Danely.

In contrast to Miura-san, Ogawa-san, a widow in her early eighties, seemed to be still feeling her way through her own narrative, trying to find the proper words to describe the interdependent relationship developed through acts of offering and memorial:

> *Ogawa*: The reason I offer flowers and remember back is because you wouldn't want to treat them [the dead] indifferently. That person—oh, how should I say it? I guess I sort of have the feeling that remembering them will make the [dead] happy. It's like, instead of just ignoring them, maybe that person [making offerings], they're thinking about themselves, I think. Offering flowers and going to the graves, *you could interpret it as being happy that you're being remembered* [by the deceased]. Maybe that's how it is. You know, because it is a spiritual world (*seishintekina sekai*).
>
> *Jason*: Spiritual world?
>
> *Ogawa*: Right, spiritual, well isn't memorial a spiritual thing? That's why that's—how would one say it? It's comforting, isn't it?

Ogawa-san's intuition seems to be that memorial involves a reciprocal recognition between the living and the dead ("being happy that you're being remembered"), and this is what makes it such a comforting experience. For Ogawa-san, the practice of making offerings entailed a strong sense of identification with the spirits and an intimate knowledge of their minds and emotional states in response to her own (Astuti 2007). Finally, memorial offerings are seen not only as signs of thoughtfulness, but of remembrance. Memory and spirituality both contribute to a sense of one's place in the life cycle.

Conclusions

My purpose in exploring Japanese formulations of the life course is not to reject, but rather to expand, our existing models in light of different cultural perspectives on temporality and spirituality. Yamada and Kato's conceptualization of *ryōkō* and the Generative Life Cycle Model, for example, affirms some of the distinct qualities of time as experienced in Japan, but in many respects, it also resembles Erikson's assertion that old age involves reengaging with identities and crises of earlier life stages (see Bateson, this volume) and reweaving them into a kind of integrated life-course narrative. Furthering our comparison, developmental psychologist Carol Hoare keenly explains Erikson's perspective on the life course as one in which memory and moral continuity are indelibly linked in the formation of adult identity: "By moving through developmental time, by weathering personal and social changes, and by seeing backward over a variety of cumulative and altered roles, requirements, contexts, and commitments, each person develops a sense of moral continuity. Thus, for each person, there is a sense that 'What I am in space, changes in time; what I was is now in me; and what I become is more than the sum of all that I have been'" (2002: 74, with quotation from Erikson 1974: 90).

In this chapter, I too have considered experiences of developmental time as recollections and aspirations that construct a sense of moral continuity framed by spiritual time. As Japan's population ages, aspirations to live a long life come to entail possibilities of loss and dependence that are tempered by alternate life-course scripts such as living out one's natural life (the life one has been given and which will return to the social system). This social interdependence, or ethic of mutual care, creates a comforting sense of continuity akin to Dōgen's understanding of "being as time." While this orientation towards "being as time" cannot be directly mapped onto Erikson's virtue of "wisdom" in old age, it does find much in common with the late-life crisis of "integrity versus despair" (Erikson 1963 [1950]: 268–69). Yamada's Generative Life Cycle Model offers a promising blend of Eriksonian developmental principles and Japanese cultural psychology—a blend that bears greater critical examination and elaboration in light of ethnographic research.

Understanding how people relate themselves to time is essential to the development of phenomenologies of aging and the life course. In Japan, recollection and aspiration are processes of exploring "the possible" at different points in life (Han 2011). Temporal and spiritual practices of mutual recognition and reciprocal exchange with the spirits of the dead offer conceptual resources for grounding lived experiences within broader cultural narratives of the moral life cycle. Within the phenomenological world of these practices, elders consider questions such as: "Why do I live as long as I do?", "How much longer should I live?", or "What will become of me after this?" Perhaps these questions are not meant to be completely resolved, but for time to tell. "Will time say nothing but I told you so? If I could tell you I would let you know."

Acknowledgments

In order to protect the identities of the subjects, all names of institutions and informants have been changed to pseudonyms. Research for this chapter was conducted with funding from the Japan-U.S. Exchange Commission and the IIE Fulbright Program. I also thank the Center on Age and Community Post-Doctoral Fellowship Program at the University of Wisconsin, Milwaukee for its support for the initial draft and presentation at the Meeting of the American Anthropological Association in 2009. Thank you to Caitrin Lynch, Samantha Solimeo, and Robin Danely for their time, insight, and close readings of earlier versions. Finally, my deepest thanks go to the participants in this research at the Takara Day Center and throughout Kyoto for generously donating their time.

Notes

1. "Villanelle" is the title of an Auden poem but also a poetic form in which the first and last lines of the first tercet alternately reappear as the last lines of the middle four tercets, and again as the last two lines of the final quatrain. The portion from "Villanelle" at the head of the chapter is the first tercet of his poem. Thus, the repeated lines are "Time will say nothing but I told you so" and "If I could tell you I would let you know." I interpret Auden's poem as a meditation on the ultimate mystery of time and loss. This is perhaps not so different than what Amano-san is expressing. In thinking of the conversation with Amano-san analogically as a villanelle, the repeating "lines," such as "How old do I look?", are not redundancies, but add value.

2. After *kanreki* (60), which symbolizes "rebirth" after one has passed through the twelve-year zodiac cycle five times, Japanese recognize and celebrate the ages 70 (*kiju*), 77 (*koki*), 88 (*beiju*), 90 (*sotsuju*), 95 (*chinju*), 99 (*hakuju*), 100 (*hyakuju*), 108 (*chaju*), and 111 (*kōju*). This tradition originated with the celebration of court nobles' birthdays (Tsuji 1997: 198). The words for these age markers are commonly used by the elderly, but unlike *kanreki*, there is no specific meaning attached to each of them.

3. The number 10,000 itself is not meant to be literal, but is a synonym for a very large number of something.

4. As of 2009, the Japanese Ministry of Health, Labor, and Welfare calculates the life expectancy at birth for a Japanese person as 79.59 for males and 86.44 for females. However, it estimates the years of life expected for those currently aged 60 as 22.87 and 28.46 for men and women respectively (Kōseirōdōsho, Abridged Life Tables for Japan 2009).

5. In this chapter, I use Japanese naming conventions (surname followed by given name) for all Japanese authors. Therefore, when a Japanese author's full name is given, the bibliographic entry can be found under the first name that appears in the text.

6. This use of the word "occasions" is a reference to philosopher Alfred North Whitehead's *Process and Reality* (1929) and *Adventures of Ideas* (1933) in which Norimoto sees a similar use of time free of spatialization: "Whitehead ... regards all things as occasions. God is a series of occasions; man a series of occasions; matter a series of occasions. And occasion is a concept denoting time. Here Whitehead seems to aim at avoiding spatialization in describing the interweaving of all things" (Norimoto 1962: 55).

7. Although the GLCM concentrates on the project of "generativity," which Erikson associated with Adulthood, Yamada's data comes mainly from college undergraduates and has, to my knowledge, not been used in any studies focusing on old age. For more on the GLCM and her experimental methods, see Yamada 2003 and Yamada and Kato 2006.

SECTION IV

FAMILIES

8. "I HAVE TO STAY HEALTHY"

Elder Caregiving and the Third Age in a Brazilian Community

Diana De G. Brown

WE WERE SITTING AT DONA *Eulália's kitchen table talking about her life and her family. I had asked her if her parents were still alive, and she explained that after her father died, her mother had come to live with her, and shortly after, when Eulália was just sixty, her mother got Alzheimer's and for seven years Eulália cared for her at home. At the beginning, she was still working in domestic service; she would care for her mother in the morning, make her breakfast, give her a bath, wash her clothes and her bedclothes, prepare lunch, and feed her. Then she took the bus to work, often without time to eat her own lunch. Her husband, retired with disability, cared for her mother during the afternoons, and she took over again when she returned at night from work. On weekends, her sons and their wives would help with the cooking and housecleaning. Dona Eulália told me she contracted an ulcer as a result of these difficult caretaking responsibilities.*

This narrative, and others that I will shortly recount, capture my concerns with filial obligations of older women caregiving for dependent elders, the intimacies and pleasures of such care, its social and health costs, and its intergenerational mobilization of family members. Set in a neighborhood in the southern Brazilian city of Florianopolis, in the state of Santa Catarina, these narratives dramatize a situation common among Brazil's "*classe popular*" (popular class), a term that refers collectively to less affluent working- and lower-middle-class sectors of the population. Here the combined pressures of greater longevity, chronic disease, and the absence of public-sector infrastructural support places the burden of caregiving for dependent elders squarely upon their families, especially women. The women whose caregiving activities I discuss here are members of a distinctive local population whose history and current circumstances place particularly intense obligations on their family caregiving activities. I met them in 2002, through our common membership in a local "Third Age" (*Terçeira Idade*) group, one of many in Florianopolis, where I am conducting research on aging, gender, health, and beauty. Since this group serves as the source of my subjects and of gossip and information on caregiving in this local community, I offer brief initial comments on the Third Age in Brazil. I then elaborate on caregiving activities and the local moral imperatives that keep them in place. Finally, I return to the Third Age group itself and consider the ways in which these caregivers enjoy and engage with the activities and resources offered, and at the same time, serve the concerns and interests of the neoliberal Brazilian state.

The Third Age in Brazil

The "Third Age" (*Troisième Age*), a term that originated in France in the 1970s, proposes a "new" age category for the post-retirement period of the life course that embraces healthy individuals through the period of their continuing good health and celebrates their health, vigor, vitality, capability, independence, self-realization, and empowerment (Debert 1999; Laslett 1987, 1991; Robbins, this volume). This new category distinguishes them from what are seen as the negative connotations of "old" as dependent and declining in health, a subsequent "Fourth Age" of decrepitude and infirmity. The Third Age is thus an effort to collectively reimagine post-retirement years as productive and to redirect societal discourse and practices to focus on the capabilities of post-retirement life. It seeks to provide positive images of aging and promotes the formation of groups and activities to realize these ideals.

The Third Age recognizes a distinction long noted in the American literature on cross-cultural aging that is based on functionality and distinguishes between the physically and mentally able—the "intact" old—and the dependent or "decrepit" old (see Glascock 1982; Glascock and Feinman 1981; Simmons 1945, 1960). In France, Third Age was conceived expressly to address the aging of the world's population and the burdens that longer-living elder citizens place upon younger working generations whose labors support their retirement, upon their families, and upon state healthcare and pension systems. These new ideas, with their promises of greater autonomy, independence, and health for older citizens through educational, recreational, and health-promoting activities, spread quickly through Europe and by the early 1980s were arriving in Brazil and Latin America (Cachioni 2003). The concept of the Third Age has been adapted in different national and cultural contexts to address particular concerns and challenges posed by growing numbers of elder citizens. For example, in France, where the concept originated, it was intended to reconfigure the self-image and leisure activities of middle-class retirees (Laslett 1991; Peixoto 2000). In Germany, Third Age discourse is currently being mobilized in a situation of severe decline in the available labor force and the growing economic burden on retirees to argue for their continuing value to the workforce (Greenberg and Muehlebach 2007).

In Brazil, the concept of the Third Age has been deployed by many sectors of society to address similar problems related to the rapidity of population aging. One of the heaviest burdens related to increased longevity is the extended elder health care required to treat the chronic diseases of aging in the face of an already inadequate public health service (Chaimowitz 1998). Healthy aging and individual health-promoting activities have thus become a central concern in Brazilian Third Age groups. Workers in government health and welfare agencies, together with gerontologists, members of the business community, the media, and consumer marketers have actively promoted the concept of the Third Age, which they refer to as "Terçeira Idade," and have sponsored the formation of Third Age groups. Directed at those age sixty and above, Third Age groups are now found throughout Brazil. The city of Florianopolis, with a population just over 400,000, currently has 107 such groups, most sponsored by the mayor's office, ranging in size from 20 to 100 members and diverse in their gender and class composition and their activity focus. While initially following the French model of university-based elder education programs, most of the groups in Brazil now concentrate on social activities, exercise programs, excursions, and attract mainly women from the popular class.[1]

The local neighborhood Third Age group that I discuss was officially organized by members of the neighborhood in 1999, and its leaders are elected from among the members. It is registered with the mayor's office, from which it receives small funding. Its forty-five members, an average size for such groups, who range from sixty to ninety-five years old, participate in weekly exercise classes; gather once a week to socialize, gossip, consume coffee and cake, demonstrate their needlework skills, and play bingo; go on occasional excursions; and attend yearly citywide Third Age meetings. Group members range from poor to affluent, but most are from the *classe popular.*

The Neighborhood and Its Inhabitants

The majority of the participants in this particular local Third Age group identify themselves as *"nos d'aqui"* (we who come from here) or "Nativos" (Natives). They are members of a distinctive local group little known outside of southern Brazil who trace their ancestry to the Portuguese Azores Islands and are now known in the city as *"Açorianos"* (Azorians). In this neighborhood they form a tightly knit community whose members continue to hold common values, such as intergenerational and gender reciprocity, which is embedded in historical memories of the land and their former lives. I sketch their background here, since it is central to the value placed on their caregiving activities. These derive from generations of residence and intermarriage among small, isolated rural communities. The ancestors of this population were brought by the Portuguese Crown in the mid-eighteenth century to settle the southern coast and to help protect the area from depredations by the Spanish. They were given land grants and most families remained on this land as subsistence farmers and fishermen. The older women with whom I am working were born, grew up, married, and raised their own children in this same coastal region, most in this same neighborhood of Florianopolis. The women farmed, their husbands also fished, and they ran their cows and gathered wood for their farinha (manioc) mills on the commons. Until the late 1960s, there was no electricity or running water, no paved roads, no public transport for several miles, and travel was on foot and by canoe. There was no health post, the Catholic Church was a several-kilometer walk, and the local school went only through second grade.

Then, during the 1970s, the city expanded, and the coastal areas were rapidly urbanized and settled by middle-class Brazilians from neighboring states (Fantin 2000). The neighborhood is now one of many that crowd the coasts of this island capital. The areas on and near the beach have been appropriated for tourism, and the Nativos now live clustered along an inland secondary road, along the dirt roads extending up the hills, and at the margins and in the interstices of the new commercial establishments and luxury apartment houses. Gradually, over the past forty years, members of this Nativo community have abandoned subsistence agriculture and fishing to become part of the contemporary urban world of literacy, wage labor, and consumerism associated with a post-industrial service economy. Yet their community has remained vital. Though poor, few are impoverished. Most have been able to retain at least some of the properties of their lineal ancestors, own their own homes, and have small incomes from retirement benefits and government pensions. Many now work for the wealthier "outsiders" (*gente de fora*) in domestic service, in construction, and in small commerce. They have become part of the *classe popular,* and some of their upwardly mobile children have joined the middle class. They have accommodated to this new world.

The women with whom I have been working are healthy and long-lived, including several in their nineties. I consider all of them here as a cohort, as co-members of this local Third Age group. They are also members of a generation, in the broad sense of that term, "a group of people who have lived through a time period together and have developed some kind of shared consciousness" (Lamb 2001). Most continue to live in family residential compounds (*segmentos familiares residenciais*) (see Motta 2002; Rial 1988), in nuclear family households on family-owned plots and adjoining properties granted by usufruct to their ancestors, which now contain several houses, and may include lineal relatives of three, four, even five generations on a single property. Kin ties are dense and overlapping. They structure much of daily life, relationships, and activities, and are omnipresent in conversations. Mention of any particular member of this Nativo "community" to another is likely to evoke a long, spontaneous, and very precise recitation of the multilayered consanguineal and affinal relations between them. Frequent intermarriages within this and to other neighboring Nativo communities over many generations have produced a tightly knit community whose values they struggle to transmit to their children and grandchildren (see also Motta 2002; Rial 1988). These values emerge often in conversations about caregiving. People discuss their own health, gossip about who is ill in their families and in the community, and linger on long recitations of conditions, symptoms, treatments, exactly who is caring for them, and the quality of that care.

The Caregiving Narratives

The caregiving narratives I discuss here were related directly to me by the caregivers, or emerged through ongoing collective narratives gathered from various sources as the caregiving episodes themselves developed. The narratives reflect the involvement of these elder Third Age Nativa women in caregiving within their families and their sense of a moral obligation to do so. I opened this discussion with Dona Eulália's account of her care for her mother with Alzheimer's, her mobilization of family members to help her, and her own illness as a result of her caregiving activities. All of these points form common denominators in the narratives. These are older women, Third Agers themselves, caring for ill and dependent elder Fourth Age spouses or parents in their own homes, assisted only, though very ably, by a multigenerational network of kin members who live nearby.

When the ill elder has no spouse or child to care for her, a sister may step in, as happened when Dona Joana's sister, a childless widow in her early eighties, was diagnosed with colon cancer. Joana, seventy-three and already caring for another ill relative, took over her sister's care, bringing her to live with her, and taking her to the hospital for her operation. Then, busy with her own life and her other ill relative, Joana paid a neighbor to stay with her sister. When her sister rejected this woman, complaining about a stranger taking over her intimate bodily care, Joana turned to her own daughter and granddaughter who live in a neighboring district of the city. Her granddaughter, who was unemployed at the time, arrived at 8 A.M. to prepare her great aunt's meals, wash her, change her diaper, and keep her company throughout the day. In the evening, Joana's daughter arrived to spend the night, and Joana's son helped out with the driving and purchasing of medicine. Joana remained in charge of organizing the caregiving, mobilizing a network of intergenerational collateral kin.

Another narrative registers general community dissatisfaction with the way tasks and responsibilities for caregiving are allocated, and illustrates the strong sense of a daughter's obligation to care for her ill mother and the moral weight placed upon her failure to do so. Until 2009, Dona Edí, a widow of ninety-five, had been a vigorous and active member of the Third Age group, participating in almost all of its activities. That year she developed colon cancer, requiring a rectal colostomy, and returned home weak and confined to her bed with a colostomy bag. Of her three children, only one daughter, Helena, sixty-three, is still alive. It is well known in the neighborhood that Dona Edí and her daughter do not get along, and there are many conflicting stories as to why that is the case, with some stories placing blame on one or the other or both. When I first met Dona Edí she was living in a damp apartment, in a row of cement block apartments behind her daughter's large and comfortable house. Many believed that her daughter should bring her mother into her house to live with her. But she did not. Dona Edí subsequently moved up the street to another more comfortable apartment, but after her operation she was forced to move back into the same damp apartment. Since her daughter Helena refused to be her principal caregiver, her grandson, José, who was around forty and lived next door with his family, assumed that role. José was on vacation when Dona Edí was discharged from the hospital, and he spent a great deal of time with her, including changing her diaper and emptying her colostomy bag, which (as they both commented to me) felt inappropriate and highly embarrassing to both of them.

When José had to return to work, caregiving tasks were divided with some reluctance among his wife, his brother, and his brother's wife, who took over the task of bathing and changing her, though in the middle of the night when her bag became disconnected and spilled all over her and the bed, her grandson was once again called in to clean it all up. José also contracted with a neighbor, another member of the Third Age group and thus a colleague of Dona Edí, who was paid a small sum to come in four days a week to make lunch, clean her apartment, and keep her company in the afternoon. José, his brother, and their wives alternated in sleeping in her apartment in case she needed anything during the night.

Virtually all members of the Nativo community agreed that Helena should have assumed primary care. She came in sometimes to make lunch and took her turn sleeping in her mother's apartment at night, but although retired and available, she remained very much at the periphery of her mother's care. She was extremely reluctant to speak with me about this matter, avoided me when I came to visit her mother, and under my direct questioning muttered only that she herself was not well enough to care for her mother. I discovered that she did have a heart condition, but this was not generally accepted within the neighborhood as a sufficient excuse since, as several people commented to me, it was not serious enough to prevent her from traveling often to São Paulo (10–12 hours each way by bus) to buy clothing that she then resold locally.

Neighborhood opinion is very vocal on this case, as is clear in the following comments, which reveal clear norms and expectations for intergenerational obligations and duties, and resonate with comments we hear in Gamburd's chapter on Sri Lanka, in this volume:

> "Helena should have taken responsibility for her mother's care—imagine a man changing her diaper and taking care of her colostomy bag."
> "How appalling that Helena didn't take on caring for her mother."
> "How could anyone do this to their own mother?"
> "Helena should have brought her mother to live with her; it's scandalous. But if she had done this, she would have had to assume more of her mother's care, instead of having her sons do it, and she didn't want to do this."

Dona Edí's sister, who lives in a neighboring district, is reported to have been asked why she herself did not take over her sister's care, to which she replied, "Look, if my sister has a daughter who lives next door to her and could take care of her, why should I, who am ninety-three and live in another district, have to do this?" Dona Edí herself laments that she does not really have a daughter—that Helena doesn't do any of the things a daughter should do for her mother when she is sick, and that she herself did for her daughter when she was a child. Some say that Helena is "nervosa,"[2] while others call her "a very difficult person." A few stand up for Helena; one told me that this daughter had tried many times in the past to help her mother, but that nothing she did ever pleased her mother—not her cooking, not her care—and that this has been true since she was an adolescent. This rupture of reciprocal household intimacies had begun much earlier in this family. It also occurred in a community in which mothers' relationships with their children are customarily closer than husband-wife relationships, and where, at least in older generations, knowledge about and execution of household tasks such as cooking, cleaning, childcare, and training in caregiving is a domain of women, and is passed on from mothers to daughters. Helena's current refusal to care for her mother was just another of many such ruptures.

In highlighting what is regarded as a breach of proper family caretaking, this example underscores the unwritten gender and kinship rules that govern community expectations about who should properly serve as the main caregiver for a dependent elder family member (see Gamburd, this volume). Care for Dona Edí, in the absence of a spouse, should fall on her daughter. Dona Edí's sister also agrees and uses this argument in her own refusal to care for her sister, rather than saying that she is too old, at ninety-three, to assume care. The caregiving then falls upon the second descending generation, and since there are no female grandchildren, draws on a grandson as the principal caregiver, and he and his brother and their female affines must perform intimate care for the grandmother.

This model of what is considered to be proper intergenerational care within the family is exemplified in Dona Luiza's comment to me one day after the weekly Third Age meeting. A widow of seventy-eight, and a pillar of the Nativo community, she lives surrounded by her children, their spouses, her grandchildren, and great-grandchildren. We were discussing her family, and she said to me, pointing to the grass at our feet in front of the Third Age meeting place, "Yes, I can die happy. If I were to fall here in this grass right now, in a few minutes my family would be here to care for me. Thank God, they are all very close to me, very concerned about me, and I know that they will care for me very well."

When I asked her who would assume the main burden of care for her, she replied: "Ah, my daughters." And when I asked her why her daughters but not her sons she gave me a look indicating that I was being particularly dense—"Because I took care of them when they were children. Now it is their turn to take care of me.[3] And because they are women, and they know how to do these household tasks, and to take care of us [elders], because they have already taken care of their own children, isn't it so? And my sons, ah, they will also help out." Here, Dona Luiza enunciates the ethic of intergenerational reciprocal care, and with it, the outlines of a gendered division of labor and gender complementarity that is found within this community and in other Nativo communities in Florianopolis, especially among older generations (see Motta 2002). Women are expected to be the caregivers for the elderly ill: wives for their husbands, who usually predecease them, and daughters for their parents. As indicated in the case of Dona Edí, whose primary caretaker was her grandson, gender flexibility is severely taxed in the care for the elderly; it was considered highly inappropriate that a grandson—a male, even though he was close kin—should take over caregiving.

These narratives of caregiving conform to a pattern often cited in the health science literature in Brazil. The elderly are cared for by their families at home, and caregivers tend to be close female kin who live nearby and have affective ties to the dependent elder (Caldas 2002; Mendes 1998; Nerí 2006; Santos 2006). As has been seen in the example of Dona Edí, in the absence of such affective ties, a daughter may not become the primary caregiver. Sílvia dos Santos has likened caregiving networks to "the ballet corps of a grand ballet of caregivers" (Santos 2006: 100). In this local Nativo community, however, the ballet corps of caregiving networks is almost exclusively composed of kin, and includes few of the volunteers and paid professional caregivers referred to in this literature on caregiving. Rarely in this community have I found non-kin caregivers as regular members of any caregiving network. Few families have the financial resources to pay for such care, and the notoriously bad conditions in public nursing homes make them unacceptable alternatives to home care. While cultural imperatives to caregiving within the family remain strong in Brazil, they are challenged both by the Brazilian healthcare system's failure to provide any kind of professional home caregivers, or even train family members for this job (a situation the health researchers cited above strongly criticize), and by the erosion of families' capacities for such caregiving, particularly in urban areas, due to shrinking family size and reduced numbers of potential caretakers (see Neri 2006; Santos 2006; see Lamb and Gamburd, this volume, for responses to similar pressures in India and Sri Lanka, respectively). In contrast, this Nativo community's overall stability, and its stable multigenerational residential arrangements, must be seen as crucial to the continuing support of its extended kin networks of caregiving.

These elder caregivers agree that daily caring routines, often undertaken over periods of several years, are exhausting, and many have suffered illnesses as a result of their caregiving activities: ulcers, high blood pressure, nervosismo (being nervosa), stress, exhaustion, and depression.[4] Yet they state unequivocally that they have undertaken their caregiving activities out of love and that they have found them to be immensely gratifying. As one woman said to me about caring for her mother: "I felt the greatest satisfaction I have ever had in my life caring for her. I felt very happy caring for her, and I felt great love and affection for her." Close family members of these women admiringly agree that their caregiving was performed with much patience and affection, and they receive high praise and respect in their families and the community for their selfless caregiving. One woman was even hailed as a "heroine" by other members of her family for her self-sacrifice and suffering during her years of caring for her mother.

Within this devoutly Catholic community, references to women's self-sacrifice and suffering recall the sufferings of the Virgin Mary, as suggested in political scientist Evelyn Stevens's discussion of *marianismo,* which she construes as an ideal female gender role among Latin American women (Stevens 1973; see also Miles 2010). At the same time, these women are expected by their families and their community to offer this care, as women and in reciprocity for the care received from their parents. With their children, daughters as well as sons, employed outside the home in wage labor, they are often the only people available to their extended families for elder care and a variety of other activities such as caring for sick children, babysitting, retrieving children from school, and doing myriad other bureaucratic errands and services. Thus these elder women are crucial to the social reproduction of their families, a role that continues as long as they remain healthy. While it is easy to see them as victims—of family and community pressures, as women without agency—their situation is more complicated. Growing from infancy within their families and community, they have learned to feel love as well as obligation; they exercise agency in choosing to care for family members, find rewards in doing so, and do not see themselves as victims.

The Third Age Group and its Impact on Caregivers

Earlier in this chapter, I outlined the general orientation of the Third Age movement in Brazil and explained that my sample of caregivers was recruited from a Third Age group of the type focusing on social and recreational activities. I now want to consider briefly the ways in which these caregivers draw upon this local Third Age group: how Third Age discourse and practices have entered into their daily lives, and in what ways these discourses and practices may have influenced their experience of aging and caregiving. Participation in this Third Age group puts these women in direct weekly contact with ideas and activities designed to emphasize their capabilities as elder citizens, to stimulate a new awareness of the positive aspects and possibilities of being healthy and active.

Members respond very positively to this message. When I asked a group of women if they thought that their group had influenced the way they thought of themselves, one replied: "Yes. It helps me to stay healthy and to think young [*pensar jovem*]," and the group members listening agreed. "Aging is easier now," volunteered another woman. These women identify themselves, and each other, as active and healthy, and pride themselves on their ability to do stretches, bends, and fast walking in the exercise class, to be lively in the social meetings, and to maintain good humor and endurance on long tourist trips. They also pride themselves on their busyness, how busy they are with caregiving and other services to their large families. Busyness appears to be a mark of their positive identity within their families as members who are still vital and depended upon, "givers" of services rather than dependent "takers" of them. The exercises, the socializing, and the trips provided by the Third Age group provide pleasure and an appreciative audience for demonstrating their continuing vitality.

Group members feel recognized as an active age group by city authorities and feel new visibility within their own community and families for their Third Age group activities—their weekly exercises, their tourist excursions, their attendance at municipal meetings in the city. They feel that these activities give them increased status, both as elders and as women. Moreover, participation in the Third Age meetings seems to give them new courage to undertake their strenuous caregiving duties. "I have to come to the exercise group," said one caregiver to me. "It's the only way I can stay healthy to take care of my bedridden husband." Support for the maintenance of their own health provides them with a form of social capital within their families and community. The local Third Age group provides a collective, non-familial support group for their endeavors as caregivers and sympathy for the many challenging moments they experience. The group also provides social solidarity, helping to strengthen and celebrate their identities as caregivers while providing them with rare and treasured moments of leisure, conversation, and laughter. In its emphasis on health and activities, it strengthens their identities as strong, healthy women. Like membership in the local Catholic chapel, participation in the local Third Age group acts to reinforce bonds within the community.

These women have shaped this Third Age group to their own purposes, using it as a local resource: a community center, a source of tourism, a health resource, and indirectly, a resource that helps them sustain their own physical powers, and through this, their status within their families and community. But at the same time, this Third Age group is part of a government-driven initiative to address the burdens of an aging population, and in this sense it can also be seen as mediating between the interests of the Brazilian state and the *classe popular*. This group, and the Third Age movement more broadly, may be seen as efforts within a neoliberal government to shift the burden of healthcare from the state to individuals and to make health an individual moral responsibility, a process Guita Grin Debert (1999) refers to as "the reprivatizing of aging" (*a reprivatização do envelhecimento*) (see also Stucci 2000).

Health and the importance of exercise are promoted in exactly this way in this group. The instructors (interns in physical education at local universities) who lead the exercise classes encourage members to take responsibility for their own health, sometimes very pointedly. One exhorted us on the eve of a two-week vacation: "You need to keep doing these [exercises] at home while we're on vacation—even in two weeks you can lose a lot of muscle tone. Remember, you don't want to land in a wheelchair." His exhortation served as a reminder that the proximity to a state of dependency, the Fourth Age, is never far away. In promoting elder health, the Third Age group also, at least indirectly, supports government health initiatives in another way. The government Laws for the Elderly (*Leis dos Idosos*) at the federal, state, and municipal levels mandate families to take responsibility for the care of their own elderly, and stipulate that state assistance will be provided only when the elderly person is without family (Caldas 2002; Prefeitura de Florianopolis n.d.).[5] In promoting a neoliberal agenda of responsibility for personal health and strong support for family caregiving, this local Third Age group provides further reinforcement for the values of moral obligation and reciprocity in caregiving to the elderly ill, values already present within this distinctive local population.[6]

It is ironic that the concept of the Third Age, one of whose initial central themes has been the provision of leisure activities, is in this instance also serving as a support for continued labor, reinforcing these women's abilities to undertake unpaid family labor and thus to carry out the state's interest in placing the burden of responsibilities for the elderly ill on families. Debert (1999) has worried that the focus of public attention and support for the Third Age will lead to further neglect of individuals of the Fourth Age. This may well be true. But in this community, at least, care of the dependent elderly seems to depend importantly on the continued health of Third Age caregivers, and thus the promotion of Third Age health helps to provide family caregivers for individuals of the Fourth Age.

These Third Age women's managerial work in mobilizing kin networks of caregivers—members of their own nuclear families, both lineal and collateral relatives, affines spanning several generations, and men as well as women—exemplifies their continuing authority in the family and their important roles in the intergenerational transmission of reciprocal kin obligations. The intergenerational nature of these networks establishes that members of younger generations are drawn into caregiving obligations: grandchildren are drawn into caring for grandparents and great aunts, and they thus receive early training both in the practices and the obligations of family care. Caregiving acts to bind the generations together and to transmit moral values from one generation to the next. It is a "local moral world" (Kleinman 1992) where health and illness are constructed within a context of shared experience that mediates macro social forces, shaping their specific local effects.

This research captures a moment in the historical process of transformation within this group when family values, community values, and state policies are aligned to place a huge potential burden on older women to serve as caregivers. These women may find both intense personal pleasure and community praise for undertaking these duties, and may do so voluntarily, but nevertheless they do so within a situation that seems to be overdetermined at the family, local, and the national levels. Older Nativa women are from a generation rurally born and raised. Many of these women never worked for wages and have thus been "available" in emergencies. In their children's generation, in which most women as well as men are salaried workers often unavailable to participate in or direct networks of care, whatever their sense of filial obligation, they may have to replace their own familial labor with paid care. This may act to shift patterns of elder caregiving from an almost exclusive dependence on networks of kin toward the use of more paid, informal caregivers, thus bringing caregiving in this community closer to what I have observed among non-Nativa families in the "popular classes" (see also Lamb and Gamburd, this volume). It is also possible that pressures on government from health professionals may lead to the provision of some kind of assistance to elder caregivers from community health services, which would alleviate to some degree the all-consuming duties of the caregiving experiences I have related here. In the meantime, a paradox is apparent: the Third Age movement for this community reinforces and legitimizes traditional practices as modern answers to an inadequate health service for the popular classes.

Acknowledgments

I thank the Brazilian Government for a CNPq (Conselho Nacional de Pesquisas, National Research Board) grant as a Visiting Researcher in the Anthropology Department at the Federal University of Santa Catarina (UFSC) from 2005–2007, and Bard College for a Professional Development Grant in 2002, both of which financed this research. Jean Langdon, Cleidi Albuquerque, and Maria Amélia Schmidt Dickie provided helpful suggestions and commentary during my research, and Jason Danely and Caitrin Lynch very expertly tamed what started out as an unwieldy manuscript. Mario Bick, with whom I have shared Third Age activities and danced the Quadrilha, has been a constant companion and my best critic. My greatest debt is to the members of the Third Age group who welcomed me, and especially to the caregivers who so generously shared with me their experiences.

Notes

1. Social groups of the type studied here are called "Grupos de Convivência," and are found mainly in the popular class, in contrast to the more middle-class activities of the Third Age universities (Universidades da Terçeira Idade) (Alves 2008: 132; Britto da Motta 1999: 220–21). There is a tendency toward gender complementarity between Third Age groups, which attract mainly women, and retirement politics, principally a male activity (Debert 1999; Leibing 2005).

2. "Nervoso, -a" is a popular illness, much discussed in Brazil, which can refer to a range of organic and mental conditions, from bouts of irritability, anxiety, stress, or undefined unwellness (*mal-estar*)—all of these give the sense in which it is used here to characterize Helena—in contrast to what might be labeled serious psychiatric problems (Silveira 2000). Silveira's discussion of nervos, nervoso, and nervosismo is an appropriate reference here because she worked with a Nativa population in another part of Florianopolis.

3. This expressed sense of well-being that her daughters will care for her when she becomes dependent is very different from the situation described by Lee and Elithorpe for the U.S., where close kin relations and care in general, and care by children, in particular, are found not to be relevant to the morale (the subjective well-being) of older persons (Lee and Elithorpe 1982: 222). See also Lynch (this volume) for a discussion of how some older workers in the U.S. may find ideal "family-like" relationships in the workplace rather than among kin.

4. Dwyer, Lee, and Jankowski (1994) writing on caregiving in the U.S. indicate that primary female caregivers caring for their mothers experience significant "stress" (both psychological and emotional) and "burdens" (disruption of daily routines, social relationships, and other activities); that co-residence lessens these for the daughter but also decreases the mother's feelings of psychological well-being, as she feels herself a burden on her daughter.

5. Keith et al. similarly noted in the conclusion to their cross-cultural study of aging that in Hong Kong, "government policy seems to be built on the assumption that care from kin is a substitute for public resources" (1994: 329).

6. Keith et al. also note that especially in communities with residential stability, kin participate more heavily in caregiving, but in all of the sites in which they did research, the elderly "rely on close kin and relatives for care and support when ill or affected with chronic health problems" (1994: 293).

9. GRANDMOTHERING IN LIFE-COURSE PERSPECTIVE
A Study of Puerto Rican Grandmothers Raising Grandchildren in the United States

Marta B. Rodríguez-Galán

An individual's life course is entrenched in and shaped by the times and places in which the person lives, including the geographical and cultural context (Elder, Johnson, and Crosnoe 2003). As immigrants, Latina grandmothers in the United States are set on a different path from their own cultures of origin, and they are loosely tied to the age norms of the host culture.[1] Moreover, the timing of grandmothering typically starts earlier and takes on different meanings from those of the Anglo majority. To analyze the decisions made by low-income Puerto Rican women to assume their "mother/grandmother" role on the mainland, and ultimately to make sense of the meaning of this role in the larger picture of their own lives, we must examine the intertwined relationships among timing (when the entry to the role occurs), historical time (late twentieth-century foster care policies), and place (mainland Unites States, low-income public housing, U.S. Latino culture). In this chapter, I examine how Puerto Rican grandmothers integrate the meanings of the mother/grandmother role into their life-course narratives, grounding my discussion in ethnographic vignettes from research among Puerto Rican grandmothers raising grandchildren in the Boston metro area. I pay particular attention to these grandmothers' adherence to (or contestation of) age norms, cultural meanings of the mother/grandmother role, and its implications for how they construct and achieve "ego integrity" (Erikson 1959).

The goal of my larger study is to offer a comprehensive portrait of Puerto Rican custodial grandmothers, including how they negotiate their role, its perceived psychosocial impact, and the physical and social context in which the caregiving experience occurs. I first became interested in the topic of grandmothering while conducting ethnographic interviews as a research assistant for the NIH-funded Boston Puerto Rican Center on Population Health and Health Disparities from 2005–2008. This work helped me identify forty-seven potential subjects for my investigation in 2009 of surrogate grandmothering. I was able to reach fourteen grandmothers from my master list of potential subjects and I recruited them via telephone. I used semi-structured ethnographic interviews, field notes, and observed and recorded details about the availability and quality of services, use of public spaces, and characteristics and type of housing where grandmothers live. Because of my previous ethnographic work in Boston, I had lived in several of the same neighborhoods as these women and had become very familiar with the Puerto Rican population there. In the following sections, I examine how Puerto Rican grandmothers construct and integrate the custodial grandmother role into their life-course narratives.

Custodial Grandparenting in the United States

Low-income grandmothers raising grandchildren in the United States present a compelling case study from a life-course perspective because the mother/grandmother role does not fit neatly into the classical U.S. life-course narrative. Over the past three decades, social scientists have documented the increase in the number of grandmothers raising grandchildren, their patterns of family care, their roles within the extended family, and quality of life issues, particularly among African-American and Native-American families (Burton 1995; Burton, Dilworth-Anderson, and Merriwether-deVries 1994; Dolbin-MacNab 2006; Goodman and Silverstein 2002; Minkler and Fuller-Thomson 2005; Weibel-Orlando 2009). In the United States, grandmothers of all ethnicities typically take on the responsibility of raising grandchildren due to several factors, among them a deceased parent, child abuse, neglect, or other problems such as drug addiction in the biological family (Roe, Minkler, Saunders, and Thomson 1996). A similar trend is also observed frequently among Puerto Rican women, who euphemistically refer to such issues in reference to their children as "*cometió un error* [my daughter made a mistake]," "*estaba descarriada* [she had strayed away]," and "*hubo un incidente* [there was an incident] and the police had to intervene." Oliva is a 53-year-old grandmother who has two adolescent custodial grandchildren and provides care for several others. Consider the following exchange between Oliva and myself:

> *Marta*: And what caused you to take custody of the child?
> *Oliva*: Well, my daughter *made a mistake* and she had to go to prison.[2]

Like many other Puerto Rican grandmothers, Oliva offers only a vague and sketchy picture of her children's illegal or immoral behavior, most probably because in Hispanic cultures this behavior brings much shame, not just on the individual, but on the entire the family. Similarly, Amarilis, a 44-year-old grandmother raising a seven-year-old grandchild, alludes to her daughter's involvement in what Amarilis believed to be an immoral and irresponsible lifestyle: "I obtained the [legal] custody for him [the grandson] because his mother had him when she was fourteen and she was *descarriada* [she had strayed away], living a life of vice, she was not capable of keeping him ... very *desatendida* [careless]; and then because I did not want the child to go to a foster family that has nothing with me [no kinship ties] ... because this is my first grandson ... then I decided to talk to her." Her daughter's irresponsible behavior goes against the cultural values that Amarilis adheres to, such as being a responsible mother and taking good care of the child. In order to lessen the shame of her daughter's *descarriada* life, Amarilis draws on ideas of kinship-based ethics when she makes the decision to become a custodial grandmother.

Although this family trend cuts across class, ethnic, and gender lines, low-income single grandmothers of color are overrepresented in the United States among grandparents raising grandchildren (Caputo 2000; Fuller-Thomson and Minkler 2000). Researchers often conceptualize this growing family group as a social problem in the United States (Grinstead et al. 2003; Pruchno 1999). Because custodial grandmothering is usually an unexpected role, it is assumed to create disruptions in women's life courses, which in turn increases the likelihood of deleterious effects on the women's health, such as higher levels of stress and burden (Burton, Dilworth-Anderson, and Merriwether-deVries 1994). Although studies on Latina grandmothers are still limited, research shows that African-American and Latina grandmothers experience lower levels of stress and burden than Anglo white women (Grinstead et al. 2003; Pruchno 1999). In many societies, grandmothers have played an important role in their grandchildren's lives, even taking on the responsibilities of surrogate motherhood when necessary. For example, among North American Indian groups, grandparents play multiple normative roles in the community that include the role of custodial grandparent, the fictive grandparent, and the cultural conservator (Weibel-Orlando 2009). Similarly, because of Hispanic grandparents' (grandmothers in particular) importance in family decision-making, the role of the custodial grandmother may be a natural extension of the culturally normative roles of Hispanic women. Thus, grandmothers raising grandchildren in Hispanic cultures, or raising other children who are not their biological children, should not be seen as an abnormal or even an uncommon family arrangement in the way that this has been construed in the United States. Melba Sánchez-Anyendez (1988), for example, found that among Puerto Ricans in the Northeast, surrogate and foster parenting are culturally proscribed and linguistically acknowledged as roles in the vernacular. Several of the grandmothers I interviewed had already mothered other people's children whom they referred to with the native idiom *"hijo/a de crianza"* (reared son or daughter). Often these have been a niece/nephew, cousin, or even a non-kin child. Furthermore, some of these grandmothers have been foster mothers in the United States. In general, the transition to the role of grandparent seems to be more important in Hispanic families than in the Anglo majority, as Hispanic grandparents are often expected to be more involved in the caring and socializing of their grandchildren than are Anglos (Valle and Cook-Gait 1998).

In her study of African-American surrogate mothers, Linda Burton (1995) has argued that although this role may bring several rewards to the women, it commonly causes stress if it is perceived as being an "off-time" social role or the result of non-normative life events. However, the assumption that the mother/grandmother role is an "off-time" life event with deleterious consequences for grandmothers may not apply to many low-income Latinas. Furthermore, a significant portion of these grandmothers highlight the psychological gains derived from the caregiving experience, such as companionship, purpose, and new forms of social support (see Brown, this volume, for a discussion of the different meanings of family caregiving in a Brazilian context). Additionally, the meaning and interpretation of the mother/grandmother role may be shaped not just by life stage, but by such factors as chronological and functional age and class and culturally based views on gender and the life course. Although the Spanish term *abuela* translates literally to "grandmother," its cultural interpretation differs from the Anglo role construction, as these grandmothers often share more of the duties of a mother. Moreover, for Puerto Rican grandmothers, their legal immigrant status (the majority of the Puerto Rican women were born on the island) and culture of origin shape their grandmothering experiences and interpretations of their role in many other significant ways.

The Mother/Grandmother Role among Puerto Rican Grandmothers

Hispanic families in the United States have typically included at least three generations in the same household, and they have placed great value on the notion of *"respeto,"* or feelings of deference and obligation towards elders based on age hierarchy. *Respeto* for the mother figure is especially valued.

Often, the mother assumes the pivotal role in the family, and thus mothers enjoy great symbolic power among Hispanics. In this regard, all the Puerto Rican grandmothers in my sample—regardless of their age—felt that they were first mothers to their grandchildren, but also felt that the grandchild ought to know who his or her biological mother is and respect the biological mother, even when she was not a fit parent and could at times be hurtful to the grandchild. Paquita explains how the importance of *respeto* remains, even in spite of a biological mother's faults: "Well, I raised him [her grandson] since he was a baby, and for me he is just another child of mine; but in my subconscious I have always known that he is my grandson, and I have never hidden the fact that she [her daughter] is his mother ... my daughter, that no matter what she is, he owes her *respeto.*" Although grandmothers not only fulfill the role of mother, but also identify as mothers, they are not necessarily accredited with the same cultural value of *respeto*—a situation that in some cases leads to a sense of role confusion, in other words, the grandmother may feel unsure as to exactly what role she should play.

Seventy-three-year-old Paula, for example, has cared for her seven-year-old granddaughter since she was an infant and has only temporary custody of her. Paula's daughter, who lives with her two other children in a different part of town, refuses to allow her to gain full custody, in spite of the fact that she (Paula's daughter) does not contribute in any way to the child's caregiving. In the following quote, Paula describes her struggle over feeling both as a mother and as a grandmother, and she expresses her inability to fully separate these roles or to reconcile her experience with the cultural ideals with which she is familiar: "[I am] a mother because ... in fact, I am a mother, even before I had her, and because I have her since she was so small here, in her Pampers, ... and rearing her ... I feel more like a mother, imagine that! [laughter] But ... both things came together, that of mother, and that of grandmother, I cannot ... I do not know! I cannot separate ... I do not know how to separate it."

While almost anybody can be a biological mother of a child, grandmothers often state that it is the person who raises the child who is the "*verdadera madre*" or "true mother" (i.e., the social mother). Furthermore, they see themselves as playing multiple roles in relation to their grandchildren, and although they perceive the identities of grandmother and mother as fluid and inseparable, they are also aware that they do not fit the ideal normative view of the family and the life course. Thus, because their social identity as "mothers" is legitimated neither by their own families nor by the state, they must ensure that the grandchild understands that special (i.e., non-normative) relationship. When grandmothers do not have legal custody of the child, they fear that the child can be taken away from them at any time. In addition, they fear that if the grandchild does not know that the grandmother is not the biological mother, it will create confusion in the child's mind that may lead to the development of recurrent inner psychological turmoil—or "evil thoughts." Graciela, sixty-seven, explains this dilemma in the following conversation:

> *Graciela*: No, I am his mother! And his cousin is his grandmother … and she is 25 years old—that [sic] she is my granddaughter—and if you ask him he says "that [his cousin] is my grandmother" and for me he says that I am his mother.
>
> *Marta*: And how do you see yourself? More like a mother or a grandmother or?
>
> *Graciela*: Both.
>
> *Marta*: Could you explain how that is?
>
> *Graciela*: Well, I love him with all my heart like a son, and I am his grandmother. But sometimes, once in a while, I tell him "I am not your mother, you have another mother," because I want him to start getting it, because he needs a psychologist, but … because if I start telling him "I am your *may* [vernacular for mother], I am your *may*" then I am hurting him, do you understand?
>
> *Marta*: And why do you think that it is important to make that distinction clear?
>
> *Graciela*: Because it is possible that his mind may start doing *maldades* [having evil thoughts], because I would be to blame if he would start doing that, and it is better to start talking to him from an early age.

Graciela's case also illustrates one of the strategies deployed by low-income Puerto Rican grandmothers, who overwhelmingly live in public housing, to circumvent housing policies that are informed by U.S. normative life-course views and conceptualizations of the family. Graciela has multiple health problems and lives by herself in subsidized housing for seniors and people with disabilities. The grandson whom she cares for is the son of her son, who is the legal custodial parent, but who suffers from depression and cannot take care of the child. Thus Graciela has arranged for the grandson to attend school very close to her apartment, and she takes care of him. However, the grandson must go to her daughter's house in a different part of town to sleep because Boston public housing codes do not allow family members who are not on the lease to sleep overnight.

Hispanic elders tend to live in proximity to children and other family members, and, on average, they have a larger number of children than non-Hispanic whites. The relatively larger family size increases the possibility of the frequency of interaction and of intergenerational solidarity (Valle and Cook-Gait 1998). Nonetheless, there has been an increase in the like-lihood of independent living among unmarried elderly Hispanic females since the 1990s (Burr and Mutchler 1992), a phenomenon that has the potential to decrease the frequency of interaction with children. This trend applies particularly to Puerto Rican populations. Because of their U.S. citi-zenship, Puerto Rican elders can be eligible for subsidized senior or low-income housing. In my observations, many middle-aged and senior Puerto Rican women reside in this type of housing, while still living in the same neighborhood, and sometimes the same building, as their children, siblings, partners, ex-spouses, and other extended family members. However, those living in public housing are constrained by what is available. Policies that promote independent living for aging individuals, as constructed in the U.S. model of promoting independence from family, stem from a particular nor-mative understanding of the life course and the historical emphasis on the nuclear family in the United States (Lamb 2007).

These policies have important implications for the informal and inter-generational social support available to the increasing number of older Puerto Rican women living alone with their grandchildren. The limited availability of housing options may at times interfere with the Puerto Rican indigenous model of family organization, which includes extended family members and an emphasis on intergenerational solidarity. Thus, it does not seem farfetched to hypothesize that the adaptation to this form of living ar-rangement may contribute to diminishing involvement of immediate and extended family members in raising a grandchild, especially when relatives do not reside in the same neighborhood.

Older Puerto Rican grandmothers and great-grandmothers who reside in senior living arrangements face additional challenges in carrying out their "mothering" duties. In the Boston area, for example, senior public housing codes do not allow grandchildren or other relatives to stay over-night. Therefore, grandmothers who have primary or partial responsibility for grandchildren, but who do not have legal custody, must find alterna-tive sleeping arrangements for their grandchildren, or else they must hide them from management and risk eviction. Even if these grandmothers have access to senior housing, accommodating grandchildren may pose problems for custodial grandmothers because these buildings are not de-signed to house children, and grandmothers must deal with problems such as cramped spaces, the small availability of larger units in the same build-ing, and the prohibition against school buses stopping at their building. Moreover, when Puerto Rican grandmothers need a larger apartment for their children and themselves, they may be reluctant to move to a different apartment complex because they have already developed supportive relationships with other Spanish-speaking seniors living in the same building. Those who live in majority English-speaking communities report experiencing greater social and linguistic isolation.

Grandmothers raising grandchildren in Hispanic cultures both inside and outside the United States do not see this as constituting an "abnormal" family arrangement. Many of the women I interviewed took on the responsibility of grandparenting in their early forties, before the advent of menopause, and interpreted this act and new role as "normal" or "natural." Indeed, they consider this role equivalent to raising their own biological children. In their explanations of the "naturalness" or "normalness" of the role, Puerto Rican grandmothers allude to the idea that becoming a grandparent and a custodial or main caregiver did not mark the entrance into a different life stage; therefore they raised the child as one of their own. Amarilis, the 44-year-old grandmother raising her grandson, felt just like a mother again when she adopted her grandson, especially because of her own relative youth and the fact that she cared for and tended to the grandson since he was an infant. "[I feel like a mother] because, even though I am a grandmother, I feel like I have started again, like having a child, because— as I told you—I had always wanted to have a boy, and I had three girls, and the first grandson was a boy and I felt like I was the one who had given birth, because I was in bed, waking up every two hours to give him milk, and I did not let my daughter touch him. I was so excited about this boy."

Although for young grandmothers assuming the mother/grandmother role may not mark entrance into old age, their new grandmother-raising-grandchildren role is not exactly a continuity of mothering either. Puerto Rican grandmothers like Amarilis interpret the mother/grandmother role as a second chance at motherhood, and as an opportunity to maintain a younger functional age, that is, to remain physically and mentally active in order to delay or avoid the appearance of functional limitations that may come with aging. In a sort of paradoxical twist, being a mother/grandmother may serve as a way of restoring or maintaining youth. Grandmothers also feel that they have arrived at a point in their lives at which they can offer more support to their children, since they benefit from greater maturity and wisdom, more life experiences, and time to devote to the child. At sixty-six, Carmina, who is raising an adolescent granddaughter and her grandson, relates this idea: "I feel more now ... better taking care of the grandchildren, *fíjese* [look here]! ... I have more experience ... because the daughters are always working and going out, and because I am already getting old ... because it is always said that when you get old you may start feeling down.... I do not want to reach that point yet, I want to keep moving here and there ... in order to feel better." For Carmina, having the company of her grandchildren and great-grandson and keeping busy by caring for them helps her to maintain a high morale and delay as much as possible the feeling of being "old." (For the role of paid work in creating meaning and a sense of "busyness" among older adults, see Lynch, this volume.)

Why Puerto Rican Grandmothers Become "Mothers"

In the social science literature, grandmothers raising grandchildren in the United States has been constructed as a new social problem whose exponential increase has been linked to the crack-cocaine epidemic (Roe et al. 1996). The Puerto Rican grandmothers whom I interviewed in the Boston area reported problems with their own children as the main reason for assuming their custodial role. In some cases, the daughter may have lost custody because of neglect or abuse of the child that was often associated with drug use or with an abusive relationship with an intimate partner. Other times a son—whose partner may be incapable of taking care of the child—asks his mother to assist him in taking care of the child or assuming the custodial role. Yet, quite often, the mother of the child is simply too young, a minor, or lacks the mental maturity to take good care of the newborn ("*no tenía la capacidad*," "she did not have the maturity/wisdom to do so") at which point the grandmother feels compelled to intervene. In the following quote, Ramona, a 67-year-old grandmother and great-grandmother raising children, illustrates this scenario: "Well, I became a grandmother when I was forty, when I had my first granddaughter, and then I did not have the custody, but I was taking care of her, I had to take care of her, because the mother was very young.... My daughter was fifteen years old, and then I had to help her because *ella no tenía la capacidad.*" Because childbearing has typically started at an early age (often before age twenty) for the custodial grandmother, the daughter, and sometimes the granddaughter, it is common to find not only grandmothers raising grandchildren, but also great-grandmothers like Ramona, who are also raising great-grandchildren.

In a similar case, Paquita, a 61-year-old grandmother, whose grandchild is 21 and still living with her, explains that her 34-year-old daughter is addicted to drugs and has already given birth to 13 children because "she does not have respect for her body" (*no respeta su cuerpo*). Paquita also shares with me that her daughter has "given away" all her children; in other words, she has given them either for adoption or foster care. Photographs of all of these grandchildren decorate a wall in the grandmother's living room. Here she explains the reasons for assuming custody of her first grandchild while she was still living in Puerto Rico: "[I assumed custody] because the mom was a minor [fourteen years old], and because she was a minor, I had to be the guardian of the child until ... the mother took responsibility, but she never took responsibility as a mother. So, all along I was the grandmother and the mother." Sometimes when a grandmother is raising a granddaughter (at times with other grandchildren), that granddaughter becomes a teenage mother while still living with the grandmother. Therefore, it was not at all unusual to find that several of the women I interviewed simultaneously were custodial grandmothers and great-grandmothers.

In spite of the growing numbers of Latina grandmothers raising grandchildren, very few studies have been conducted on this population, and ethnographic accounts are especially lacking (Burnette 1999; Goodman and Silverstein 2002). Puerto Rican grandmothers present an interesting case study because of their particular historical idiosyncrasy compared to other Latino and non-Latino groups. In 1917, Puerto Ricans were granted U.S. citizenship. Since that time, large communities of Puerto Ricans were formed primarily in New York City and secondarily in other Northeastern areas, including Boston. Unlike many recent low-income Hispanic immigrants who may face problems obtaining services due to their legal status, Puerto Ricans have access to basic U.S. entitlement programs, such as affordable housing, Medicaid, Medicare, Supplemental Security Income (SSI), and food stamps. Their legal and constitutional ties to the United States also allow them the right to assume custody of grandchildren in the United States. Although Puerto Ricans can move freely from the island to the mainland, they are culturally distinct from the mainland majority, and, like other immigrants, undergo a similar process of social and cultural adaptation. This immigration experience shapes the life course of first-generation immigrant women and their offspring in many significant ways. For instance, low-income immigrant women often move to the United States in search of a better quality of life for themselves and for their children and families, *"pa tirar p'alante"* ("to move ahead," in Puerto Rican vernacular), and they normally form a protective shield against potentially adverse situations. When their children find themselves in a life crisis or at a "stressful point" in their lives, many Puerto Rican women feel obliged to sacrifice themselves in order to offer their children or grandchildren better opportunities in the United States. Oliva, quoted in the beginning of the chapter, exemplifies this scenario. She is a single mother of five daughters, custodial grandmother of two adolescent grandchildren, and occasional caregiver for several other grandchildren: "When I came here, I came with the desire and the idea of *superarme* [bettering myself], to learn English, to work ... and then my oldest daughter got pregnant, and she was in school, and so, *este*, I stopped going to school [she was taking English courses], because I wanted her to study. And this was bad because I was still young ... but, so, *este*, I always wanted my daughters to study, because I did not study, because I came from a humble family ... and so I dedicated myself to taking care of the baby."[3]

Oliva's decision to migrate was motivated by a desire to become more educated and to have a second chance in life; she was hoping for the opportunity to move out of poverty in the United States. However, she had to "stop" her own aspirations in order to take care of her grandchildren and allow her five daughters to educate themselves and improve their life chances. Subsequently, she was also simultaneously taking care of her own mother who had Alzheimer's disease, and whom she brought from Puerto Rico to the mainland. In my observations, I have often found that Puerto Rican women's sacrifices involve taking the responsibility for a grandchild, while allowing their children to attend college or some form of educational training, search for employment, find better housing, overcome a financial crisis or a health problem, or resolve marital conflicts.

Puerto Rican Grandmothers' Role Strain

Some Puerto Rican women experience role strain, in other words, the role expectations and obligations of being a grandmother raising a grandchild may exceed their own abilities and/or desires. They become preoccupied with their grandmother responsibilities when the grandmother-raising-grandchildren role becomes recurrent and/or they start feeling "*cansada*" (tired), when they have health problems, when they experience "role conflict" brought by the competing demands of taking care of ill spouses or parents, or when taking care of their own health issues. Rafaela is sixty-seven and the grandmother or great-grandmother of thirty-two children, and the mother of eight children (seven of whom are alive). She has had a happy family life but had to work very hard both inside and outside of the home to support such a large family. She began experiencing role strain when her husband, with whom there was a twenty-year age difference, became ill. Rafaela's husband had been very supportive in raising or helping to raise her children and grandchildren, and when he became ill, she felt that she could not do it all. Moreover, she was simultaneously taking care of her own ill mother whom she brought from Puerto Rico. Rafaela described her experiences in this way: "It was not easy ... a soap opera could be made about it ... because it was not easy. I have worked very hard in this life, and now I already feel *cansada* [tired], because I do not have the same strength that I had before." Rafaela explains that she went through a severe depression after the death of her husband, and that because she neglected herself during this period of mourning, she developed diabetes and other health problems. For all these reasons, she now feels that she does not have the same strength to care for small children as before.

Another woman, Mercedes—who had already raised a grandson and was hoping to move back to Puerto Rico—explains that becoming a caregiver for her grandchildren has been especially difficult because she suffers from depression. Mercedes, who is fifty-six, has already raised a grandson alone and is currently raising three grandchildren (by the same daughter) ages four, three, and two, while her daughter receives medical treatment for hepatitis. As she said, "It is affecting me, but I must do it, because she [my daughter] is sick; because if she was not sick, I would not have done it, because at my age ... but I try, until one day I say 'Well, I cannot do it any longer.'" Even though Rafaela and Mercedes both experience role strain and suffering when they see their own children and grandchildren in dire circumstances, for the majority of Puerto Rican grandmothers, this caregiver role seems to enhance their sense of life purpose and connection to society. As Latina women aging in the United States, they have few opportunities for socialization outside of the family. In this context, becoming a caregiver allows these women to gain a feeling of social visibility.

Conclusion: Grandmothering and the Life Course

The ordering of family and domestic life is increasingly becoming more diverse and less predictable (Phillipson and Allan 2004) in the United States. The life-course trajectories of many low-income immigrant Latina grandmothers and their offspring do not fit the normative pattern of the majority U.S. non-Hispanic white population. Therefore, the application of normative theoretical models to the explication of the custodial grandmothering phenomenon could have only partial success at best.

Psychologist Erik Erikson, in his model of psychosocial development, describes the last developmental tasks of "integrity versus despair and disgust" as a period in which "only he who in some way has taken care of things and people and has adapted himself to the triumphs and disappointments of being, by necessity, the originator of others and the generator of things and ideas—only he may gradually grow the fruit of seven stages" (1959: 98). Erikson's developmental emphasis on "taking care of things and people" is relevant to the many low-income Puerto Rican women who have had very limited resources and opportunities for integration in mainstream U.S. society over their life course, and for whom becoming a custodial grandmother represents a second chance at parenthood and a way of making an impact on the lives of their families and, by extension, on their particular communities. Moreover, the older Puerto Rican women I spoke

with find the experience of custodial grandmothering psychologically re-
warding, especially because they perceive old age in mainstream U.S. society as a lonely and isolating experience. Carmina, sixty-six, explains this
idea: "I feel happy, because I still have a full house. I have not experienced
loneliness, thank God!" Similarly, Graciela appreciates the companionship
and support of her seven-year-old grandson:

> *Graciela*: He loves me; he asks me "*Mami*, did you take your pills?" Then, I
> cannot have depression in spite of all the illnesses that I have, because I have
> to be taking care of him, and I have no time to be thinking about everything
> that is happening to me, do you understand?
>
> *Marta*: So, because of your health problems you think that without the
> grandchild ...
>
> *Graciela*: Exactly! And I am alone! And then I start to think.... But with him
> ... no.... When one is alone, one sits down and then you feel all the aches and
> pains, all the illnesses coming to you ... and I ... I am sick because of my age,
> but I do not feel sick.

Thus, the grandmothers' caregiving role keeps them and their household
at the center of family interaction, helps them remain socially active, gives
them a reason to stay healthy, and even furthers their gender-derived social
power within the family (see Lynch, this volume, on a similar benefit of
paid work among some Anglo-American older adults). This suggests that,
like Gamburd's findings in Sri Lanka (this volume), cultivating intergenerational exchanges of support may be seen as beneficial to aging individuals.
Ego integrity may be achieved by being able to see many generations of their
family and their role and impact on so many lives. In the following quote,
Rafaela, sixty-seven, describes this feeling of having successfully completed
the life cycle: "I feel satisfaction and pride that The Lord has allowed me to
see my grandchildren and he has allowed me to raise grandchildren and
great-grandchildren." In essence, this mother/grandmother role facilitates
the achievement of ego-integrity for low-income Puerto Rican women in
spite of their socially disadvantageous position. As Erikson explains, "the
possessor of integrity is ready to defend the dignity of his own life style
against all physical and economic threats" (1959: 98).

Being a caregiver is central to these women's own social identity. In
many cases, not only have their family lives shaped an identity that is tied
to "mothering"—whether by taking care of their own children or siblings
from an early age—but these women's work experiences have also been
linked to social reproduction. Several Puerto Rican grandmothers were
employed as housemaids and nannies while living in Puerto Rico when
they were as young as twelve or thirteen years old. Moreover, many Puerto

Rican women became foster mothers in the United States and take great pride in the social "mother" role they performed. Hence, continuity can also be achieved through the mother/grandmother role. As in the case of aging women from the "*classe popular*" in the state of Santa Catalina, Brazil (Brown, this volume), their role in social reproduction remains so long as they stay healthy. Ultimately, in trying to comprehend the meanings of the grandmother's caregiver role in the U.S. mainland, one needs to elucidate the dynamic and complex intersections of state regulatory powers and definitions of family; old cultural notions and new hybrid immigrant adaptations; and the connections between these and Puerto Rican women's own life histories, social locations, and personal meanings.

Acknowledgments

Funding for data collection on Puerto Rican grandmothers raising grandchildren in Boston was provided by the Bingham-Young Faculty Grant, Transylvania University for research during summer 2009. I wish to thank the Boston Puerto Rican Health Center at Northeastern University for collaboration in helping me identify potential subjects. Finally, thanks also to Jason Danely, Caitrin Lynch, and anonymous reviewers for their helpful and insightful comments and suggestions.

Notes

1. Although some scholars make ideological and political distinctions between the terms Latino and Hispanic, I use them interchangeably in this article. "Hispanic" generally refers to a person who traces his/her origin to a Spanish speaking country, whereas "Latino" (in the U.S. context) refers to a person who traces his/her origin to Latin America.
2. The names of all the grandmothers quoted in this chapter are pseudonyms. All interview quotes were in Spanish and translated by me.
3. The term "*este*" indicates hesitation, as in "um" or "ah."

10. CARE WORK AND PROPERTY TRANSFERS

Intergenerational Family Obligations in Sri Lanka

Michele Ruth Gamburd

SRI LANKANS CURRENTLY FACE CHANGES in crucial contextual circumstances, including the aging of the population and the prevalence of transnational migration. In demographic terms, Sri Lanka's total population is stabilizing, but its population structure is changing rapidly, from a pyramid with many younger people and few elders, to the column that characterizes most developed nations (de Silva 2007; World Bank 2008). Simultaneously, Sri Lanka's global economic integration is growing. Since the late 1970s, increasing numbers of guest laborers have migrated to work in the oil-producing nations in the Gulf (M. Gamburd 2000). In 2009, over 1.8 million Sri Lankans (8 percent of the island's population of 20 million, and 24 percent of the total number of employed Sri Lankans) worked abroad and remitted funds to Sri Lanka (SLBFE 2009: 140). Because more than half of these migrants are female, the number of locally available caregivers has been significantly reduced—while simultaneously the number of truly needy elders has begun to increase.

Usually depicted in statistical summaries, these large-scale trends in aging and migration affect people in personal and intimate ways. Acting in family units, people cooperatively allocate care work and make decisions about migration. Kin relationships carry social force because they entail moral obligations (Stone 2010: 5) and impose intergenerational rights and responsibilities throughout the extended family. (For discussion of the impacts of kin relationships on intergenerational rights and responsibilities, in this volume see Brown's discussion of Brazil and Guyer and Salami's discussion of Nigeria.) To understand the local impact of global and national trends, scholars must explore the cultural rules, expectations, and emotional ties that govern kinship obligations.

In this chapter, I examine how Sri Lankan families handle intergenerational transfers of property, money, and care. Through ethnographic methods, I explore the current norms and expectations that govern the treatment of elders, including the care of distant relatives. I examine local debates over acceptable and unacceptable forms of elder care, including conversations about newly emerging old age homes (see Lamb 2009 and this volume). In the process, I consider people's understanding of duty, their calculations of risk, and elders' strategies to minimize the possibility of neglect and to leverage attention and care. I also investigate how family members grapple with conflicting values when the gap between expectations and reality is not easy to bridge. I conclude with some thoughts on how the demographic transition and current migratory patterns may challenge and change cultural norms about kinship and care.

Research Methods

Naeaegama[1] is a village of Sinhala-speaking Buddhists near the coast in southwestern Sri Lanka. I have performed ethnographic research in this village of 1,100 people since 1992. In 2009, I undertook two months of research on the topic of intergenerational family obligations surrounding aging and the life course. I gathered the data discussed here from twenty-nine Naeaegama informants interviewed individually or in groups of two or three. Some informants (eight) were in their sixties and seventies but did not yet need care. Others needed some extra care (four) or had experience as caregivers for elderly family members (seventeen).

My long-time research associate Siri and I quickly realized the difficulty of broaching topics of intergenerational obligations and eldercare directly. Such queries probed intimate emotional and financial matters. After nearly two decades of developing rapport with members of these families and learning Naeaegama norms for appropriate interactions, bluntly asking questions about these topics would have seemed inexcusably rude and intrusive. Therefore, Siri and I employed an indirect approach. We asked all of our interviewees to comment on a series of twelve fictional scenarios that addressed the ethical dilemmas and choices we wished to explore. (Three scenarios dealing with intra-family exchanges of care work and material assets are discussed here.) We asked that for each scenario, our interviewee discuss what he or she thought the people in the scenario should do, and why they should do it. We asked this of all interviewees. When we felt it was appropriate, we asked whether the interviewee knew of any actual cases of this sort. In some circumstances, people volunteered information about a situation in their own family; in such cases we let people provide as much or as little information as they saw fit. Using this strategy, we garnered rich data without strong-arming our informants with bad-mannered demands

FIGURE 10.1 Women worship during a ceremony at the Buddhist temple in Naeaegama. Photo by Michele Ruth Gamburd.

for private information, and our interlocutors could avoid what they perceived as sensitive subjects without discourteously refusing to answer a question.

As a research technique, the use of scenarios has both advantages and disadvantages. An advantage is that scenarios trigger trenchant conversations and elicit nuanced replies with lower risks of bias because interlocutors can be objective in their responses without the fear of having their private lives intruded upon. However, a disadvantage is that this approach is likely to generate normative responses. As ethnographers commonly note, what people say they would do in an ideal case can be at odds with what they actually do when confronting a real situation. Therefore, I present some actual cases from Naeaegama, as well as villagers' discussions of the scenarios.

The Intergenerational Transfer of Property

Elaborate and widely accepted cultural rules about the reciprocal exchanges of property and eldercare shape how elders and their heirs transferred these valuable goods and services. To elicit discussion of these rules, Siri and I crafted a scenario involving an elder who has considerable property. We described the fictitious family's finances and then asked our informants, "Should the elder 'write' the land to an heir? If so, when?" Writing the land could consist of signing a deed over to the heir, or writing a will through which the original owner maintained a life interest in the property but designated who would be the next owner upon his or her death.

Unless someone has left explicit instructions to the contrary, the current inheritance law leaves half of a deceased person's property to his or her spouse. The other half is divided equally among all of the deceased's legitimate children. If a widow, widower, or unmarried person passes away, his or her property is divided between the children or reverts to next of kin. If someone passes away without leaving a will, the estate can get mired in a costly and drawn-out court case, with agents of the state becoming involved in tracing kinship links, tracking past sales of land shares, surveying the property, and dividing the land.

When asked how an elder with property should pass it down to heirs, the majority of our informants felt that the elder should write it early for the sake of the entire family. In separate interviews, several village residents imagined in vivid detail the disputes that could arise in the event of the sudden death of a property owner who did not have a will. Amerasinghe, eighty-eight and the father of four grown children, said, "If you keep it in your own name and die without writing the land, then there will be a big problem. The kids and also outsiders will blame the elder." Titus, a man in his forties with three sons, concurred, noting, "They will fight about who gets which piece, the piece by the gate or the piece with the jack tree." Lalith, a cinnamon peeler in his late thirties from a large family, made a similar comment: "The landowner needs to distribute it, or else the kids will go to the court. There will be a war for the better half of the land." He then pointed toward his own family property, and said, "Take us as an example!" He laughed. "In our case it would just be a question of whose fist would win. And the family would be destroyed. We would end up with two brothers dead and the third in jail for murder!" Legally binding instructions for the distribution of property can and do help families avoid such fragmenting confrontations.

In discussing this scenario in separate interviews, several neighbors and relatives mentioned the case of Padmasiri, a recently deceased elderly man with three sons and three daughters. Padmasiri held two acres of land, with three houses and a small business. The two married sons and their families each occupied a new house, and a divorced son had been living in the original family home with his father. The three daughters were married and lived elsewhere. After Padmasiri's death, his three sons claimed that their sisters had no right to the land, even though their father had not officially deeded or willed his property exclusively to the sons. They claimed that one sister in particular had no right to a share in the land because Padmasiri had already written her the deed for the land on which she and her husband lived. Padmasiri's sons refused to let their sisters exercise their legal right to pluck coconuts from the land. In anger, the sisters filed a court case and refused to take part in the almsgiving honoring the three-month anniversary of their father's death—a solemn moment for the public display of family unity and respect for the departed elder (see Figure 10.2). Villagers cited this case as a prime example of the damaging family disputes that could arise over parental failure to distribute property.

Speaking of his three sons, Titus perceptively isolated the root issue: parents need to obtain property for all of their male children. Although sons and daughters inherit property equally in this part of Sri Lanka, the dominant, preferred, and most prestigious post-marriage residence pattern is virilocality: a daughter at marriage receives a dowry and moves to her husband's property (G. Gamburd 2010). Thus parents often assume, as one informant put it, that "sons need land but daughters don't." Titus felt

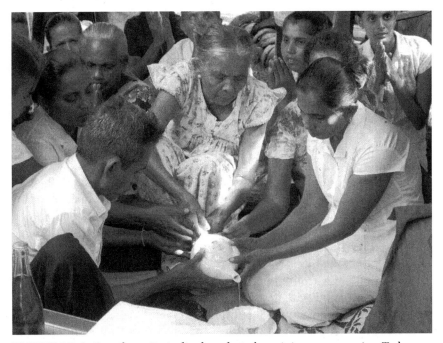

FIGURE 10.2 Family unity is displayed at almsgiving ceremonies. To honor a deceased relative, family members collaboratively pour water out of a pot. Photo by Michele Ruth Gamburd.

that all but one son should receive property elsewhere, and the youngest son should inherit the family home as well as responsibility for caring for his parents. This pattern of ultimogeniture (Strathern and Stewart 2011: 18) reflected a common ideal in the village.

Enacting the ideal of ultimogeniture could cause problems, however, if these arrangements were not formalized in writing. For example, Darshani, a woman in her mid-forties, had looked after her father-in-law until his unexpected death. She continued to look after her mother-in-law, who suffered from dementia. Her husband, the youngest son in the family, had *de facto* inherited the family home, and Darshani as his wife was fulfilling the expectation that care would be provided for the elders. But the father-in-law had passed away without deeding his land to anyone, and the mother-in-law was no longer capable of making out a will. Officially, all of the siblings owned equal shares of the land. Because the other siblings already owned land and houses elsewhere, Darshani hoped that they would not demand their shares of the small property or payment for their portion of the family home from their youngest brother when their mother passed away. Nevertheless, Darshani and her husband were in a precarious situation, having already provided long-term care for the elderly couple, but having left implicit the arrangement about property inheritance.

Although in Darshani's case an explicit agreement about property would have been welcome, in other cases informants saw a danger in formalizing the inheritance. Deeding a bigger share of the property to one particular individual might obligate that person to do more care work, but doing so did not guarantee care, and it could alienate those who did not stand to inherit property. For example, Ramani, thirty-seven and the mother of four children, noted: "If the parents don't distribute the money and property equally, then the ones who didn't get any will say, 'You gave us nothing. We won't help you. Tell the one to whom you gave the land to help.' If the parents give to everyone, then no one can say, 'You didn't give to me.'" Deeding all of one's property to one child implicitly relieved the other children of some of their obligations to provide care.

Although most people said that it was better to formalize the inheritance, a small but vocal minority of my informants felt that the landowner in the scenario should hold on to the property until he or she died, lest an ungrateful heir take the inheritance and fail to provide care. For example, Rukmini, a middle-aged widow with two daughters, worried that, "If you write your land to your kids, you can't say whether they might abandon you once you have written it." Renuka, a widow in her early fifties, felt the same way. She instructed the elder in the scenario: "Keep the power in your own hand. Some people support elders only until the land is written to them." Similarly, Virasena, a man from a large family in his late fifties who had cared for his aging mother, felt that someone should "after getting help, give the property at the last minute to the person who provided care. It's not good to write the land earlier." In these situations, the elder could direct the inheritance after some or most of the care had already been provided.

Anura, a 35-year-old former policeman and current stay-at-home father, considered the timing of writing property to reflect the degree of trust between parents and children. He said, "If you believe in your kids, you can give the land at the time of marriage. Then the father is happy and the kids are happy. The father can take a risk. If you write it at the last minute, it means that you don't trust your family. If you hold the property too long, the children will think 'the old man doesn't trust any of us.'" Anura then related to us a story that he had heard from his grandfather:

> There once was an old man who had three sons. He gave them most of his property when they got married. He kept only his own house. His three sons came to do their duty. They brought food. Things went along well for some time. Then the man decided to divide the remaining property. He did so. For about two weeks, things continued as they had before. Then gradually there were a few shortages, like not as much food and care. Things got worse and worse, to the point that the old man had to go to his sons' homes to ask for food. If the sons were at home, he would get food, but if it was just their wives, they didn't take much care.
>
> So this old man was very sad. He went out on the road to a beggar's shelter. There he met an old friend from his school days who worked as a carpenter. That friend took him home and gave him tea and heard the whole story. That friend was smart. He made for the old man a good wooden box and filled it with ceramic pieces that clinked like coins when they shifted against each other. He told the old man to keep that box with him all the time, even when he went to the toilet.
>
> The old man went home. He kept the box with him all the time. His eldest son saw that he was home, and he came to visit. He saw that his father had a box. The other sons came, and they also saw the box. They heard that something in the box clinked, and they assumed that the box was full of valuable coins. Then that old man got very good treatment from all his sons! The old man kept the box with him until he died. After the funeral, his sons opened the box—and found only broken pieces of pottery![2]

Anura's story implies that one can trust one's children, but only so far. An elder needs to hold something in reserve, as the man in the story did with his box that clinked as if it were full of coins. Naeaegama villagers with considerable assets seemed to agree implicitly with this point. At the same time, they saw the need to distribute some property in advance. For example, Sumitha was a retired schoolteacher who came from a rich family. Sobered by the recent death of their younger brother at age sixty-five, she and her surviving siblings were in the process of dividing their ancestral properties. She planned to give her share of these properties directly to her children, while continuing to live on and retaining ownership of the land her home was on. Another wealthy villager told Siri and me that he had already deeded his property to his children. He received a pension, however, so he still controlled some income.

Despite the accompanying uncertainties, the majority of my informants thought it was better to distribute their land before they died. Janaki, a retired schoolteacher and mother of four grown daughters, recognized the risk that the heir might cast out the former landowner after he had signed away the property. Another elderly woman cynically remarked, "Well, if they abandon you after you write the land to them, then you know that they were just helping for the property!" Emaline, a widow in her late sixties, speculated, "At least the children will help a little bit, even if not 100 percent perfectly. And if a death occurs, the kids will do the funeral." Most informants thought it better to risk some neglect from their children than to endanger the future of the family over a property fight.

The above village cases and reactions to the first scenario reveal a number of key points about intra-family exchanges of homes, moveable assets, money, and caretakers' time. In Naeaegama as in many other areas in South Asia, the general parameters of intergenerational obligations outline clear expectations that parents will provide an upbringing for children, giving dowries to daughters and properties to sons (Jeffery and Jeffery 2010). In exchange, adult children (particularly the youngest son and his family) will look after the parents until their deaths. In such long-term, extended cases of intergenerational reciprocity, however, it is impossible to keep exact track of who owes what to whom, particularly because the obligations surpass mere economics and involve strongly felt emotions (Magazine and Sanchez 2007). In fact, *not* keeping exact track of debt and obligation is precisely the nature of generalized reciprocity characterized by family interactions (Cronk 2008).

Within the general expectation of trust and love, however, lurk areas of risk and fear. By formalizing large financial interactions such as the inheritance of property, elders could simultaneously reward those who provided care and alienate the family members who did not inherit. Some elders held off on writing their land in order to leverage attention from a wide range of kin and minimize the risk of neglect. At the same time, failing to formalize property arrangements could lead to expensive court cases and family-destroying fights, which elders sought to avert. The cultural traditions of virilocal residence and ultimogeniture provided a template for handling the transfer of property and the provision of care for the aged. Within this framework, elders agentively negotiated interactions with their kin with varying degrees of trust, retaining or relinquishing control over money and land depending on individual personalities and family circumstances.

The Duties of Distant Relatives

Kinship structures endure in the face of poverty and hardship; indeed, kin operate as a social insurance scheme when all other resources are exhausted (Blackwood 2005; Stack 1970; Weismantel 1995). Villagers uniformly stated that "of course" children should take care of their own parents regardless of financial transactions. But who was responsible for unmarried aunts and uncles? By presenting informants with a scenario of a somewhat attenuated kin connection, Siri and I hoped to get at the sentimental and economic interactions that cemented care relationships between more distant relatives. In our second scenario, we described an elderly, childless, unmarried woman who lived with her married younger brother. We asked, "When she grows frail, who should assume responsibility for her care?" Key points that arose in discussing this scenario included obligatory kinship duties, the emotional quality of past interactions, temporal duration of cohabitation, and the degree of exchange of time and other resources between the elderly aunt and members of her household.

Kinship ties created a duty to share housing with the elderly aunt. In the Naeaegama area as in the rest of rural Sri Lanka, women of all ages must live within a multi-person household, preferably with a resident adult male relative; it is not acceptable for a woman to live alone or with only small children as company (Hussein 2000: 17; Marecek and Appuhamilage 2011). The aunt's brother and his children were deemed responsible not only for her housing but also for the care that she might need as she aged. One informant suggested that the brother's family was more responsible for her because she was unmarried than it would have been if she had been wed (in which case some responsibility would have passed to her husband's family). She was considered "one's own blood" or "one's own person," for whom individuals had a compulsory duty to care.

In discussing the scenario of the childless aunt, a number of informants imaginatively fleshed out the interpersonal relationships in question. For example, Anura noted: "An elder woman like that can become like a grandmother to her grandnieces and grandnephews. But she needs to have done stuff for that family, without fighting with her in-laws. Her brother loves her, but she needs to be careful also not to fight with her sister-in-law. And if the aunt has helped with the tuition fees for the nieces and nephews, walked them to school when they were young, and washed their clothing, then those kids have to help her out. If she has properties, they will expect to inherit them. They will look after her if she has laid the groundwork correctly. But the unmarried one needs to take care of it carefully in advance." He concluded, "You harvest what you sow." Similarly, Dayawansa, a 73-year-old retired schoolmaster, noted that the woman's brother would certainly look after her; her nephews and nieces should, but might not, do so too. He said, "Her brother is the closest relative, and it is compulsory for him to help. But his wife is looking to the other side [toward her own kin]. And his kids are not such close relatives." In this case, informants felt that to ensure support, kinship duty should be bolstered by positive emotions and a history of generosity.

A number of villagers asserted straightforwardly that material exchanges were important in cementing the care relationship. For example, Sumitha assumed that the childless aunt in the scenario had lived with her brother's family and helped them in the past. She concluded, "Those kids love her. If she has property, she will probably leave it to them. So they will help her." Perera, a 59-year-old house painter, asked Siri and me about this elder woman: "Does she have land?" We imagined that she did. "Then they will come and wash her feet until she dies," he opined, and we all burst into laughter at the image of a sodden elder receiving unending service of the greatest symbolic value, akin to that offered to Buddhist monks, bridegrooms, and visiting dignitaries. Perera cautioned, however, that this old aunt should be careful to distribute her assets equally to all of her kin, lest some feel slighted and refuse to help.

To complement the scenario discussions above, consider the actual case of three unmarried Naeaegama siblings who had lived until their deaths in a large joint household with a number of nephews and nieces and their families. Members of the sandwich generation had distributed the responsibility for the three elders between them; several of the responsible relatives no longer lived in the village but sent funds to support their aunts and uncle, while those living locally took care of day-to-day needs. This care included help with medical issues, food, other maintenance, and finally the performance of the funeral. As part of the relationship, these nieces and nephews received their elder charges' shares of the family property.

Several informants speculated on what would happen to an elderly woman who had not lived with a sibling. When Siri and I were deliberately vague about the living situation in the scenario, Ramani noted: "It's important to know how this aunt lived and who she helped and whether she had a job. That would help me to figure out the family obligations. If she was just living alone doing a job, she should know to save money so that she can hire a servant in her old age." Ramani suggested that an individual should plan on purchasing care for hire if she has not been able to cultivate a relationship with her nieces and nephews and their children, "mixing" with them repeatedly over the years in large or small but deeply meaningful ways that merge their lives together and cement her place in the center of the family (Trawick 1990: 83–8).

Kin relationships give individuals a claim on the time, space, and material resources of their relatives. But when people are busy, houses are crowded, and families are poor, individuals must negotiate their particular obligations to closer and more distant relatives. Childless elders can strategically reinforce kinship ties by cultivating emotional closeness, investing time and other resources in their junior kin, and amassing assets to pass on to heirs.

Having sufficient money, space, and time could make kinship duties easier to fulfill, and several informants remarked that educated and wealthy people were more likely to shoulder the responsibility gracefully. For individuals with ample schooling and funds who were short on time, however, other conundrums could arise, as the following scenario illustrates.

Acceptable and Unacceptable Forms of Elder Care

In her elegant discussion of the rise of old age homes in urban Kolkata, Sarah Lamb explores Indians' valuations of such institutions as on one hand enabling independence and freedom, and on the other hand leading to alienation and abandonment (Lamb 2009: 56; see also Lamb this volume). Lamb's informants credited the rise of old age homes to a number of modern trends, including the breakdown of the extended family, women's entry into the workforce, children's migration to foreign countries, and a "westernization" marked by more money and less time (Lamb 2009: 68). Examining comparable values in Sri Lanka, Siri and I explored acceptable and unacceptable forms of eldercare, focusing on the cultural norms that stigmatize residence in old age homes. To accomplish this, we crafted the final scenario discussed here, in which an older man, whose son is a doctor, resides in an "old folks home" (to use the local term).[3] We described the fictitious situation and asked our informants, "Do you think that the father will talk with staff, fellow residents, and visitors about his son? In particular, will he tell people about his son's job?"

Issues of eldercare resonate with deep emotions, including trust, love, and pride, as well as fear, shame, and anger. One key element of this scenario is the conflict between the pride a parent feels in a son's accomplishments and the shame that both son and parent are culturally conditioned to feel about placing an elder in a care facility. As illustration, consider this interaction between Naveen (in his twenties) and his mother Indrani (fiftynine), who had cared for her mother-in-law until her recent death.

Upon hearing the scenario, Indrani surmised, "The father won't tell, to protect the son's reputation."

But Naveen thought that the father would talk about his son because he was proud. "Of course he will talk about his son," Naveen exclaimed. "His son is not a robber!"

"That's true," Indrani replied. "But he's not helping his father! Couldn't a doctor at least hire a servant for his father, rather than putting him in a facility?"

"Some people want to go to old folks homes rather than having servants or troubling their kids," Naveen asserted.

"I can't think that way!" Indrani protested. The conversation had gotten heated by this point, and Indrani turned to Siri for support. She asked, "Wouldn't it be embarrassing for your son if you were in an old folks home?"

Diplomatically, Siri agreed that his son would be too embarrassed to put him in a facility, but also noted that some residents entered old folks homes willingly. Naveen agreed vehemently with this point, noting, "It's like when someone who is in a bad argument at home goes to the temple for relief."

Informants discussed a number of conflicting emotions in relation to this scenario. Sumitha noted, "Some fathers will tell, because they are proud; others will tell because they are angry. Some won't talk about the son's job, because it is a disgrace to the son." Mahanama Thero, the Buddhist monk at the local temple, opined that a parent might speak out of pain, rather than staying silent out of shame. Retired policeman Anura suggested, "If the father says that his son is a doctor, then the people can understand that the son doesn't love the father and the father doesn't love the son. If the son and father are okay together, then the father won't tell anyone that his son is a doctor." Informants frequently noted that it was an "embarrassment" or a "shortfall" to put a parent in an old folks home. Such an "ugly" act was the opposite of treating one's parent with respect. Opinions varied over whether the shame belonged only to the son or also to his father and the rest of the family. Most informants felt that the parent bore no blame in the matter but did partake of the overarching stigma that attached to the family reputation.

In addition to examining the conflict between pride and shame, villagers who took more nuanced positions about old folks homes brought up a second set of possible conflicts. This discussion focused on the difference between having taken a parent and left him or her at an old folks home by force, which informants universally deemed wrong or a sin, and turning a parent over respectfully to a high-quality institution for care, which informants deemed acceptable under certain conditions, though rarely optimal (see also Lamb 2009: 94).

Exploring this scenario with her 43-year-old daughter Shivanthi, Emaline said: "Some parents will have been brought to the old folks home by force, angrily. They will talk. They will say of their children, 'This one is like this and that one is like that.'" The conversation continued:

> Shivanthi chimed in to say, "If children put their parents in a for-pay facility, not a free one, it is better." A short discussion of various for-pay facilities in the area followed.
>
> Emaline agreed, saying, "The for-pay places are okay. If the kids are busy with their jobs, they can pay and keep their parents in that sort of place comfortably." She compared elders who went to an old folks home "happily" with those who were left there against their will. She felt that those who went happily would not speak badly of their children, especially if their children visited frequently.
>
> I asked, "Is it shameful to put parents in a facility?"
>
> Usually informants answered this question with an unconditional "yes." In this case, however, Shivanthi nuanced her reply. She said, "It's not a shame if they went happily and they are in a for-pay place."
>
> But Emaline added in a whisper, "No parent really wants to go to an old folks home. Even if they go to a better place, a for-pay place, parents might be angry. I myself would prefer to stay in my own house even if I have to sleep on a mat on the floor and go without eating, rather than to leave. At least my kids will help me with food." After a thoughtful pause, she continued, saying she did not want to make problems for her children. "It's not just the kids' fault that parents go to old folks homes. The parents are also sometimes at fault. When you are old, you need to obey your children and be satisfied with what they give you."

In this discussion of the scenario, Emaline and Shivanthi spoke about trade-offs: the expense of a for-pay facility can remove some of the stigma of placing an elder in an institution, but the luxury of aging in a familiar context can offset less-than-perfect care. As Emaline and Naveen sensitively pointed out, emotional factors can influence difficult decisions, and elders become vulnerable to unwelcome changes as they relinquish authority to the next generation.

A third set of conflicts brought out in this scenario concerns the sort of care that relatives could provide. In separate conversations, two local men discussed this issue. Perera made the following point: "If you can't afford to feed someone, then by putting them in a free facility you *are* taking care of them. You are sending them somewhere where they can eat! Sometimes it is like a punishment to put someone in an old folks home. But sometimes it's a necessity." Atulasena, an unmarried 62-year-old mask-maker, echoed these sentiments in a different exchange: "If you put someone in an old folks home after doing everything you can for that person, then it's okay. If you put someone in a for-pay place because you can't take care of him, it's okay." About this specific scenario, Perera felt that it would be acceptable for the doctor to put his father in a good-quality, for-pay facility, especially if the doctor's wife did not want to do that work. "If the doctor put that father in a free place, though, that's not okay. That is a shortfall." And similarly, Atulasena noted, "When parents are old, some important people will push them off to an old folks home, because they lower the household status." Although certain circumstances justified the use of a facility, he deemed this motivation improper.

Most villagers felt that elders who had children and families that had money should care for the elder at home. When we asked Lakmini, fifty-six, whether she would put her aging mother in an old folks home, she replied: "No. She has kids. This would only happen to someone without kids." For a rich person like a doctor, Sumitha felt that "it would be better to keep the father at home, according to Sri Lankan values. An old folks home is for poor people, although some other people go there too." As elsewhere in South Asia, in Naeaegama people felt that professionals owed their success in part to their parents (Lamb 2009: 181–7), whom they should repay with respect in their old age. A doctor should be rich enough to hire a servant to care for his father at home instead of placing him in a facility. In many villagers' opinion, receiving hired care was not stigmatized at home, only in an institution, and staying in the family home was the most important signifier of dignified aging.

Contextualizing Aging: Labor Migration and the Demographic Shift

As mentioned above, Naeaegama norms and values about kinship obligations, aging, care work, and the transfer of property unfold in the context of two large-scale trends: increasing transnational migration and rapid population aging in Sri Lanka.

Over the past fifty years, a steady trickle of the village elite has moved to the capital city of Colombo and abroad to Australia and the United States. In addition, beginning in the 1980s, working-class women have sojourned in West Asia in ever-growing numbers as domestic servants; these migrants' most often stated goal is to buy land and build a house to improve their family's status. Recently, members of the younger generation (often children of the older labor migrants) are going abroad, heading not only to the Gulf but also to more desirable destinations such as Korea, Cyprus, Malaysia, Israel, and Italy (M. Gamburd 2008; Wanasundera 2001), sometimes with the hope to settle permanently in their host country. As scholars have repeatedly pointed out in cases worldwide (Cole and Durham 2005: 12; Lamb 2009; Magazine and Sanchez 2005; Parrenas 2005), migration patterns affect family strategies for caring for household members.

FIGURE 10.3 A grandfather and his grandson visit the grandfather's sister. Both elders are in their 90s. Photo by Michele Ruth Gamburd.

Sri Lankan migration trends affect individuals' thoughts and plans for their future. Shivanthi, forty-three, noted, "My husband and I have no children. Now we can come and go and cook well. But when we are elderly, we will not be able to do so." She was grateful that she and her spouse would have pensions. She then remarked that she thought her younger sister's children might help her out. But Shivanthi worried, "We can't expect too much from the kids. And they might not be able to come and see us. They might live far away or go abroad, and then they would only be able to call us on the telephone." And even if an elder had offspring, it did not guarantee that he or she would live in a household with a child, particularly as ambitious and upwardly mobile members of the younger generation sought greener pastures in the city and abroad.

In tandem with extensive migration, Sri Lanka is undergoing a demographic shift. The proportion of elders is growing: the median age is projected to increase from 30 in 2001 to 43 in 2041; and the percentage of the population over 60 is projected to increase from 9.2 percent in 2000 to 29 percent by 2050 (de Silva 2007: 23; World Bank 2008: ii, 2). The demographic shift is caused by progress in a number of social indicators. It reflects declines in mortality, increases in longevity, progress in family planning, and rising rates of female education and participation in the labor force (de Silva 2007: 8–12; Gamaniratne 2007: 2–3). The causes of this transformation are positive, but the change in the population structure will create significant eldercare challenges in the near future.

In conjunction with continued transnational migration, the demographic shift is likely to exacerbate some of the difficulties that families already face in providing care. For example, consider the retired schoolteacher Janaki's rumination on the difficulty of hiring help. She said, "My daughters come home from work at 8 P.M. How can they look after me and my husband? They will have to pay someone. But you can't find a servant. All the local people are seeing to their own kids or they have gone abroad. The grandmothers are all looking after their grandkids, so you can't hire them. And those people can't put their grandkids in daycare and look after us!" Janaki's statement implicitly points out the dilemmas caused by the dwindling of available caregivers brought about by labor migration and the growing numbers of women in the workforce. As the demographic shift continues, challenges in providing care for elders and children will grow in Sri Lanka as they have in other parts of the world (see Brown this volume for Brazil; Rodríguez-Galán this volume for the United States).

The snapshot presented here of perspectives from Naeaegama in 2009 provides a benchmark from which to understand future changes in norms and expectations of eldercare. The data offer a glimpse of how families currently handle the progression of individuals through the life course, and reveal some of the values that guide them when they make decisions about employment, care work, and the transfer of property. Ethnographic materials suggest that family members will continue to care as best they can for each other, recognizing long-term obligations and duties to elders who have contributed time, money, property, and other emotional and material assets to the family. But families are not static, and the cultural rules that govern intergenerational obligations can and do shift and change over time (Bateson this volume; Collier and Yanagisako 1987; Franklin and McKinnon 2001b: 5–6; Lamb this volume). The contradictory and disputed positions and the mixed emotions revealed in villagers' responses to the three research scenarios show the difficulty of working out cultural expectations in light of actual experiences. As new generations enter the life cycle, the social values and practices that govern family relations in Sri Lanka will shift and change. These anthropological insights on social relations and the life course are important for scholars and policymakers around the world to consider in modeling future trends in labor migration and caregiving as nations grow ever more integrated in the global economy and more countries go through the demographic transformation.

Notes

1. "Naeaegama," or "the Village of Relatives," is a pseudonym. Throughout this paper, I also use pseudonyms for interviewees in order to protect their privacy.
2. Sarah Lamb relates a similar tale, in which the father's friend gives him a large, locked chest and advises him always to keep the key with him. Lamb notes, "The expectation of an inheritance frequently serves ... as a major motivator of filial service" (2008: 34).
3. Here I use "old folks home" as a translation of the Sinhala term *mahalu nivaasaya*. This phrase generally connotes a facility that provides free service for poor elders, and yet it is also used to describe quality for-pay institutions.

ECONOMIES

11. PERSONHOOD, APPROPRIATE DEPENDENCE, AND THE RISE OF ELDERCARE INSTITUTIONS IN INDIA

Sarah Lamb

One late morning in the winter of 2006, my research assistant Hena and I were chatting with Sri Ashok Bose, a warm, articulate man in his early eighties, who had been living in the Ramakrishna Mission Home for Aged People since its inauguration twenty-two years earlier in Kolkata, India.[1] We sat in his modestly furnished private room framed by two capacious windows open to tree-filtered sunlight and a pleasant winter breeze. In the room were a single bed brightly covered by a cotton hand-loomed spread, a desk, two simple wooden chairs, and a tall metal wardrobe. Sri Ashok spoke with us animatedly about how he had come to reside in the home, one of the first eldercare institutions in India.

Sri Ashok was a bachelor who had long been devoted to a spiritual life. This devotion was in keeping with this home's mission, as described by one of its directors, which is to provide "a life away from the din of family, spent in solitary religious practices." Sri Ashok had begun to lose his eyesight in his mid-fifties, but he had been able to serve out a full career as a government employee, and he now drew a pension with which he could fund his expenses. But before retirement, he had worried about how to care for himself in old age, being then almost blind and having no children of his own to depend on. He tells the story: "Then one day, I came across a notice in the newspaper that the Ramakrishna Mission was planning to start an old age home! As *soon* as I read that, I went to the [Mission headquarters]." He recalls his application with detail and emotion: "I wrote, 'If I am accepted here, then that is very good.'" He paused and continued with a full voice: "But if I am not selected, then please don't write that in a letter. Because since I am blind, someone else will have to read the letter to me, and—I won't be able to bear that.'" He then narrated, brimming with pleasure and pride, "But they wrote back in a letter, saying, 'So long you have served [*seva kora*] us [the Ramakrishna Mission and society]. Now let us serve [*seva kora*] you.'" He repeated, smiling broadly, "'So long you have served us. Now let us serve you.' And so I received admission!"

"About this ashram," Sri Ashok went on, referring to the institution throughout as an ashram or spiritual shelter/abode, "there's something you should know: we are living here *completely* without worry. *Everything* we need, we receive: the giving of food, tea, warm bath water—*whatever* we need, we receive. *Truly,* there are no worries! At *precisely* the right time, the tea comes, the food comes! Be there a strike, or a storm, whatever there is, *still* the food comes at just the right time." And, indeed, just as he was speaking, his midday meal arrived, a few minutes before noon, placed quietly on the desk-cum-eating table next to his window, as some other residents chose instead to make their way through the halls to the common dining room, several pausing in Sri Ashok's doorway to greet him as they passed.

Dr. Ranjan Banerjee, retired psychiatrist and resident of another elder residence situated on the outskirts of Kolkata amidst vibrant green rice fields, much more pessimistically reflected on the rise of old age homes in his nation:

'Old age homes'[2] are not a concept of *our* country. These days, we are throwing away our 'culture.' The U.S. is the richest nation in the world and therefore has won us over. Now we, too, are only after material wealth as a nation and have become very unhappy. Some are here [in the old age home] because their families dumped them here, and there are others whose children are living abroad and can easily afford the money [to pay the home's fees]. But 'old age homes' are not *our* way of life. My parents died *right with us....* We as a nation have become very unhappy. Material wealth used not to be the prime value in life; rather, family and social closeness were.... I myself am against the 'old age home concept'—but 'old age homes' will stay and increase in India.

These two vignettes speak to the variety and intensity of meanings accruing to the rise of eldercare institutions in India. In this chapter, I examine the emergence of old age homes in the major Indian city of Kolkata, focusing in particular on how the notion of life-long intergenerational reciprocity within the family is transforming to paying for care on the market, with concomitant shifts in ideas of personhood and appropriate dependence and independence over the life course. If one pays for care, the notion is of a more independent and individuated person. Yet forms of appropriate dependence and other core dimensions of more conventional Indian models of aging are being highlighted and maintained by those participating in market-based eldercare in India, revealing how globalizing institutions take on profoundly unique meanings and shapes across cultural, political-economic, and historical contexts.

In country after country around the world, not only in India, there has been a dramatic transformation—from the multigenerational family to the individual, the market, and the state, as the key sites of aging and eldercare. In fact, the United States witnessed in the late 1800s and early 1900s some of the same extraordinary transitions that Indians are going through at present—such as the rise of the notion of the old age home, a decline in multigenerational co-residence, and an increase in state support of the aged. Such transitions in modes of aging entail, in any context, quite remarkable shifts in understandings of the human condition, and what it is to be a person. Yet, a central purpose of this chapter is to examine how such transitions—from more family-based to increasingly market- and individual-based systems of eldercare and elder living—take on unique forms and meanings in their particular contexts. In addition, I aim to illuminate how questions of appropriate eldercare pertain not merely to the more practical matter of how to support an aging population as nations face the dramatic demographic shifts of the twenty-first century, but more broadly and profoundly, to our very understandings of what it is to be a person and how best to live.

The materials in this chapter derive from several periods of intensive anthropological fieldwork in India, especially among Bengalis in Kolkata and rural West Bengal, conducted over the past twenty years.[3] I concentrate for this chapter on Hindus and also on the cosmopolitan middle classes. This is because elder-care institutions have not (yet) hit rural Bengali villages, and the urban poor—lacking in the economic resources to pay for eldercare in any event—tend to interpret their problems of aging more in terms of timeless poverty ("my sons don't feed me rice because they don't have any money") than as the result of the social, economic, and ideological changes of their increasingly globalized nation.[4]

Aging in Families (*Samsar*): "That Which Flows Together" and Appropriate Dependence

Before I delve into the rise of market-based eldercare, I must explain the more conventional backdrop against which these new aging trends are situated—aging in families. Indians have long seen caring for aged parents in a family home as a fundamental part of a reciprocal intergenerational cycle. In fact, the majority of Indian elders today, as in the past, continues to live in a multigenerational family setting—about eighty percent.[5] Both daily and media discourses widely portray living within an intergenerational "joint family" as representing a quintessentially *Indian* way of life, morality, and tradition (see, e.g., Lamb 2009: 32–38). In a joint family system, old age is essentially a family matter. Adult children, particularly sons and daughters-in-law, live with and care for their aging parents. This is done out of love, a deep respect for elders, and a profound sense of moral, even spiritual, duty to attempt to repay the inerasable debts (*rn*) they owe their parents for all the effort, expense, and affection the parents expended to produce and raise them.

Such long-term reciprocal transactions don't always work perfectly, but nonetheless are believed to create and sustain intimate bodily ties, what Bengalis often term *maya*. *Maya* (in addition to meaning "illusion") means attachment, affection, compassion, and love, and Bengalis think of the ties of *maya* as entailing both emotional and bodily bindings (*bandhan*). A range of anthropological studies have explored how, in many contexts, Indians think of persons as relatively fluid and open, that is divisible or "dividual" in nature, in contrast to the prevalent Western notion of the relatively self-contained and bounded *in*dividual.[6] One of the most common words for "person" (*lok*) also means "world"; the most common term for worldly life and also family (*samsar*) means literally "that which flows together"— the assembly of people and things that "flow with" persons as they move through their lives. Through transactions of food, touch, objects, words, and bodily fluids, family members give and receive parts of themselves, forging not only emotional but also bodily ties. According to such conceptualizations, by co-residing in the same household, and by giving and receiving food, material goods, bodily care, and affection, parents and descendants not only meet each other's survival needs, but also sustain intimate ties of kinship and relationality. Thus, if a child were merely to pay for an elder's care, but not to co-reside with the elder, this would constitute a very different type of—and much more individuated—relationship.

From such a perspective, not only children but also elders can be *appropriately* dependent on kin for material, emotional, and bodily support, and, in fact, Bengalis often explicitly compare the acts of caring for elders and children. For instance, one middle-aged Bengali man, whose frail mother was incontinent and bedridden, reflected to me while he was cleaning his mother's sheets: "Caring for parents is the children's duty; it is *dharma* [moral-religious order; right way of living]. As parents raised their children, children will also care for their parents during their sick years, when they get old. For example, if I am old and I have a bowel movement, my son will clean it and he won't ask, 'Why did you do it there?' This is what we did for him when he was young. When I am old and dying, who will take me to go urinate and defecate? My children will have to do it." When adult children care for their elder parents, these caring practices are often labeled "*seva*" (respectful care or service)—a key concept across north Indian languages. *Seva* can refer to care offered to a guru or deity, yet is most often used to refer to respectful care offered to elders and in particular elder parents—including practices such as serving tea and food, taking care of bodily needs, and offering companionship.

In such a context, many have a very difficult time envisioning their own or their parents' aging in an eldercare institution. For instance, forty-year-old Amrita reflected on how she felt more comfortable placing her son in a boarding institution than her mother. After fifteen years in the U.K. and following a divorce, Amrita enrolled her fifteen-year-old son in a U.K. boarding school and returned to Kolkata in order to live with and care for her mother, who had become bedridden and was suffering from dementia that was perhaps Alzheimer's. Amrita feels that in her Kolkata neighborhood circles, to put her mother in an old age home "would be the *worst* thing I could do. I would lose *all* respect, more than I lost even from my divorce. Of course, I already lost all respect [in our Kolkata society] and don't care that much about it anyway." She went on (in English):

> But, I—I don't know that I could do that, put Ma in an old age home. People from the U.K., my close girlfriends there, say, "Wow, you must love your mother so much—moving back to India after fifteen years abroad, leaving your son behind in a boarding school." But they don't know—that's the farthest from the truth. I really was never *that* close to my mother. I can't say that I really *love* her so much. She doesn't even know who I am any more. So what's behind my—making me do this? It's hard to articulate. It's that she's my *mother*—and if I don't, who else will? How would I feel if I put my mother in a home and she were abused? My son can speak up if he's abused, but my mother can't.

More than "love"—here seemingly perceived as a matter of an individual-based relationship, emotion, or choice—what motivated Amrita most was a sense of profound duty and of not being able to envision things any other way.

In 2007, the Indian Parliament passed the Maintenance and Welfare of Parents and Senior Citizens Bill stipulating that children must support their parents or be subject to fines and potential imprisonment (see Lamb 2009: 237–42). This bill was passed into law in 2009 and was enacted in the context of what many within the Indian public perceived to be a broad societal decline in family-based care and respect for elders. As the bill was deliberated, the Secretary of the Ministry of Social Justice and Empowerment proclaimed decisively, "It is an established fact that family is the most desired environment for senior citizens/parents to lead a life of security, care and dignity."[7] Thus the core aim of the legislation is to ensure that "the moral obligation of children to look after their parents in their old age [is] backed by a legal obligation."[8]

To become dependent in late life, and to receive *seva*—respectful service and care, paradigmatically provided by juniors to elders—is not from such perspectives a failure in personhood, but rather an appropriate, normal, and even, in certain respects, valued part of the life course. Although to become very needy and dependent *without* kin (or others) to provide *seva* is bad, incoherent, and not in keeping with common visions of a normal, appropriate, and valued life course, dependence in and of itself is not negative when it takes place in the context of *seva*.[9]

Such a stance is similar in certain respects to how those in the United States would view children as appropriately—morally, economically, and legally—dependent on their parents. However, in the U.S. context, this might be because children are not yet considered full persons. Prevalent models of successful *adulthood* and *aging* in the United States emphasize living independently as a key feature and value. U.S. census figures are reflective of this ideal of independence: among those sixty-five and over, 30.5 percent live in single-person households and 54.6 percent live with only their spouse—so, 85 percent, a significant majority, live on their own, without children and outside of institutions, as they forge their later lives.[10] Such trends are not at all represented in ordinary public discourse as a problem. What many people do consider to be less than ideal is to be institutionalized or, especially, to depend fully on one's children. U.S. elders in general are happy to turn to children for some care and assistance—in the form of visits and phone calls, escorting to the doctor, errands, offering love, etc.; yet, if an elder requires co-residence or intimate bodily care such as help with dressing, toileting, or bathing, most U.S. elders will prefer to pay for such care rather than to have to depend on an adult child. Paying for the care is one way for the elder to preserve his or her sense of independence.

In their influential work presenting the results of a major MacArthur Foundation Study on *Successful Aging*, U.S. gerontologists John Rowe and Robert Kahn present dependence, in fact, as one of the *worst* fears and failures connected to aging. Rose and Kahn show that Americans generally associate dependence with "disability," "inactivity," and "bleak" conditions (1998: 14). Interestingly, though, people in the U.S. would never ordinarily describe a *child* who could not live completely independently as "disabled," "inactive," or in a "bleak" condition. Indians would also not ordinarily describe an elder who is living with, and receiving care from, family members as in a "bleak" condition or having "failed" at "successful" aging. These differences in perspectives on dependence and successful aging reveal very different cultural understandings of personhood, dependence, and independence over the life course.

Abandonment and Freedom:
Independence and Market-Based Eldercare

Despite the prevalence of family-based living, many in urban middle-class Indian circles are beginning to participate in a surge of market-based alternatives to family-centered aging. Most dramatic has been the rise of old age homes for the middle and upper-middle classes. Understood to be largely Western-style and Western-inspired institutions, elder residences barely existed in India until recently. However, they now number near 1,000 across India's urban centers, most having been established just since the mid 1990s and the first few years of the 2000s (Lamb 2009: 53–171; Liebig 2003). Most of these homes are run as private businesses or non-profit NGOs, both charging fees to stay,[11] and are thus predominantly for the solvent middle and upper middle classes. Indians widely view such forms of market-based eldercare with much ambivalence, interpreting them both negatively as abandonment and positively as freedom. Both narratives—of abandonment and freedom—highlight an increasingly independent and individualized mode of personhood, with associated new ways of defining old age and the project of being human.

Narratives of abandonment emphasize the "throwing away" of not only individual elders but also of culture, values, morality, humanity, and a whole way of life. As old-age-home resident Dr. Banerjee reflected in this chapter's opening, "Old age homes are not a concept of *our* country. These days, we are throwing away our culture." One middle-aged Bengali woman whom I met in the airport with her husband, on their way to visit their son settled in Chicago, commented forcefully: "'Old age homes' are actually very few in our country. Because most people think that—*we* think that—those who throw their parents away in 'old age homes' are *very* bad—'criminal,' in fact! We think that it is *criminal* to put your parents in an 'old age home.'" Her remarks were characteristic of many other encounters I had, as Indians would strive to represent to me (an outsider) a particular vision of a moral nation.

Resident Kalyani Chatterjee herself told of being "thrown away" (or *phele daoya,* the same term Bengalis use to refer to the discarding of trash) into an old age home by her son and daughter-in-law suddenly one day shortly after her retirement. She had, as is typical, co-resided with the younger couple ever since arranging her son's marriage and bringing the daughter-in-law into their family home years earlier after Kalyani-di[12] had become a widow. Three generations had shared the home, its finances, and labors until one day her son told her that he would be taking her the next day to an abode for elders. Kalyani-di had never even heard previously of such an institution. She narrated: "That this thing would happen I couldn't have ever imagined. That I would have to leave my home. Of course, even while living at home, people experience all sorts of situations and are not always perfectly happy. But I *could never have even imagined* living like this [in an old age home]. With our own eyes, we had *never even seen or dreamed* of any place like this!"

Old age homes are tied in many people's minds to India's economic boom of the last two decades (in part because it requires many more resources to live separately) and to the materialism and westernization of the younger generation. One characteristic cartoon in the Bengali daily newspaper *Sangbad Pratidin*, accompanying the story "Is it Desirable if One's Children Live Permanently Abroad?", depicts sons leaping after foreign dollars and pounds as their elder parents line up, confused and forsaken, in front of a *briddhabas* or home for the aged (Figure 11.1). In the midst of my field-work in Kolkata, I was invited to give a talk as part of a multi-disciplinary conference on "Senescence." Professors, gerontologists, and social activists from across India participated. I focused my talk on the rise of old age homes in India, and a lively discussion ensued. Then, a distinguished senior sociology professor from the University of Delhi rose to make an impromptu impassioned closing speech: "Some of this discussion has seemed to be advocating that we adopt old age homes. But we should *not*! ... The very data provided by Sarah here shows that the majority of old age homes in Kolkata are *businesses*! ... They are making *money*!—they are making *money*!—by having people in old age homes. Let's not get persuaded by the idea that old age homes are the answer. They are not! *Family* is the answer.

FIGURE 11.1 Sons leap after foreign money as elders line up outside a *briddhabas* or abode for elders (Choudhuri 2003).

We need to strengthen the *family!*" We see in these impassioned words that it is the turning of what should be a non-market-based entity (care, or *seva*) into a market commodity that is at the heart of such narratives of abandonment—that is, the commodification of care and thus the severe attenuation of family bonds. Many sitting around the conference table nodded soberly to the professor's remarks.[13]

Yet, much more positive narratives emphasizing freedom can be found quite readily among the elder-home residents themselves. In fact, most of those in the media and on the streets proclaiming moral panic stories have hardly, if at all, entered such homes. However, upon following several homes and their residents over time,[14] I learned that many residents themselves proclaim that old-age-home living enables a kind of freeing independence for both the older and younger generations, relieves daughters-in-law from the unpleasant burden of caring for and being subservient to their husbands' parents, keeps family relations easy and harmonious, fosters a healthy gendered and aged egalitarianism, allows both children and the nation to develop, and provides living options for those who are simply without viable prospects for residing with kin—such as the never married and/or childless, those whose children have moved abroad, and those for whom family relations are deeply unpleasant and strained. The homes can also be attractive for those with no sons and only daughters, as many Indian communities view it as deeply unacceptable for parents to live with and be supported by a married daughter. Some residents describe how they have come to appreciate also that it can be fun to live amidst peers in a college-hostel-like setting, gossiping in crowded dormitories as they fall asleep at night, sharing tales about their lives and troubles, and enjoying companionship over afternoon tea. Thus, although not all the decisions are perfectly easy or happy ones by any means, many residents do actively choose elder-home living for complex reasons.

Inu Ghosh, for instance, a resident in one all-women's home, told me convincingly that she was delighted and relieved to find the old-age-home option, as she was a widowed woman with only daughters and no sons. Most widowed Bengali old women with only daughters, she explained, have to live in "someone else's" home—perhaps a nephew's. She went on: "In someone else's home, I couldn't hold my head up high. If I need something, I couldn't ask. I would just have to lie in bed and wait. Here, I can live independently [*svadhin bhabe*]. I can ask for what I need with my head held high. I don't have to feel uncomfortable speaking up and asking for anything. They [the staff] are here to help me.... I am *very* happy here, *very* happy and at peace."

Shilpa Roychowdhury chose to move into an elder residence partly for spiritual reasons (which I will mention below) but also to give more space to her son and his family. She had worked all of her married life as an engineer, had been widowed before her son was married, and had decided then that upon retirement she would enter a spiritual ashram or, once she learned of their newly emerging presence, an old age home. In contrast to the rambling village family homes of old, "flats these days are small and can't be expanded," she remarked. "I wanted to give more room to my son, daughter-in-law, and granddaughter." She and her granddaughter had shared a room and bed in the two-bedroom apartment ever since the girl's birth, but Shilpa-di reflected: "As my granddaughter grew up, it would be inconvenient for her to share a room with her grandmother. I didn't want my granddaughter to resent me. This way we'll maintain a very good, loving relationship." Shilpa-di still returns to spend several days per month in the family home, and finds that she and her thirteen-year-old granddaughter have a great time chatting for these few days as they share their former room and bed.

Some Indian gerontologists are advocating for such new market-based elder-care trends—for instance, advocating the development of self-sufficiency and institutional (*non*family) means of elder support, presenting "traditional" family-centered modes of aging as "backward." For instance, S. Irudaya Rajan, U. S. Mishra, and P. Sankara Sarma (1999) recommend that the Indian government should support old age homes and pension plans, and that aging individuals should cultivate a dependence on the self—through savings, exercise, and an open-mindedness about living in old age homes—as one can no longer count on (and *should* no longer count on, if one is modern and educated) depending on children in old age. Such gerontology discourses resonate with broader international development discourses, which frequently depict family-based care as a feature of "developing" nations, while "developed" nations have "advanced" to offer individual-, state-, and market-based eldercare options (see Lamb 2009: 250–51).

The rise of old age homes in such narratives of freedom, independence, and development suggest less the sloughing off of tradition and of elders with weak ties to family, and more the emergence of a different way of managing and envisioning personhood and the life course[15]—a much more individual-centered, independent, egalitarian, and market-based way. One now has the opportunity to find and pay for one's own housing and care, living among peers and away from the family. Such a trend goes hand-in-hand with other social, political, and economic processes—including the upwelling of middle-class, nuclear-family, consumerist lifestyles amidst India's booming economy; the increase of women in the professional labor force; the transnational dispersal of families amidst global labor markets; and the emergence of broadly shared global visions of proper individual, familial, and national development and progress.

Appropriate Dependence and Meaningful Decline: *Seva*, Spirituality, and Indian Values in the Homes

If one looks beyond the surface of India's elder residences, one comes to appreciate that, in important respects, they do not unvaryingly cultivate an independent and globally uniform vision of personhood at all. After spending time in the homes over months of fieldwork, I gradually came to realize how certain key conventional Indian and Bengali visions of personhood and the life course are in fact incorporated into the homes, making them not simply or uniformly "western"-style, individual-making institutions.

One respect in which the eldercare institution is made Indian in Kolkata is in the way Kolkata's old age homes highlight the elder's ongoing appropriate dependence, especially through the instantiation of *seva*. Lawrence Cohen, too, observed how a "retirement ashram" he visited in north India fashioned itself as a "locus of *seva*" and "an equivalent space to the family" (1998: 115). Though offered by hired staff and paid proprietors rather than kin (an admittedly significant distinction), *seva*—or respectful care for and service to elders—is widely regarded by both proprietors and elder residents as one of the most central and valued features of elder-home living. Recall that when Sri Ashok gratefully learned of his admission to the Ramakrishna Mission Home for the Aged, the Mission's offer letter expressed: "So long you have served us. Now let us serve (*seva kora*) you." Indeed, many of the seventy elder abodes I visited were set up expressly to offer *seva*, and several were succinctly named Seva. Other similarly evocative names included *Sraddhanjali* (Offering of Reverence) and *Gurujan Kunja* (Garden Abode for Respected Elders). The manager of Gurujan Kunja explained the home's name: "It indicates the home's purpose: to serve and honor the old people living here. You see, they are all revered people living here." Residents who greatly appreciate the *seva* they receive in their elder homes routinely list favorably all the amenities and services offered: bed tea each morning at 5 or 6 A.M., breakfast, a full Bengali noon meal, tea in the afternoon, "tiffin" in the early evening, and finally supper; then also the delivery of warm bath water, combing of hair, massaging of tired feet, hanging up of mosquito nets, washing of clothes, and the offering of comfort and love.

The majority of elder-abode residents I encountered were, by American standards, quite "young" in both chronological years and fitness—often in their sixties and seventies and generally quite capable on their own of performing daily living tasks such as preparing tea or hanging a mosquito net.[16] But most residents and staff viewed late life as an appropriate period for receiving attentive care from juniors. So while it is true that by moving into the institution residents become independent from family, they also

FIGURE 11.2 Residents of modest, homey Loknath Old Age Home tell of greatly appreciating the *seva* offered by proprietor Pushpa (right). Photo by Sarah Lamb.

become properly and purposefully dependent on others—the proprietors, managers, and staff who take the place of junior kin by offering the residents *seva*.

Attentive and concerned children, too, can continue to offer their elders *seva* via the market, often by paying for the old-age-home care. Alpana Bardhan, a sweet and stooped 81-year-old resident, cried frequently when she spoke of her life in the home, recalling in contrast how much love and adoration she had received earlier when she was a child in her father's home, then as a new bride in her father-in-law's home, and later as an older woman in her sons' homes: "If I fell asleep early, my father would pick up the mosquito net and feed me with his own hands." "But, my sons had no choice," she conceded. Because, according to her narrative, she could no longer stay alone in her sons' homes during the day when all the others went out to work and school, her sons had had to place her in the old age home. "But still now, my sons come. My son just came and spent 4,000 rupees on an x-ray and blood test, and they come to give me medicine—1,000 rupees of medicine!" She proudly showed me several medicine containers on the crowded shelf next to her bed, along with a vitamin drink, fruit and vegetable juices, and a packet of biscuits that her sons had delivered. While money might not be as intimate a form of support as living together, feeding, bathing, or changing bed sheets, a gift of monetary support can still be perceived as *seva*. One proprietor commented, "Children these days have no time, but they can gift money. This is just a reality that must be faced."

Other elders commented that old-age-home living offers a familiar "joint-family-like" feel and sociality, less alien than living alone—reminding residents of their childhood days in overflowing households, where (in both settings) all eat food cooked from the same hearth, people sleep in groups of two to six to a room, and one almost never has to be alone. Some develop intimate, family-like, very supportive relationships over the years, especially with co-residents. And many say that living in an old age home is less culturally alien and bizarre than living alone, offering reflections such as "human beings have never lived alone" and "it is not natural for human beings to live alone." Thus, although the old age home can be a quintessential space of family absence or a marked alternative to family care and co-residence, in India elder residences are at the same time, and in important respects, an instantiation of family values, appropriate dependence, and *seva*.

Indian values enter the old age home in other ways as well. For instance, quite a few residents told me that they perceive old-age-home living as akin to the "forest-dwelling" or *vanaprastha* life phase long presented in Hindu texts as appropriate for older age, where one purposefully loosens ties to worldly-family life (*samsar*) in order to pursue spiritual awareness and a readiness for the myriad leave-takings and transitions of death. At age sixty-eight, Shilpa Roychowdhury, the recently retired engineer, is still in vibrant good health and describes her motive for choosing to move into an elder abode as preeminently a spiritual one: "If I were to stay in my family, I would become more and more accustomed to their company and would have difficulty leaving [when it is time to die]." She peppered her conversations with statements illustrative of her outlook of worldly detachment: "I came alone and will have to leave alone." "Aside from God, I have no one at all." "No one is really anyone's." "Without abandoning, nothing can be attained." In general, compared to U.S. institutions, I found the Indian elder residences to be conspicuously free of both elaborate life-prolonging medical technologies as well as life-long-learning activity programs, highlighting instead a sense of late life as a time to reflect on and meaningfully confront the fundamental transience of human life (see Lamb 2009:

FIGURE 11.3 Longtime roommates Kalyani-di and Uma-di offer each other loving support, describing theirs as an intimate sister-like relationship. Photo by Rachel Black, printed with permission.

134–142). So the elder institution becomes not simply a western invasion, but rather in certain respects, an ancient Hindu way of ordering the life course.

Concluding Reflections

The transfer of eldercare and elder living from the family to the market immediately strikes many in India as a radically different way of living, promoting individualizing subjectivities amidst remarkable social and economic changes. Yet, in some ways these new eldercare institutions in India are not so radically new and individualizing after all—serving to sustain forms of appropriate dependence via the offering of *seva,* and to become a site for meaningful decline, where ties to family, belongings, and body can be purposefully sloughed off. The older people and their communities taking part in these institutions, often with much ambivalence, are in these ways striving to maintain older values and lifestyles at the same time that they creatively embrace new ones, working to fashion meaningful lives in the present.

What key insights can we take away from this ethnography? We see, first, how seemingly similar processes can take on very different meanings and shapes across particular cultural, political-economic, and historical contexts. Although many nations have participated in a shift from family-based to individual-, market-, and state-based elder living, these shifts get played out in importantly unique ways. One of the very basic yet most profound contributions of anthropology is to document the localization of global processes and to make interventions into presumed universal frameworks—that is, to unsettle the certainties of Eurocentric models, of matters such as health, policy, and successful aging.

Further, this work suggests that we in the United States might begin to think more on how to incorporate visions of appropriate dependence and meaningful decline into our understandings of successful aging. With baby boomers hitting sixty-five, new visions of aging are becoming increasingly prominent in our public discourse and consciousness. Most emphasize an energetic, positive vision of late life, featuring independence, productivity, and activity. These visions are inspiring and exciting, and they aspire to prolong the period of vitality, activity, and productivity in the life course. But, should we not also work harder at this point on developing visions of appropriate *in*activity, human interdependency, and decline, so that decline and dependence are not simply envisioned and experienced as failures? To do so might help us better realize that not all situations of caregiving, dependence, and disability must entail a loss of dignity and a failure to age well. Debates on old-age homes in India provide us one context to consider these questions.

Notes

1. All names used in this chapter are pseudonyms. I tell Sri Ashok Bose's story as well in Lamb 2009, 53–54. Here and below, conversations are translated from Bengali unless otherwise noted.
2. I use single quotation marks to signify words spoken in English in an otherwise Bengali conversation. Residences for elders are frequently referred to by Indians in English as "old age homes," signifying the perceived Western-originating nature of these institutions.
3. See, for instance, Lamb 1993, 2000, 2009.
4. For more on the intersection of forms of class and poverty with understandings of trends in aging, see Lamb 2009: chapter 2 and especially pp. 51–52.
5. Rajan and Kumar (2003), based on National Family Household Survey data, report that 80 percent of the elderly in India live with their adult children. See also Jamuna 2003: 127–128.
6. See, for instance, Daniel 1984; Lamb 1997, 2000; Marriott 1976.
7. Standing Committee on Social Justice and Empowerment (2007–2008), Twenty-Eighth Report: "The Maintenance and Welfare of Parents and Senior Citizens Bill, 2007": p. 10. The text of the 2007 bill is available at http://www.prsindia.org/uploads/media/1182337322/scr1193026940_Senior_Citizen.pdf (accessed 12 January 2011).
8. Ibid., p. 9.
9. Nonetheless, many Indian elders I know speak of not wishing to become entirely bedridden in old age, preferring to die while their "hands and feet are still working" and before becoming absolute burdens on their children, attitudes Silvia Vatuk (1990) also finds in New Delhi.
10. "A Profile of Older Americans, 2009: Living Arrangements," Department of Health and Human Services, Administration on Aging, http://www.aoa.gov/aoaroot/aging_statistics/Profile/2009/6.aspx, accessed 25 February 2011.
11. Elder-residence fees range from about 1,000 to 6,000 Indian rupees per month (a little over 20 to 120 USD), and often require a sizable joining fee or security deposit of anywhere from about 5,000 to 500,000 rupees (or about $100 to $10,000). The monthly fees can be covered by most retirement pensions and are roughly equivalent to the cost of a full-time domestic servant in a middle-class urban household.
12. "Di" is short for *didi* or older sister. Bengalis generally find it disrespectful to refer to a senior person by first name only, so epithets such as *didi* (older sister), *dada* (older brother) and *masi* (maternal aunt) are commonly used to signify not only respect but also kin-like closeness.
13. Michele Gamburd (this volume) examines similar strong feelings of stigma attached to old age homes among villagers in Sri Lanka.
14. See Lamb 2009 (chapters 2–5) for a much more detailed examination of the rich and varied resident, family, proprietor, and public discourses and perspectives sur-

rounding elder-care institutions and people's reasons for entering them in Kolkata. In Kolkata, I visited thirty-two homes, interviewed one hundred residents, and focused most closely on six homes, participating in and observing daily affairs, and following the residents' and proprietors' lives over a period of several years, from 2003 to 2009.

15. Guyer and Salami (this volume) examine changing visions of the life course and intergenerational relations amidst widespread economic changes in rural Nigeria.

16. Thus, the majority of Kolkata's old age homes are to date more similar to U.S. assisted living facilities than to nursing homes, and many of the institutions require that residents be able to perform basic activities of daily living.

12. MEMBERSHIP AND MATTERING
Agency and Work in a New England Factory

Caitrin Lynch

MANY AMERICANS WANT TO BE engaged in work well past traditional retirement age, whether for financial, social, health, or other reasons (or a combination). At Vita Needle Company, a factory in a Boston, Massachusetts suburb, the shop floor workers are mostly older adults. Though there are some employees in their teens through fifties, the median age of the forty or so production workers at Vita Needle is seventy-four, and the eldest is one hundred and clocks in a thirty-hour, five-day workweek. The Vita Needle story illustrates the importance of mattering and membership for older adults in the United States, where older adults often feel socially marginalized and even invisible. For Vita's older workers, work means something very different than it did at earlier points in their lives. This is in large part because work generates experiences of mattering and membership that are largely absent in their lives outside of work. But the difference is also because of the feeling of "control" that work provides for older people who are often stereotyped by others as having no control over their lives (the notion being that old people are just waiting it out until the end). Indeed, some older workers may themselves feel that much of their current life is not in their control (bodies may be failing, friends and loved ones are likely to be dying). In this chapter, after briefly introducing Vita Needle and my research there, I sketch the landscape of the meanings of retirement in the United States. I then examine narratives of Vita Needle's older workers in order to discuss membership and mattering—and ultimately how these sentiments connect to feelings of control and agency.

Vita Needle Company

Vita Needle Company is a family-owned factory that produces stainless steel needles in the affluent Boston suburb of Needham. I immersed myself in life at Vita Needle for nearly five years, from 2006 to 2011 (more intensively in some years than in others), in order to learn what, on top of a paycheck, Vita Needle provides its employees. My analysis in this chapter is based on interviews but also on my own work on the shop floor during one summer. I did a variety of jobs including packaging and inspecting needles, attaching four-inch-long needles to plastic glue dispensers with rubber bands, and working on a machine that flares the ends of six-inch-long stainless steel tubes. I would work a shift, sometimes sneaking into the bathroom to take notes, but always composing field notes on a digital voice recorder the moment I stepped onto the sidewalk outside to head home—trying to retain as much as possible before my immediate memory faded.

By working on the shop floor I furthered my understanding—already developed over a two-year period of offsite interviews and occasional workplace visits—of everyday shop dynamics, the ways in which people try to live out their dreams for community and productivity at work, and how management and employees reconcile their joint social and economic goals. Insights arose from experiencing many things I had heard about in interviews and many things that had never come up. For instance, I had conversations during breaks about the effect of deteriorating eyesight (from cataracts or macular degeneration) on quality control, I heard jokes and complaints about the sweltering ninety-four-degree factory temperature, I saw great concern about unexpected coworker absences, and I got to feel what it was like to finish inspecting a batch of three hundred needles only to be given three hundred more!

My methods also included examination of particular people and situations based on long-term friendships as well as semistructured interviews (more than eighty total, including with focus groups) with Vita Needle owners, managers, employees, and family members; other local people over sixty years old engaged in paid, unpaid, or no work; geriatricians and eldercare service professionals; and European journalists covering Vita Needle for stories on the surprising success of a factory staffed by older workers. To provide the wider context for understanding Vita Needle, I also analyzed cultural material (such as retirement magazines, senior citizen newsletters, and popular books on aging) and attended events at senior centers and retirement communities.

Vita Needle has been operating since 1932 and its forty or so production floor employees are from varied work backgrounds—retired engineers, schoolteachers, realtors, waitresses, and lifelong factory workers. At Vita Needle, these diverse workers design, construct, inspect, pack, and ship hollow needles in an assortment of diameters, lengths, and sharpness levels; the needles serve in a multitude of applications that include inflating basketballs and performing brain surgery. The workers exemplify a range of personalities and backgrounds and a diversity of reasons for working. Even those who come out of financial need also seek social engagement and purpose. The production workers are all part-time (up to thirty-four hours), and none receive medical or retirement benefits—the employer banks on the employees' eligibility for receipt of Medicare and Social Security.[1] The pay rate generally starts at roughly nine dollars per hour, which is above the state's minimum wage of eight dollars per hour (in 2012). Workers typically set their own hours, and some are like Carl Wilson who arrives for a seven-hour shift at 3:30 A.M., while others might start at a more conventional 9 A.M. and clock out by 2 P.M., and yet others show up for a four-hour shift at 3 P.M. Upstairs from the production floor is the sales office, where the eight or so employees are full-time salaried workers in their twenties through fifties, more characteristic of the age of office workers elsewhere in the United States.

The owners and managers are attuned to the age-related social, health, and economic needs of the workforce, and the company accommodates this workforce in various ways. For example, managers work closely with shop workers to make an ideal flexible schedule that might accommodate grandchild care, medical appointments, volunteer work, and the early rising that is common among older adults (starting work at 3:30 A.M. is convenient for Carl, whose restless leg syndrome is a condition more common and severe among older people). Vita Needle's is a surprisingly flexible production system, in part because workers are trained on multiple jobs (someone is usually able to step in for a coworker who is absent or who clocks out early), but also because of the nature and size of its orders and the store of backup inventory. Managers communicate with families of their employees about health concerns such as memory lapses or narcolepsy. They have also been known to curtail a worker's hours at the end of the year at the worker's request if he or she is approaching the federally mandated "earnings limit"—a limit to how much money a person below full retirement age can earn before the amount of his or her Social Security benefit will be reduced.[2]

Contradictions of Retirement

For people of all ages, work provides more than a paycheck. Work can enable social engagement, provide a sense of contribution, and offer a respite from domestic troubles. In U.S. society, paid work is integral to one's sense of self-worth and value, and non-working adults often struggle to develop a sense of value that counters the cultural and economic norm. How does one respond to the common question "What do you do?" if you are a stay-at-home mom (perceived by many as non-working), unemployed, or a retiree? One sign of how Americans measure themselves by work is that retirees often ask each other "What did you do in *real* life?" The subjects of this chapter are older adults—past typical retirement age. They live at a confluence of contradictory social and economic values.

On one hand, many have long looked forward to and planned for a life-stage called retirement, a phase of life in which one is no longer ruled by clocks, schedules, and bosses. This is especially true for the many people with alienating, demeaning, difficult, or unpleasant jobs that simply have not provided meaning for them—though even here, work can be an important aspect of identity, a point vividly made by the journalist Studs Terkel in his book *Working* and in the Broadway musical based on it (Terkel 1997). This retirement phase is idealized in American society in many ways, including by romanticized images of golfing, traveling, fishing, knitting, playing bingo, and relaxing in recliner chairs. The dominant U.S. norm is that as people age, they transition from a period of labor productivity to a period of non-productivity, beginning in one's sixties (see Bateson, this volume, for further discussion of this norm).

On the other hand, many American older adults want to work in the conventional retirement years. If during the lengthy period of labor productivity, a person's value is measured in large part by the ability to earn income, how does a person measure his or her value during this supposed "non-productive" life phase? Many people want to remain busy and engaged throughout their lives, and they want to be recognized for the contributions they make. Thus, "retirement" is a complicated ideal for people across social classes (cf. Savishinsky 2002; Weiss 2005). This is not only because of the cultural connotations and experiences that accompany it, but also because of the economic position in which retirees find themselves—a position that is increasingly difficult since the 2008 global financial crisis as costs of living have increased and private and state pension payments have stayed steady or decreased.

Many Vita Needle workers were born in the 1920s and 1930s, and they are primarily white Christian men (there are a handful of women) who profited from the post-World War II economic prosperity in the United States. Most are at least high school graduates—some the first in their family to have graduated from high school—and some have master's degrees. They worked hard to live the stereotypical American dream: they married, supported children who went on to get college degrees, saved money, and owned their own homes. Much of this was financially feasible because of federal financial policies such as housing loans established after World War II. They all now draw incomes from Social Security and support from Medicare, policies adopted in the United States in the 1935 Social Security

Act, and, in the case of Medicare, with the Social Security Amendments of 1965. Many also draw income from private pensions and investments.[3]

Even though Vita's workers are not all Protestant, they are strongly influenced by the pervasive Protestant work ethic of their New England suburban community and the era in which they were raised.[4] Many refer in interviews to a "Depression ethic"—the effect of being raised by parents who struggled to raise children through the Great Depression—and they have seen that an individual's hard work is critical to success. The term "work ethic" came up in daily conversation and interviews with Vita workers. Sociologist David Ekerdt uses the term "busy ethic" to describe a concept that has arisen in response to the leisure-filled stage of life called retirement—a stage invented after the adoption of Social Security policies throughout the world starting in the late nineteenth and early twentieth centuries (Ekerdt 1986; cf. Katz 2000).[5] Ekerdt argues that in the United States, a society that values productivity and a work ethic, retirement is "morally managed and legitimated on a day-to-day basis in part by an ethic that esteems leisure that is earnest, occupied, and filled with activity—a 'busy ethic'" (1986: 239). Vita Needle employees, however, do not seek a busy *retired* life, a life of "busy leisure." Rather, they revel in a busy *working* life where one contributes to the economy and participates in an interdependent production process with peers. For them, it is not so much being "busy" that is important. These older adults value doing something that is meaningful to others, as well as to themselves (mattering), and doing it with others (membership). *Membership* refers to sociality, connection to others, a sense of belonging, and being able to point to an "us" in opposition to a "them." *Mattering* refers to the sense of relevance and value that comes from knowing one's life makes a difference to others; it provides an answer to the question "So what?" that people often ask themselves as they grow older.[6] While we can analyze membership and mattering for people of any age, by listening to the narratives of Vita's workers, we learn that these sentiments are of a different order for older adults than for younger people.

Membership and Mattering

In daily shop floor conversations, I heard older workers share with each other about the challenges of aging. I heard stories about illness and impending death and about friends and family who passed away; comments about being lost, confused, or unable to do something one used to be able to do; concern about health conditions and about nagging children; worry about having to stop work and become a burden for their children; and disquiet over feeling useless and betrayed by health and bodies with changes they cannot control, especially those related to memory loss. In a life context such as this, imagine what work must mean.

I repeatedly heard stories and reflections from some employees implying that Vita Needle was an oasis in a society that looks down upon or ignores older adults or assumes they are "the living dead" (as one worker put it). I have often heard people say that old people are invisible in U.S. society (an experience similar to being black in the United States, which Ralph Ellison so famously described in his 1952 book *Invisible Man*). An 85-year-old worker named Esther Martin was eloquent on this experience of invisibility. In the following comments, we hear Esther compare being inside and outside the workplace, and we hear her voice how her own experiences with family might not quite match up with the ideal she has of what family is supposed to mean at this life stage. For not only is retirement romantically imagined in American society as a period of non-work, it also is imagined as a time to spend with family. Listen to Esther reflect on being the only person of her generation at family gatherings:

> You just feel like you're a fifth wheel when you're with a younger group.... They don't let you join in in anything.... You're just sitting on the outside looking in. And I felt that almost the day after my husband died, that feeling. It's just depressing. I remember being over at my son's around Easter day, and my husband died in February. I remember being over there for Easter, and I was joining in, but I felt like a fifth wheel. And when you're outside, you love to be with your family too, but somehow you become closer with those of your own age group.

In this comment, Esther slides between, on one hand, a notion of inside and outside her family, and, on the other hand, a notion of inside and outside her workplace. Within her own family, she has the feeling of being outside (like a fifth wheel) the world of younger people. By contrast, when she is inside Vita Needle, among people close to her own age, she feels like an insider.

Moments earlier in that same interview I had asked Esther what she likes about work. Referring to the former company president, without hesitation, Esther said: "The friendships. When I lost my husband, Mason said to me, 'You come back to work, Esther, because it's therapy.' And it is. It truly is. It truly is." Esther next told me that a former coworker developed a severe illness after she stopped working at Vita Needle. When Esther then pronounced that "it is the beginning of the end when you stop working," I asked her why:

> Well, because it [work] gives you a reason to get up in the morning. And if you're hanging around the house all day, you know, it would be pretty bor-

ing. You can't be doing something every day. And we're all approximately the same age, so we can all talk about our aches and pains. Sing the old songs.... talk about the old times. And, when I'm with my kids, half the time I don't know what they're talking about. And I look back and now I know what my father meant when he said, "I wish somebody my age were still alive."

So here is 85-year-old Esther, working at Vita Needle five days a week, packaging needles, reminiscing with friends about "old times," and comparing notes on "aches and pains." Esther says here "we're all approximately the same age." Although the ages of Vita's workers are diverse, to Esther, Vita Needle is marked by sameness of aging experiences.

Esther prefers to work at Vita Needle rather than volunteering somewhere. She says she spent many years volunteering in her children's schools as a room mother, but she prefers the regular contact with coworkers that you get at Vita—people and the relationships are central to her assessment of the value of Vita in her life. Esther had earlier mentioned that she uses her paycheck for "my gasoline, and my groceries, and my hairdo." I asked if it is the pay that makes the difference between this work and volunteer work. "I really don't think it's the pay, I mean ... [pause], we don't get paid that much. We're not going to make our fortunes. So um, I don't know what it is really [pause]. Well, it's almost like we're a family." Esther then paused again and asked me to turn off the voice recorder. I complied and then, although we were alone in her house, in a whispered voice she told me about some of her coworkers feeling estranged from their families, feeling not welcome at family get-togethers. It was when I turned my recorder back on that she mentioned feeling like a fifth wheel. Esther's insistence that I turn off the recorder for this comment revealed her instinctive sense that describing a preference for work over family in one's retirement years was to voice something taboo.

When Esther grasped for a word and eventually said "it's almost like we're a family," she was attempting to explain what Vita means to her. She had settled on the concept of family, but then immediately contrasted this Vita family with her and her coworkers' outside-of-work families. In Esther's comparison, those kin-based families came up short. Like Esther, others confided with me about problems with family relationships, such as children's persistent worries about a parent's health and children wanting parents to stop driving or working. One man and his three brothers do not speak to each other due to a conflict over the inheritance when their parents died. Another man divulged that he was hurt when his great-grandson had a recent birthday party, in the next town over, and he was not invited. Others wish their out-of-state children would visit more often. Women are divorced. Men and women are widowed.

Even in the face of painful family relationships outside of work, Esther and her coworkers frequently use the term "family" to describe Vita Needle. This "imagined" family is the one that seemed to match their ideal of what this concept of family *should* mean, and here they were invoking an ideal with a complex and changing history in the United States.[7] When Vita's workers refer to Vita as family, it is an attempt to create and preserve an archetypical desired family that they long for even outside work. In so doing, they fight against the sense of marginality, loneliness, and uselessness that they often feel as older adults outside of work. They settle on the word "family" because this is a term readily available in their vocabulary to describe relationships of closeness—even if, in practice, families are often estranged, competitive, full of misunderstandings and argument. When we hear Esther quickly describe the pain of outside-of-work families, we see her making sense of how Vita Needle may be more like a family than her real one. Although it may seem counterintuitive (if we assume the ideal of family as the site of unequivocal intimacy, and if we assume a factory is the site *par excellence* of alienation), in some ways it is the sense of alienation in their family situations that sets Vita's older workers up for finding meaning and intimacy in work (cf. Hochschild 2001 [1997]).

When Esther describes "sitting on the outside, looking in" at family events, she evokes anxiety about a transition as one ages from being the center of society to living at the margins. She and her coworkers describe a sensation of shrinking social circles. As another Vita worker once said, "As you get older, your world gets smaller." Theater studies scholar Anne Davis Basting's work to create meaningful care environments for people with dementia includes a creative storytelling project called "Time*Slips*," in which participants jointly create stories based on visual prompts. Basting has described the end of one energizing and fun-filled session where a participant pronounced, "Hey, we're a group here! And we're really good!" (Basting 2009: 98).[8] While a dementia care facility is different in many ways from a factory staffed by cognitively intact people, the similarity in the two places has to do with what it means for people considered the "living dead" to experience a sense of *belonging*.[9] Exclaiming that "we're a group here" is an incredibly important assertion of self-awareness and agency for people otherwise written off by the society in which they live. This sense of belonging, and of connection, is what Vita Needle provides. Vita Needle means closeness, friends, and being part of a community; but it also means being needed, being relevant, and *mattering*.

Sociologist Robert S. Weiss, the author of *The Experience of Retirement* (2005), once said to me about people in retirement, "they just want to matter." This point resonates with a popular quote on "mattering" that is attributed to twentieth-century American writer Leo Rosten: "I cannot believe that the purpose of life is to be happy. I think the purpose of life is to be useful, to be responsible, to be compassionate. It is, above all to matter, to count, to stand for something, to have made some difference that you lived at all." The narratives of Vita's older workers are replete with stories of wanting to be useful, wanting to count, wanting to know their lives make a difference.

A sense of mattering came up often in descriptions of work. Mattering in part has to do with the positive influence of seeing dynamic examples among one's coworkers. When the younger of the "older" workers saw their elders hard at work, it seems that the combined sense of seeing possible futures and continued productivity enlivened the younger workers. As 74-year-old Jim Downey once said in reference to the 100-year-old woman who is the factory's eldest worker, "seeing [her] makes you feel alive." I would also hear about feeling valued because of being productive, and feeling like your work in an assembly line process influences the next person's. As Jim once said, in reference to squaring needles (grinding a batch to a common length): "I used to get these comments back from Ruth after I'd square stuff. She said, 'You do good work,' and she ... has the next step of sandblasting. If it's badly done she can tell right away." Workers commonly invoke the concepts of interdependence and common purpose in the production process. Coworkers help each other out: they fix someone else's crooked needles, pick things up off the floor, carry boxes, find missing parts. Coworkers, managers, and owners have a strong perception of mutual obligation to each other and address each other on a first-name basis, a linguistic gesture of equality and common purpose.

While it is evident that work provides a sense of membership and mattering for Vita's workers, one might counter by saying work does that for many people across the life span. However, one's place in society influences how one feels about work, and mattering feels different for older adults than it does for younger people. Vita's older workers describe how work enables a feeling of control and of agency in a life phase assumed by others (and often by older adults themselves) to be devoid of both.

Agency and Control

Jim Downey is a 74-year-old retired architect who has worked at Vita Needle for nine years, since shortly after he retired from thirty years at a Boston architecture firm. A busy man, involved in many volunteer activities, civic organizations, and social groups, committed to his family, and a frequent traveler, Jim came to Vita Needle for "meaningful interaction." He is candid that he is not at Vita Needle for the money, though he likes the extra cash. He works at Vita Needle five hours a day, five days per week. Jim sent me these thoughts via email, after reading comments about Vita from my students who had been surprised that anyone would find working in a factory to be an ideal retirement activity. "Each of us has a different set of needs—personal, economic, and social—that might be met in a con-

FIGURE 12.1 Photo by Caitrin Lynch.

ducive workplace. But the value of time is different for retirees and young people, where the investment in work may interfere with play, or workouts, or whatever social milieu provides more satisfaction. Yes, the job is much more than money, but how many young people actively seek to meet so many of their needs at work?" Jim was responding to analysis by eighteen-

FIGURE 12.2 Photo by Caitrin Lynch.

and nineteen-year-old students, and so he interpreted their thoughts in terms of differing age-perspectives: he emphasized how work feels different for people depending on their age.

Vita workers are varied in the extent to which the paycheck is important to their everyday survival. Jim is one extreme; on the other end of the spectrum are people who are struggling to make ends meet despite these paychecks and their income from Social Security and Supplemental Security. In between are the many people for whom the Vita paycheck is a supplement to various other forms of support and who may use it for groceries, but also for grandchildren gifts and vacations. Regardless of the significance of the income, all Vita workers describe work today as different now than at earlier life stages, and—as with Jim—*time* is a recurring motif in workers' narratives. Key features of work for Vita's older workers have to do with how they choose to use their time, and it often comes down to notions of freedom, flexibility, and choice—in short, it is about *agency*, being in control.

Agency and control: these adjectives may not typically be associated with older adults in American society. Whereas they are important values in the United States, Americans seem to assume stereotypically that old people do not have agency: their bodies are failing, they are not in control, their life choices have already been made, and they are just finishing up their years.

Many Vita workers are doing work that is entirely different now, in their "retirement" years, than the work they did as they raised children, paid off mortgages, saved for college educations. Vita employees were often eloquent on how work today feels much different than before, when there was a heavy sense of obligation about the role work had in terms of supporting a family. Pete Russell, eighty, is just one example, and he refers to a sense of contribution but also of freedom.

> *Pete*: What I do, I like to do. And, I feel like I'm contributing and I feel appreciated. And if they don't like it, they can [laughs a bit, as he obviously omitted a curse]. But, I have the freedom to say, "see ya." [Pauses.] But, the obligation to be there and to do the work is still there, but I can always get out of it. It's not like there's seven kids going to college. Or anything.
>
> *Caitrin*: Oh, so earlier, when you did have seven kids who needed to go to college, work felt different?
>
> *Pete*: Ohohoho, yeah. [Laughs.] Work felt like "huuhuhuh." [Makes a groaning sound.] Like that.

Here in the interview Pete indicated that something is bearing down on his head from above, and he is fending it off—like the world is going to fall on his head. Pete was emphatic that today he could get out of the work if he wanted to; yes, there is an obligation to show up, since the employer and coworkers expect him. But this internally chosen obligation is much different from the obligation to work when raising a family. Choice and control are key to Pete's assessment of his job.

In narratives I gathered from Jim, Pete, and others, the recurring themes include their willingness to be here, the lack of obligation to family members (they no longer have kids to support), their ability to quit if they want to, and ability to use their time as they choose. In these claims about work, they repeatedly pronounce how they are individuals, obligated only to themselves, making choices of their own free will. This is a vision of old age so stark in its contrast to stereotypes about aging as diminishment of possibility and control, the inability to make decisions and to lead independent lives. For these workers, the freedom their work enables is a symbol of the freedom they have to live their lives as they wish.[10]

I often heard workers say they do not want a job that they have to "bring home" and that causes them stress. As one worker put it, the minute he steps onto the sidewalk he forgets about work—and that is how he likes it. Another told me that his ideal retirement is what he has at Vita: "It's to have ... employment, during acceptable hours, without a lot of stress, job stress, let's say, in a collegial atmosphere. And I guess with a certain amount of flexibility in regard to time." Vita workers want to be in control of their time, they want to be able to clock out in a moment of frustration, or when a grandchild needs them, and the production manager has expertly designed the production process to allow that (a surprising feature of an assembly facility). As one worker said, referring to the owners and to himself: "It's a win-win. For them, for us, and I get a little extra money, and I don't use up all my time." Unlike many of their previous workplaces, where work used to take them away from their families, this work brings these (mostly) men to a new and in some ways more ideal family. Yet it also allows sufficiently flexible scheduling so the workers can (when they choose to) be with their non-Vita families for babysitting, accompanying a spouse to the doctor, school performances, birthdays, illness, holidays, funerals, and the like.

Allen Lewis, a lifelong factory worker who considers himself "semi-retired" at eighty-four, found he had to buy a "retirement clock" (which shows the days of the week but no times) because, "I was just having trouble remembering which damn day it was." He told me that one day he had gone to work to find the door locked, and he then realized it was a Sunday. Regarding scheduling flexibility, Allen told me the managers allow him to choose when to arrive and when to leave: "But most of the people there, if we know something is needed, we'll work on it.... The other day, I saw a job was there and I knew they didn't have anyone who was going to do it so I came in and took care of it. So it, it works out. They're reasonable. We're reasonable. You know, and we get along fine." When Allen ended by saying both parties are reasonable and "get along fine," he described a situation where both worker and employer are "reasonable" about their expectations, obligations, efforts, and hours.

For Allen, there was an obvious positive valence to schedule and task flexibility, so I asked him about the downside to flexibility, that workers might not be able to rely on steady work—as critics of flexible labor often note. I also asked him if perhaps the workers are being exploited by only being given near-minimum-wage-level work at part-time hours. To this Allen was adamant in his reply: he argued that the scheduling flexibility that this job enables justifies the relatively low wage, with some people starting at minimum wage. "Take Esther. She sits there and mostly she is just putting needles in the box. She's talking.... She'll get a phone call. Her daughter-in-law wants her to babysit, sometimes during the day. She'll just punch out and go along, you know. You pay for these things. The convenience of just being able to drop your work and go baby-sit for your daughter-in-law and then come back the next day and go to work." Allen ended this story of Esther by saying, "There are no chains on the seats." He added, to explain the analogy because I had misheard him, "slaves chained to the oars." For Allen, it was important to emphasize to me that everyone is here on their own free will, and that they are making conscious choices about what is important to them: flexibility, yes; high pay, no.

Workers' comments about flexibility invariably cite the concept of flexibility in positive terms, whereas flexible labor is the subject of considerable analysis by labor activists and scholars who are concerned with businesses' increasing reliance on flexible labor forces. These are people who can be hired part-time or temporarily, who are easily fired, and who therefore cannot rely on regular work, are not eligible for health and retirement benefits, and are unable to negotiate for better working conditions (see, e.g., Freeman 1998; Patterson 1998; Susser and Chatterjee 1998). But Allen argues, and we hear this in other ways from his coworkers, that they are willing to "pay for" their flexibility—they will sacrifice higher wages and other benefits if they can maintain a lifestyle where work is qualitatively different than it used to be for them.

Flexibility of their current work allows both the fostering of family and social ties at work, and the flexibility to be able to spend more time with their "real" families outside of work, but when they, as freely acting agents, choose to do so. They like flexibility because it also allows them to engage in activities they used to not have time for, and especially because they feel like they are *in control* of their time. In this way, they distinguish between their current work and work earlier in their lives, sometimes using the terms "career job" as opposed to "retirement work," but often not even describing their jobs at Vita as work. As 72-year-old Charles Young commented to me one day when I was coiling tubes at a table near him: "I think of this as a men's club. You come in, get some exercise, talk, do something, and get paid." A nearby coworker retorted, "You don't get paid at a men's club," to which Charles quickly replied and smiled at me, jabbing his calipers in the air for emphasis, "It's *better* than a men's club!"

Conclusion

We learn from Vita's employees that work means something different to people at different ages—and that agency can be a critical reward of work, even in a factory that we may at first glance envision to be a stereotypically alienating setting. We have seen Vita's older workers endeavor to articulate how work feels different now than before, in a range of ways including freedom and flexibility of scheduling (time itself feels different). We also have heard of a pervasive sense of responsibility and duty to self only, and not a world-is-falling-on-my-head responsibility to provide for a family. These workers articulate a sense of acting and being for themselves, with the power to quit, to say no, or to choose a new path if they so desire. There is a certain independence in their conception of work, but also running through their commentary is a pride in helping others succeed. In these many ways, Vita's workers voice a desire for membership and for mattering. Their comments echo those of Weiss who another time said to me, about the people at Vita, "you don't want to retire to a rocking chair, you want to continue to matter, but you also don't want to continue to be out in the competitive world scrambling to make a living."[11]

Vita's workers are not alone in seeking meaning in retirement. A sense of purpose appears to unite many people's motives to work in retirement. The organization Civic Ventures is spearheading the creation of opportunities in the United States for people to do meaningful work in their conventional retirement years. Marc Freedman, Civic Venture's CEO and founder, identifies a number of elements that older workers value. One he refers to with the phrase "people and purpose." As he says, older workers value "connections to others committed to similar goals, and a reason to get up in the morning" (Freedman 2005: 4). Another element Freedman identifies as valuable to older workers is that they want their work to have social impact. Freedman describes this as "work that is not only personally meaningful but that means something important in service to the wider community." Freedman's comments about the importance of people-contact resonate with psychologist Mihaly Csikszentmihalyi's insights that the happiness achieved in an optimal experience provides a sense of purpose, and such happiness is also often found in the company of others. As Csikszentmihalyi notes, "Everyone feels more alive when surrounded with other people" (2008: 165). He adds that being with others can help people focus their thoughts and not, for example, obsess over problems (2008: 169). This point certainly reminds me of comments I would hear often from Vita workers about how working at Vita keeps them busy, and, as Charles once put it, "keeps my mind off my aches and pains." (Though we earlier heard Esther say working gives her and coworkers a chance to commiserate over the same.)

By attending to the meanings of work for older adults in this suburban Boston factory, we can gain insight into the changing meanings of work at different stages of the life course. In 1997, the sociologist Arlie Hochschild argued in *The Time Bind* (2001 [1997]) that there has been a gradual process since the late 1960s in which home has become work and work has become home. That is, people want to go to work to relax and escape the chaos of a home stocked with crying children or a nagging spouse. An important difference from this wider U.S. social phenomena is that in the case of Vita workers, the people who feel that work is a sanctuary experience themselves as marginalized, or even invisible, in society. Charles told me in an interview: "One of the nice things Vita Needle has is that it's sort of a *refuge for older people*. We come there, we can talk to each other, we can kid each other.... We can make money at the same time." So when Esther, Charles, and others use analogies such as refuge, family, and club to describe their workplace, they are expressing how their workplace matches their desire for a place to go where there are people with whom they feel close, where they belong, where they have something in common with others, where they matter, and where they are in control. In their current stage in life, they do not find all of this in any single place outside of work.

While the experiences of Vita Needle's workers enables us to see how work means different things to people at different stages of the life course, it also leads us to ask questions about the nature of the capitalist work environment itself. Using data from her study of workers at a large corporation in the American Midwest, Hochschild argues that these workers use work as a way to escape from home problems, "never quite grasping the link between their desire for escape and a company's desire for profit" (2001 [1997]: 174). So, in parallel vein, how do we weigh the Vita workers' desire for membership and mattering and the company's desire for profit?

Vita managers depend on workers' flexible labor and they design the workplace in a way that accommodates their older workers' physical and scheduling needs and abilities. If their policies and practices translate into worker loyalty, in whose interest is that loyalty? Does loyalty look different if some workers clearly self-identify as having no sense of belonging anywhere else in their lives or if they crave the freedom of a flexible schedule? Vita's example suggests that a practice that can be good for business can *also* be good for workers—it is not that flexibility serves management's interests *rather than* those of workers. The Vita example does not lead to an argument for flexible labor across the board—and especially not in situations of dire financial need, vulnerability, and desperation. But what makes flexibility acceptable to these workers is how the successful building of community (membership) and creation of purpose (mattering) provides for a sense of agency and control otherwise difficult to attain.

Acknowledgments

Research for this chapter was made possible in part by financial assistance from the Ruth Landes Memorial Research Fund, a program of The Reed Foundation. Additional funding was provided by the Research Fund of Olin College (2006–2011) and by the National Endowment for the Humanities Summer Stipend Program (2009). This chapter is based on work that appears in my book *Retirement on the Line: Age, Work, and Value in an American Factory* (Cornell University Press, 2012). Thank you very much to Jason Danely, Elizabeth Ferry, Sarah Lamb, Smitha Radhakrishnan, Cinzia Solari, and the press's anonymous reviewers for feedback on this version. In order to protect the privacy of the research subjects, I have changed the Vita Needle workers' names and some identifying features (such as age, family details, previous occupation, and current role at Vita). My greatest debt goes to the workers, managers, and owners of Vita Needle.

Notes

1. According to Massachusetts universal health-care requirements, "full-time" means thirty-five or more hours. This is an obvious boon to the employer, a point I discuss at length in *Retirement on the Line* (Lynch 2012).
2. See SSA 2011, which states, "Under federal law, people who are receiving Social Security benefits who have not reached full retirement age are entitled to receive all of their benefits as long as their earnings are under the limits indicated below [chart appears below original text]."
3. On the postwar "golden age of capitalism" see Marglin and Schor 1992.
4. On the positive moral value Americans tend to place on the intrinsic value of hard work, see Weber (2008) and Lipset (1992). A helpful review is Roger B. Hill's "History of Work Ethic" website: http://www.coe.uga.edu/workethic/history.htm.
5. An old-age social security program was first developed in 1889 by Germany's Chancellor, Otto von Bismarck, and was set at age seventy (http://www.ssa.gov/

history/ottob.html). In the United States, the age was set at sixty-five when the program began in 1935 with the Social Security Act (http://www.ssa.gov/history/).

6. For this, I am partly thinking of Erik Erikson's (1997) discussion of the self-reflection in later life stages.

7. On the changing concept of "family" in the United States, see Coontz 2000; Gillis 1997; Lasch 1995; and Stacey 1997.

8. See also http://www.timeslips.org/.

9. For the pervasiveness of this concept of the "living dead" in reference to people with dementia, see Taylor (2006) and Basting (2009).

10. Of course, I realize that one person's freedom may be another's exploitation. Yet, I argue for the importance of listening to how these older workers imagine and make sense of the role of work in their lives. While we may suspect that they are simply reproducing a set of understandings about the relationship between their work and their lives that perpetuates exploitative work arrangements, there is something much more complex at play here, as I discuss in *Retirement on the Line* (Lynch 2012). I do not consider these concepts of membership and mattering to be a disguise for capitalist interests; they are genuine feelings that propose a different set of relationships and values in the workplace.

11. Personal communication, email, 28 April 2009 (quoted with permission).

13. LIFE COURSES OF INDEBTEDNESS IN RURAL NIGERIA

Jane I. Guyer and Kabiru K. Salami

People make financial commitments at several successive stages of life. Each commitment usually has a time horizon: a date or stage of life when it either expires or comes due and is repaid. The further the time horizon into the future, the greater the possibility that the personal situations of the parties will change and repayment will become uncertain. Three temporal horizons coexist in people's lives: the present moment, with its cultural repertoire of possible commitments; the passing years of the life course, with their varied and unpredictable impact on personal situations; and historical change, with its irreversible shifts in circumstances for everyone. When the financial commitments link the generations to each other, more generalized questions can be invoked, about what, exactly, is "owed" between youth and elders, in light of what principles, and in what amounts. Do fifty-year-olds keep commitments that were made when they were twenty, and do they expect the current twenty-year-olds to behave as they did thirty years ago? The terms of repayment can become unclear.

In this chapter we examine economic commitments across all three temporal horizons of the life course in a rural town in western Nigeria, where some commitments are explicitly between equals, oriented to a closer horizon, and others are explicitly hierarchical, oriented to a more distant horizon. It may sound complex to analyze, but these are the mundane realities of life, especially over the recent decades when changes in global markets for goods, urban labor markets, and financial innovations also accompany cultural shifts and religious conversions. (See Lamb and Gamburd, this volume, for discussion of cultural shifts about aging and intergenerational obligations that accompany changing economic circumstances in India and Sri Lanka, respectively.) We students of these changes need to be as patiently attentive as the people themselves to the subtle techniques through which life courses and intergenerational relations are continuously reframed and the commitments on which social life depends go forward. We have to ask ourselves: towards which aspects of the lives of others does the concept of "life course" orient our attention?

The study of West African societies was the source of major initiatives in the anthropological understanding of the life cycle and the developmental cycle of domestic groups (Goody 1962). Ethnography showed how the domestic cycle reflected the kinship system, which in turn, was an aspect of the political and administrative system, so there were wide variations between societies. Fortes's classic (1970) article on "Time and Social Structure" used cross-sectional data on rural and urban populations to suggest how the matrilineal Ashanti cycle was likely to change: in this case in favor of the greater prominence of fathers in their children's lives as society moved towards the "modern" urban setting. For Africa, we have sparse longitudinal data to test out such hypotheses. From oral history and the occasional document, Jane Guyer has reconstructed the slow and diffuse change in bridewealth payments, food prices, and land use for the people of western Nigeria on whose lives we concentrate here (Guyer 1994, 1997). For the many urgent daily matters and longer commitments, however, systematic data may barely exist for the past, and people's memories may not be exact or consistent. During the longer arcs of people's commitments to each other, such as debt, the way may be strewn with disappointment and experiment, escape and return, retribution and reconciliation. New mediations are created. Old authorities intervene in new ways. New religions provide exemplary parables. In small communities, there may even be particular individuals who step forward to bear the intellectual and organizational brunt of defining, coaxing, and monitoring obligations, old and new. (See Gamburd, this volume, on the at-times uneasy emergence of new concepts of intergenerational obligation and property transfers in Sri Lanka.) The memory of how this was done at the time can fade as people accept an innovation and move on.

If our research methods have already missed these moments of imagination and mundane struggle, we miss the active voice in history, the imaginative moves by which debilitating downward spirals are evaded and commitments are unmade and remade by resetting the time horizon or revising who is bound up and who is released. Ideally, the study of debt would be based on continuous records that people had kept for their own purposes or, for a non-literate population, continuous monitoring through research. This is obviously impossible to carry out over generations. What we take advantage of here is the unusual opportunity to use data collected in several different studies, in the same place, spanning forty-two years, and to combine the insights and expertise of a foreign scholar (Jane Guyer) and a trained sociologist from this very community (Kabiru Salami). Since we still keep in mind the need for a much vaster record on the "portfolios of the poor" (Collins 2009), we note our leaps of interpretation as we go.

Sites and Methods of Study

The rural Yoruba town of Igbo-Ora is the site of the economic anthropological fieldwork of Guyer in intermittent periods since 1968. It is the hometown and—since 1999—the focus of research of Salami. During her broader studies of the economy in 1968–69 and 1987–88, Guyer documented ceremonial expenditure, much of it for life-course rituals, from two samples of farmers: sixty-six in interviews and sixteen in continuous record-keeping of work and budgets. In his study in 1999, Salami focused on savings and credit in general and later narrowed down in 2001 on the access of youth to their first sources of money to launch their occupational careers. A survey was carried out among 612 youths, half male and half female, whose ages ranged between seventeen and twenty-seven years. In 2009–10, Guyer focused on the institutions through which money circulates: credit association, moneylenders, hire purchase operators, and so on. Salami has been a collaborator in this work. By combining the studies we can examine the changing nexus of monetary debt.

Studies elsewhere in Africa have shown how the rebellious youth of one generation become the elders of the next phase of history (Mandala [1990] for Malawi). Lisa Cliggett shows for Zambia that powerful resentments can build up as one generation tries to hold onto commitments made to them that are impossible for the next generation to honor (2005). Our chapter suggests a process that seems specific to this community in western Nigeria, but whose counterparts we might find elsewhere if we searched more closely. The old system of commitments already contained nearer as well as further horizons of commitment and repayment, in combination. We examine the two most prominent here: the two that were explicitly generational. One was based on the equality of age-mates and the other on the seniority of intergenerational relations. Rather than seeing a single encompassing change over time, we argue that the two have been selectively transformed. In the moral economy of commitment, age-mate equality has been increasingly emphasized by comparison with intergenerational hierarchy. An important source for indicating these long shifts in the life course of debt is the finance of the ceremonial life course, from birth to death, so we turn to these data first.

Budgets and Social Payments, 1968–69

One main finding of Guyer's budget study was that the governance and ceremonial nexus deeply influenced men's most mundane daily work lives and money management. On average, a third of all monetary expenditure was devoted to gifts and redistribution at rites of passage: naming ceremonies for newborns, marriages, apprenticeship graduations, title acquisitions, and funerals. However, within each ceremony there were at least two types of transaction at work. First, there was stepwise pooling, up a precise hierarchy of seniority: from younger to older sibling, then up the generations to the oldest of each senior sibling cohort in the kin group on a lifetime cycle of contribution and inclusion. There was no short-run accounting or any expectation of precise reciprocity. Each member's money gift was remembered only within the group. The total was calibrated according to the importance of the occasion, and the leader distributed the collected amount in the name of the whole group. This kind of contribution was most important when the governance of the whole community was at stake: at death and succession, when the leadership was turning over. Second, there were simple person-to-person gifts, by friends and age-mates, to be reciprocated on future, comparable, occasions, in slightly higher amounts than the original gift. Finally, a celebrant's *egbé* (association) collected money from each member and gave as a group. Everyone belonged to *egbé,* where they were treated as social equals by virtue of the principle of organization: shared occupation, religion, age, and any other common feature or purpose they had chosen to organize around. The ethic of mutuality in dyadic and *egbé* giving worked alongside the ethic of respect of the pooling system.

The hierarchical mode did affect individual economic style in one particular way: not in the monetary transactions and debt commitments themselves, but in each person's planning for the responsibilities that they could envisage for their own social futures. In the budget study, elders in leadership positions were working less and spending more than other adult men. Their farms were small: due to advanced age; due to the considerable time they had to devote to public life; and due to their ability to come up with large contributions to any ceremony, through pooling rather than from their own work. By comparison, adult men who occupied junior positions in their sibling and kin groups ran mundane, average farms. Their budgets balanced income and expenditure, and they showed no specific signs of ambition, no larger farm size, no substantial saving nor spending. It was certain young and adult men in senior kinship positions who were creating short-run surpluses, high ceremonial giving, and substantial savings, all at once, from the produce of their larger farms. These men were the oldest of their sibling groups, within important compounds, and thereby in line to aspire to titles in town government as they matured. Long-term ambition seemed to drive their more vibrant economic lives. Finally, and by contrast, there were some very weak performers amongst the youth: men with small farms, low incomes, and low expenditure. One was the youngest of four brothers from a small compound, and therefore with very low potential for social prominence in the future.

There is a life course implied here, which also influenced the higher dyadic and mutual giving of the more prominent youth. Although all young men started out working for their fathers, who then paid their bridewealth, once established in young adulthood, the oldest sons of sibling groups paid up their kin group contributions while also building personal networks through generous dyadic and association gifting during ceremonies for social equals. They worked harder on their larger farms to generate these funds, seemingly positioning themselves for rising status and responsibility, at which point the pooled assets of the seniority model would eventually fall to them to manage.

By the time of the return study in 1988 (twenty years later), several parameters had shifted, effectively reducing quite dramatically the proportion of monetary expenditure that passed through the ceremonial nexus. The proportion devoted to production was increased, so the annual debt cycles of production came to the fore. Money-lending and other debt institutions expanded, along with mutuality on the nearer time horizons, leaving the longer horizon of obligations over the life cycle and between generations to a religious nexus that itself was changing through the steady advance of Islam and Christianity. The short-cycle social obligations and the dyadic model moved forward, while the hierarchical, life cyclical pooling model became less clearly influential on the day-to-day considerations of economic life.

The Monetization of the Farming Year, 1988: Everyone Needs Cash

By 1988, urban demand for crops was rising in the great cities to the south, and the traders' transport fleet had greatly expanded. Farmers were somewhat better off. The real value of their incomes (discussed in Guyer 1997: 181 and Appendix B) rose by thirty-one percent, or twenty-one percent net of the increased input costs. Tractors for hire had been introduced into the rural economy. Migrant farm laborers were coming in larger numbers from greater distances. The finance of farming changed accordingly. Tractor clearing had to be paid up-front, in February and March, when the work was done. The laborers were taking on more tasks than in the past, so they were costing more money to farmers.

The following abbreviated analysis of farmers' expenses compares the six months of March to August for 1969 with the same months in 1988. Proportions of total gross expenditure are indicated in Table 13.1.

The rise in living expenses was accounted for by food, household, school, medical, and transport costs. The rise in production costs was almost entirely for tractor hire and payment of migrant labor. The decline in ceremonial costs is the largest single proportional change, downsized just as incomes were rising. The numbers of contributions had declined as well as their size per occasion. (A more detailed breakdown is shown in Guyer 1997: 183.)

This budget profile, however, needs to be seen in a life cyclical as well as cross-sectional light. Life was becoming much more expensive at the beginning of every farming year, and especially for the young as they started out in their careers. By 1988, a new style of farming had been established by the younger cohort. Many young people were planning to farm as what Guyer calls "sideliners," having trained in other crafts or tried urban jobs. Nearly all these young people wanted to farm on large, tractor-cleared fields with mono-crops cultivated at low labor intensity and with the output destined primarily for the market. The apprenticeship system also expanded. With the arrival of paved roads, new types of vehicles, and the expansion of urban markets, many people started to train for occupations in transport: mechanics for cars, motorcycles, and tractors; repairers for different kinds of tires; commercial drivers for pick-ups and motorcycles. With new opportunities, those who could afford to do so left farming while others combined farming with another occupation. We are reminded of the lyrics of King Sunny Ade, the internationally-known Nigerian jùjú musician, which reflects on this moment of shifting generational patterns of work, "there are no more farmers in the farm, villagers have returned home to the town" (*kò*

TABLE 13.1 Samples of Farmers, March to August, Cash Expenditures by Destination

Year	1969 (N=12)	1988 (N=19)
Living expenses	46 percent	57 percent
Production costs	6 percent	19 percent
Ceremonies	35 percent	15 percent
Associations	13 percent	9 percent
Total	**100 percent**	**100 percent**

s'ágbè mó l'óko, ará oko ti d'arí wale). For those who remained in agriculture, starting a new farm of one's own became much more expensive. Parents became reticent—or simply unable—to support these added expenses for their children. This was captured in the well-known saying, "Fathers work for their sons" (Berry 1985), which was originally a political slogan critical of the moral decline of modern life. A gap in the economics of the life course had opened up: the large cash outlay needed to start up a new style of work for the young, and the life cycle commitments between generations started to diminish.

Youth, Cash, and Tradition: Starting a Career in 1999 and 2001

Tradition hardly covered the investment levels that were now required. The Yoruba saying, "a child should own his personal hoe when he reaches the time" (*t'ómodé bá tó l'ókó, kó l'ókó ni*) indicates that there is a time for transition from stage to stage in life and that, by implication, the expense of graduation and setting up in business—the modern version of launching a child into full adulthood—was expected to be borne by the family. Children and followers had been a sign of success for elders, a means for building the inclusive kin hierarchy, the base of the pooling pyramid, and a matter of honor (Iliffe 2005) and pride, as well as a support to production. They still were, but at a new cost. The generation that had come to adulthood just before the growth of larger scale farming and the expansion of apprenticeship, who had worked on their fathers' farms, and only gradually built up their social and financial resources, now had adult children for whom they had no obvious means of filling the cash investment gap that they themselves had not needed in their own youth. Parents started failing in their responsibilities. Sometimes they adjusted the customary approved patterns, such as by adjusting the list of bridewealth components downward, or they provided a patch from the family land without, however, contributing to any of the other start-up costs. They were seen by the youth as defending their old prerogatives. The saying "before a child eats twenty, I will eat thirty" (*k'ómo tóó jo'gún ng ó jo'gbòn*) became the slogan of the day; in fact some people even twisted it to "before a child eats twenty, I will eat a thousand" (*k'ómo tóó jo'gún ng ó je'gbèrún*). In response, the youth came up with the slang "You are tied to farming" (*O s'oko*) to tease their peers: as the land remained family property, farming tied them down to the family. In the light of low support from parents relative to need, the youth tried to operate with as little control from their parents as possible. They changed from planting long-term food and cash crops like cocoa and cassava to watermelon that can be harvested within three months. And they devised independent businesses like charcoal making (Salami and Brieger 2010–11) and taxi-motorcycle riding (*òkadà*).

By the early years of the twenty-first century, a marked preference by the youth for quick money had emerged: short season crops, the quick turn-around of charcoal production, daily income from the transport business, and downsized marriage payments financed by themselves. The whole temporal framing of economic life shifted away from the longer arc of the life cycle and its component step-wise sequences. The new sayings became, "a child's hand cannot reach the fanlight, while that of the adult cannot enter the gourd" (*Owó omodé kò tó pepe, t'àgbàlagbà kò wo kèñgbè*), that is "one does what the other cannot" which, by implication, means "*only* what the other cannot." Our studies have not yet refocused on the elders and the economy of their ceremonial life in the present. This needs to be done. But our sense is that the recuperation of life-cycle ritual by church, mosque, government (as for title succession ritual), and individual invention may show that there has been a relative attenuation of the longer arcs of resource commitment and social mnemonics.

Specialized money management institutions have moved into the spaces opened up by the relative evacuation of the longer temporal cycles in which small transactions were embedded. Some of them already existed: the *àjo* (contribution), cooperatives, *s'ogúndogójì* (a kind of money-lending, literally "turn twenty to forty," or return double the loan), and hire purchase (down payment plus installments). There are other money management institutions that may survive like *iwòfà* (debt labor service, which was outlawed under colonial rule) and *èdá* (a kind of emergency loan given under urgent circumstances, to be repaid in up to double the amount, but on no fixed time frame). Ephemeral fads have surged through from time to time, such as *Kadel*, a contribution organization, which turned out to be a pyramid scheme. Different credit associations have different rules, comprise different networks, and offer different opportunities to "jump the queue" by negotiating with a mate in the association to release (*ìyòñda*) his turn in advance.

All of these financial institutions are based on individual responsibility. To prepare for the future, young people create their own portfolio of money sources by belonging to several financial organizations, including their own peer group contribution clubs, networks of friends, work groups, or memberships with people working in the same market, where the financial operators concentrate their businesses. Belonging to several financial organizations helps youth to avoid the risk *kò s'ówó nílè* ("there is no money on ground"), that is, of being caught unaware when in need of money urgently. In the process, debts have been reinvented in a new, often peer-specific form, patterned after the dyadic social equality model of the past.

Some who were involved in *owó èlé*—money on interest—explained the advantage of hire purchase (lease to buy), in which a moneylender completes the down payment for the good (usually a vehicle) or an implement, and even to finance the farming year. Then the borrower pays back in installments that cover both the down payment and the remainder of the price. A guarantor is always required. In one of our discussions in the field, one person noted that people may even forego food in order to be able to keep money and avoid default, so as not to spoil things for future borrowers.

If we move forward in time, to 2010, many youth obtain individual loans to buy motorcycles for the *òkadà* business (motorcycle taxi-driving). Young people also mentioned ceremonies as a reason to take out a loan, as they would never have done in the past, since it would be very unlikely for a young person to run his—or even more rarely—her own ceremonies. So this study of youth and debt discovered whole areas of individual young people's borrowing and lending that did not exist in the 1960s, yet many had grown from the mutual and association models that already existed in the past.

The shift over forty years, or about two chronological generations, is a complex one, involving changes in production techniques, in religious life, and in the cost of creating a career, each placing its own pressures on the nested temporal cycles of mutuality. Yet the changes are not all in the nature of innovations. There were always the short cycles of interdependence and reciprocal dealing over money embedded within the ceremonial system. The social categories that have emerged most powerfully in the present are those, like *egbé* membership, that presume equality of status, at least for the specific purposes of debt and repayment. For example, credit associations, peer-guarantorship (*onídúró*), and the timed transactions, such as delayed payment (*àwìn*), of wholesale market sales. The balance of emphasis has shifted away from the status-specific transactional lives of the 1960s and yet it is not a complete departure from the moral and temporal economy of that earlier time. From the continuing study in 2010, we can extract a brief depiction of life in the short term, on the basis of collective interviews with several groups of ten to twenty men, out of the perhaps three-or-more thousand young men, of this town of about 70,000, who now make a living in the transport sector.

Conclusion: Life in the Short Term, 2010

The surge in the employment of youth in transport has continued and expanded since the 1980s. The needs of life require daily money. Up to around thirty years old, they take apprenticeships and occupy lowly functions as vehicle packers, fare collectors, and òkadà drivers. Beyond that age, they are drivers, mechanics for all kinds of vehicles, tire repairers, "panel-beaters" (dent-repairers), and other specialists of the road and the market. By counting the number of òkadà gathering-stations in Igbo-Ora, and estimating the number of motorcycle drivers per "park" (parking station), we estimated that there must be several thousand youth making a daily living from òkadà driving. While most of them stress the crucial factor of at least breaking even on a daily income, they are often also in debt for the motorcycle's hire purchase.

The logic here is incontrovertible. The amounts of money paid by passengers are very small, so almost nobody defaults. The whole business then rests on the volume of activity, which is not hard to generate in a spread-out urban community where people are ferrying themselves, their children, and their goods back and forth all the time. There is a large market at one place or another in the town every day. Churches, mosques, clinics, and schools are well attended. Kin are dispersed across town. Doubtless there could be a saturation point for taxi service, but it does not yet seem to have been reached.

These young òkadà drivers do engage in some longer-term debt, of the kind that Salami's study drew attention to ten years ago. In addition to borrowing to purchase a vehicle, quite often they have not been able to save for larger eventualities, so emergencies throw them into the money-lending markets. They say that fathers no longer want to pay bridewealth at all, and they themselves cannot necessarily afford the cost. It would take a longer study to identify trends, but there may well be a decline in formal marriage and a rise in conjugal unions that eventually entail parenthood as well. Even without a statistical study, we can listen to how the current youth depict their own economic lives and their expectations for their own children. The following are excerpts from the transcript of a recorded discussion with a group of about twenty òkadà drivers in 2010. They give their monetary calculations in naira, the Nigerian currency.

Òkadà work brings money much faster than farming work.... Is one going to wait for three months to take food? But if we take òkadà out for work within the next one hour one would surely make at least N100. Òkadà riding is also easier than bending down, hoeing, or weeding in the farm. Farming work is also more expensive [because] the laborers and tractors will claim their own share [and] at the end of the day one may not realize as much as the amount invested.... And by the time you harvest "there may not be market." For instance, there is no market for cassava now, it doesn't attract good sales. You cannot predict the market. Sometimes you may be thinking that you will sell your product at the rate of N10,000 but realize that it is not more than N2,000 in the market. And the government doesn't give any support to the farmers. We are satisfied with *òkadà* work because what we realize is okay. For instance from here to Òfikì River [in the rural hinterland] we take N500 and after returning to town we can still work within the town collecting N30, N40, N50 or more per trip. If we carry loads from Òfikì as well, then we collect more money because the payment for a load is different from payment of passenger alone. Most of us ride for the *òkadà* owner; they pay for minor repairs and pay N500 per day.... Those who manage their own motorcycle make nothing less than N1,200 per day, and more on a good day. They may avoid bad roads.

Some of us are thinking of saving to get another *òkadà* but others have school children and need to pay school fees and buy books. We don't want our children to fall on our own path and face similar problems to those we face now.

We also have small acres of land to support ourselves, which gives us more money during [certain seasons].

There are risks in *òkadà* riding: chest pain, cold, insects in the eyes, sometimes pneumonia. We also have accidents but not many. The police may trouble us for licenses, helmets, and [other problems]....We discuss the risks in our association but there is no solution yet.

Nobody works for any parents any more. Everybody works on his own. Everybody takes care of his parents. If a child is getting married it is the parents—[now us, as parents of the next generation of youth]—that take care of it. We pay for ourselves, our parents are already old. Most of our fathers are dead. Everybody takes care of his own family, working twelve hours, seven to seven daily.

There are several surprises here: *òkadà* drivers are now older than the "youth" of the 2001 study, and they have taken up the responsibility for daily care of their now-elderly parents from their earnings in their occupations. With the rise in farming costs and the decline in labor service from the youth, income-earning from farming by older people is limited to those who can raise capital, and those who reside in the countryside and have maintained their own strength. Some of the latter—as we saw in rural visits in 2010—also have small-scale specialty crops such as local tobacco and stands of cocoa. We are not sure how these intergenerational flows are now framed in moral terms, and especially for ceremonial life. Nor do our methods allow any speculation about the importance of remittances from kin in the cities. But one thing is clear: within the local economy, the most powerful interdependencies for the economic viability of life are now framed in the context of *egbé* and mutuality. The associations try to mediate occupational risks; they run their own contribution and loan societies; they discipline their members' behavior; and members may stand ready to be guarantor (*onídúró*) for another's individual debt. With all this, the members respect the elders for their daily needs, but perhaps less so for the great ceremonies of the past.

Such large commitments were made in the past, but within the ceremonial system. Perhaps they have simply been transposed from kinship to *egbé*, rather than invented from scratch. Has this transition and transformation been contentious, the subject of intense moral commentary, as the pragmatics of life has shifted? We might suggest that the apparently profound changes have, in fact, just extricated, elaborated, and passed through into enhanced local financial institutions the shorter-run phase in the life cycle of indebtedness that was always present. This shift in emphasis from the long temporal arc of debt to shorter temporal arcs allows the familiar moral framing of at least one temporal nexus to be retained and respected. This kind of change may not necessarily bring social peace, but it may keep controversies and confrontations within known frameworks.

The changes that we discern by pausing over the full spectrum of indebtedness, over forty years, return us to the first question of this chapter: What *is* a life course? As our predecessors argued for the domestic cycle, there is not a generic human, or natural, life cycle and neither are there unchanging cultural models. A life course of obligation and indebtedness in Igbo-Ora was always built up through multiple reciprocal relationships. Over the past forty years the long term became indeterminate, whereas in the past it was predictable according to status and seniority, and men could prepare for a long career from their early years. The short term has surged forward with its ancient, but now retooled, rubrics for a dyadic moral economy of mutual commitment for specific exchanges for specific purposes. The future that now needs study is the fate of elderhood: the current generation who would have presided over the pooling of money commitments; the adult generation moving towards elderhood, though now placed between a dependent parental generation and a very demanding youth: the new youth. Do the new youth envisage a horizon of elderhood at all?

Afterword

ON GENERATIONS AND AGING
"Fresh Contact" of a Different Sort

Jennifer Cole

> We leave childhood without knowing what
> youth is, we marry without knowing what it
> is to be married, and even when we enter old
> age, we don't know what it is we're heading
> for: the old are innocent children of their old
> age. In that sense, man's world is a planet of
> inexperience.
> —Milan Kundera, *The Art of the Novel*

THE ESSAYS IN THIS VOLUME are part of an emergent body of work that illuminates contemporary processes of aging. They explore the different ways in which people recognize aging, the opportunities and problems they associate with it, and the solutions they arrange using the cultural and social resources they have at hand. They also use aging as a prism through which to illuminate more general aspects of social and cultural life. Building on sociology's traditional concern with how people occupy particular social roles, psychology's concern with life stages, and anthropology's concern with cultural difference, the essays consider the process of growing older in the context of culturally shaped intergenerational relations. At the same time, the chapters document the process of aging in the years following the turn of the millennium: they are each located in a specific place and time. They draw attention to the intersection between the individual unfolding of the life course and the way that unfolding intersects with broader cultural and historical processes.

With its accretion of different meanings, the concept of generation is well suited to addressing this double-pronged problematic. In the early half of the nineteenth century, "generation" was used mainly to indicate the relation between fathers and sons on the one hand, or among peers on the other. In the later half of the nineteenth century, it was used primarily to characterize the relationship among peers (Wohl 1979). Today, "generation" carries both meanings, drawing attention simultaneously to people's structural positions within families and to shared historical experience. But the term also entails important representational effects, partly shaping the experience of the group to which it is applied, as we shall see.

There are good reasons for contemporary interest in how people grow old and in how aging shapes, and is shaped by, the wider social, cultural, and economic context. These days the question of how to move successfully from youth through adulthood and into old age seems omnipresent. In Europe there is increased public concern about how to care for an aging population given dwindling state resources. Meanwhile, economic malaise and blocked opportunities have both contributed to young people's participation in the Arab Spring and prompted increased migration out of Africa. In the United States, a new generation of "boomerang" kids is so-called because they move back in with their parents after college rather than establishing independent households of their own as was previously expected.[1] The signs of upheavals in the once-taken-for-granted life course are everywhere.

Although the experience of growing older and the reciprocal bonds that tie children to parents and grandparents are intrinsic to human life, the meanings and practices surrounding these bonds and experiences vary across culture, class, and historical period. So too, the extent to which aging and intergenerational relations become the focus of public attention fluctuates with time and place. The rise of the welfare state in much of Europe and North America may have been a highly contested process, but over the course of the mid-twentieth century, it nevertheless instantiated a vision of the social contract where the state took over many of the tasks associated with social reproduction, whether socializing children or caring for the elderly. It created institutions like schools and social security to attend to the age-specific needs of different groups. It also enabled the growth of specialists like gerontologists and child protection caseworkers who were supposed to administer and care for these age groups. The emergent science of human development, which sought to identify the age-specific needs of different groups, provided the scientific justification for these professions. The institutional arrangement created by many modern states, in turn, reflected underlying conceptions of the relationships among different generations. In the United States, for example, debates around social security focused on the idea that *individuals* contributed to public institutions during their working life, and hence deserved support as they aged (see Lamb 2009: 256ff.). But we can also see these forms of social security as part of a *generational* contract in which adults work and contribute to social life, with the expectation that their metaphorical (and real) children care for them in old age through their support of public institutions.

Toward the mid-twentieth century, several aspects of the institutionalization of the life course gradually converged to reify discrete age categories and the normative stages of human development. Among these factors were that large-scale institutions, rather than families, played an important role in socializing the very young or caring for the very old; that public discourse focused on distinct age groups; and that bodies of experts devoted themselves to age-specific suffering. Scientific knowledge, explanatory categories, and policy reciprocally fed off each other. These specialized institutions, and their accompanying ways of knowing, made bureaucratic sense. After all, if one views aging in terms of institutional categories, one can more easily examine and administer to different segments of the population: like a butterfly stuck upon a pin, one can parse out the component parts and perhaps create policies aimed at changing them. But this bureaucratic lens also drew both public and scholarly attention away from the temporal nature of aging and the importance of intergenerational relations.

To be sure, there have been some kinds of analyses that have withstood this pigeonholing. Scholars of the life course, for example, have long argued for a perspective that attends to how large-scale events impact individuals, and how individuals, through their responses and adaptations, shape larger patterns in turn, a perspective that resonates with practice theory (Bourdieu 1977; Elder 1999 [1974]; Kertzer 1983). Historians, too, have traced the emergence of age categories, often illustrating how changes in legal definitions and public policy concerning one phase of life affects others (Fass 2008; Hareven 1995). Family systems theorists have also sought to understand individual health and wellbeing in terms of broader familial contexts. In fact, even as recently as 1996, scholars argued that most care still took place within families, as it had across much of history, despite media representations to the contrary (Pike and Bengston 1996). Nevertheless, the general tendency within academic studies of aging has been to separate and classify, rather than looking at aging as involving the intertwining of generations with each other and with broader historical processes.

In the last thirty years, this distinct bureaucratization and compartmentalization that synchronized movement through the life course has begun to unravel amidst far-flung demographic social, economic, and political transformations. Around the world, and particularly in Europe, the United States, and Japan, low birthrates and higher life expectancy have combined to increase the numbers of elderly. As economic disparities between the global north and south have sharpened, so too have the numbers of people who migrate transnationally (Ehrenreich and Hochschild 2002; Goldin, Cameron, and Balarajan 2011). Many migrants are women; generally, women's participation in the workforce has grown. Would-be caretakers more frequently live scattered across vast distances, far away from family members they would normally have cared for, or they may have local jobs that prevent them from being able to care for older family members' daily needs. At the same time, social and economic conditions in many places have made it increasingly difficult for youth to obtain jobs or the economic means to support a family—the conventional markers of adulthood in many parts of the world. The two ends of the life course appear to be disintegrating, leaving an ever-smaller proportion of active adults—what Deborah Durham (2012) has ironically referred to as "elusive adulthood."

These social and economic changes have renewed journalists', scholars', and policy-makers' concern with processes of intergenerational transformation. They have also been accompanied by a rich array of cultural narratives seeking to interpret and explain these changes. With respect to aging, for example, policy analysts often frame the current demographic situation in ominous terms. They note that those who are younger than eighteen or older than sixty-five, and hence considered to be dependent, outnumber those between eighteen and sixty-five years old, considered the productive part of the population (Tuljapurkar, Li, and Boe 2000). They see this as creating a so-called crisis of care.[2] As the blurb for the book *Gray Dawn: How the Coming Age Wave Will Transform America—and the World* (Petersen 1999) describes the problem: "There's an iceberg dead ahead. It's called global aging, and it threatens to bankrupt the great powers. But we are woefully unprepared. Now is the time to ring the alarm bell." In this apocalyptic scenario, written by a former chairman of Lehman Brothers just a few years before the financial crisis in 2008, the world's aging population leads ineluctably to an economic and political crisis of global proportions.

Popular representations of youth are no less dire. Whether referring to the United States or Africa, analysts now talk about a "lost generation," a term that was originally coined to capture the predicament of young people after the trauma and disruption brought by World War I (Uchitelle 2010; Wohl 1979; for Africa see Cruise-O'Brien 1996). As one recent commentator remarked: "What is the most dangerous force in the world? Answers that might come to mind are al-Qaeda-inspired terrorism, or the threat posed by Iranian and North Korean nuclear weapons. These are indeed dangerous, but the most pervasive threat is *the large number of unemployed youth throughout the world*" (Morgan 2011, emphasis mine). The growth of digital technology, such as the Internet and social networking, which foregrounds aspects of social life associated with youth and makes visible their role in social movements like the Arab Spring or Occupy Wall Street, heightens the widespread perception that unemployed young people represent a "lost generation" and potential political threat.

If recent social and economic transformations have arguably thwarted youth's aspirations for adulthood and older people's ability to marshal care in their old age, generating widespread media debate, it has provided scholars with an opportunity to rediscover how children, youth, and the aged shape social and cultural life. Nowhere has this rediscovery been more visible than in writing on youth. Whether based in Africa or India, Latin America or Europe, many studies have moved away from older developmental models, which tended to treat young people as set on a path that led automatically toward adulthood. Instead, more recent studies analyze young people as active historical agents whose efforts to achieve social adulthood in difficult circumstances inform wider cultural patterns. They have untangled how young people shape and transform social and cultural life through their engagement of existing cultural resources, including their consumption habits, use of technology, and participation in new religious movements (Cole 2010; Honwana and DeBoeck 2005; Lukose 2009; Mains 2011; Weiss 2009). Anthropologists, in particular, have also become increasingly interested in the role of age in constituting specific kinds of subjects.[3] They have shown how attention to age categories provides a powerful window onto more general cultural processes (Durham 2004).

Curiously, however, this anthropological rediscovery of the generative nature of age-related social differences and perspectives, so powerfully visible amongst those who study youth and children, has been less evident for the topic of old age. This volume makes an important step in that direction by exploring how aging takes place in and through culturally shaped intergenerational relations (for early path-breaking work see Cohen 1998 and Lamb 2000; see also Livingston 2007). Read together, these essays reveal how one might view the process of intergenerational transformation from the point of view of those moving from later adulthood toward old age. In what follows, I draw from my prior work on generational change among youth to make two arguments, one with respect to the process of moving toward old age, the other regarding the scholarship—especially the anthropological scholarship—on aging. I suggest that just as youth moving toward adulthood participate in a process of intergenerational transformation, so too, do older adults moving toward old age, though these processes are not entirely alike. I further argue that the difference between how generational change occurs in youth and how it occurs in old age illuminates why, despite the evident visibility of the elderly in contemporary social life, they have not inspired the same scholarly effervescence. To develop this argument, I start with how generational transformation takes place as youth move toward adulthood.

Representations and Generational Change, Young and Old

The process of generational change that occurs as one moves from the relative dependence of youth toward the increased autonomy associated with adulthood takes place through a combination of selective acquisition on the one hand and selective rejection on the other. As young people take the many small steps that lead toward social adulthood, they acquire tools from the world around them such as language, gender norms, the ability to negotiate cultural assumptions of various kinds, and so on. Young people are, as anthropologists say, "socialized." Socialization is not a passive process. Rather, it is one of active and selective acquisition as young people seek out and absorb aspects of their environment and what they imagine to be—or are told to be—the tools for adult life. Think, for example, of the ways in which children and even adolescents perceive adult status as desirable because it connotes power and autonomy. Yet because this process of acquisition is not passive, but occurs in the give and take of social life, and because it is cross cut by complex hierarchical relations, it is always uneven. It entails both the active rejection of past practices and their selective forgetting in different measure.

The process of generational transition, as Karl Mannheim (1993 [1927]) noted, is one of "fresh contact," in which people coming of age reevaluate their social and cultural inventory. It is a process that allows people simultaneously to "forget that which is no longer useful and to covet that which has not been won" (Mannheim 1993 [1927]: 369). Mannheim's metaphor of "contact" allows us to imagine young people's movement toward adulthood as comparable to an encounter between different groups. Much as new migrants come armed with prior understandings and tools with which to make sense of their new environment, so too, youth coming into adulthood must navigate a new social and cultural terrain. This is not to say that young people have not been steeped in the practices of the culture in which they live. But when they engage in existing cultural practices with newly acquired status, or from the perspective of actually having to independently negotiate them as opposed to being dependent on others, they gain access to new interpretations and experiences. They draw on old tools or invent new ones. Using these tools to negotiate their present historical circumstances, they selectively reshape the existing social and cultural terrain. Ultimately, they craft partially new ways of being.

Generational formation, however, is always piecemeal. The "Achilles heel of generational theory," Wohl (1979: 208) notes, is that even its proponents have difficulty specifying what a generation actually is. In response, Wohl (1979: 210) argues that "a historical generation [is] not a zone of dates; nor is it an army of contemporaries making its way across a territory of time. It is more like a magnetic field at the center of which lies an experience or a series of experiences." Similarly, building on Wohl, Katherine Newman (1996) suggests that the idea of a "fuzzy set" best characterizes the degree to which members of a given generation actually share common characteristics. Like life stages that are always heterogeneous because people never evenly embody iconic characteristics, so, too, with generational formations. While everyone goes through similar processes of biological maturation, not everyone who is born sharing the same time, and even the same place, face exactly the same problems or opportunities. Nor do they find exactly the same solutions. There is no simple correspondence between when people come of age and how they inhabit a particular cultural moment. It is for all of these reasons that generations, whether in terms of predicaments, styles, or values, are always uneven and partial.

This partialness points to the importance of thinking about generations in terms of synoptic illusions, a concept I elaborate in my book *Sex and Salvation* (Cole 2010). Generational change does not take place in lockstep as armies of contemporaries move into the future. Instead, it is shaped by selective narratives about what an imagined entity called a "generation" is doing. In other words, other people, whether predecessors, contemporaries, or successors observe what a given age group is doing and construct a story about them. Such narratives create a synoptic illusion: they take a great deal of actual heterogeneity and simplify it, making a subset of highly visible practices stand in for a more complex whole, a process common to many domains of social life. The idea of the "millennial generation," the "lost generation," the "baby boomers," or "the hippies"—all these generational monikers never map onto more than a subset of people born in a particular time period. Once we think of generations as representations as well as groupings of people who partly share a common historical experience, we can begin to understand that there is a politics to how representations and perceptions of the life course work. After all, any representation is partial, revealing some dimensions of social life and occluding others.

Selective representations of what it means to belong to a given generation have effects. Representations of generations do not exist separately from the social world: they have consequences for how people experience their lives and how they act. Individual change over time—what it means to be an adult or a child, to belong to the baby-boomer generation, or to move between one life stage and the next—creates a powerful, naturalized link between time and the body. In their everyday lives, actors draw on the metaphors of human growth and change to interpret and transform their historical circumstances and life trajectories. Although such representations oversimplify what is actually taking place, they also create models to which other people relate. They create particular stereotypes that make some structures of feeling, some ways of interacting with the world, and some ways of confronting dilemmas more visible and available to be taken up by and inhabited by others. In the case of young people seeking adulthood, the synoptic illusion—whatever its content—propels them forward. It becomes a tool through which young people of a roughly similar age can imagine who and what they are, thereby imagining an unknown future. By imagining an unknown future and acting in its terms, they make their futures.

Generational Change and the Movement toward Old Age

What happens when we start to consider the process of generational change from the point of view of people moving from later adulthood toward old age? In part, we see the same kinds of processes, both those that ensure continuity and those that contribute to cultural innovation and change. But we see them from a different perspective. Some facets of the process change valence, while others remain relatively stable. Taken together, these transformations reveal how aging and the process of movement toward old age elaborates, perhaps even accentuates, patterns of generational change begun in the movement from youth toward adulthood. Considering generational change from the perspective of old age further reveals the potential negative effects of synoptic illusions, not only for aging people, but also, as I discuss in the conclusion, for the scholars who study them.

If young people engage in an "inventory of experience" as Mannheim puts it, learning to shed that which is not useful and to "covet that which has not been won," then people moving toward old age may often seek to preserve that which they *have* won. Such conservation is particularly visible at the level of individual identity as people find themselves confronting aging bodies and needing to recalibrate their sense of self in keeping with what are often diminished physical capacities. As Bateson notes in her chapter in this volume, older adults may experience a phase akin to the identity-formation that takes place in adolescence, as they reflect on where they are, where they have come from, and where they want to be (see also Kaufman 1986).

We see acts of conservation and reinterpretation, for example, in the chronic pain patients documented by Martin. These people suffer from the pain caused by accidents as well as difficult life circumstances. In learning to deal with their changing physical circumstances, they also seek to narrate an understanding of who they are and what has happened to them that preserves their prior sense of self. But such processes of preservation also take place at broader cultural and national levels. Lamb shows that as younger Bengalis move abroad, or more women work outside the home, it becomes harder for them to care for their aging parents who move to old age homes instead—in many ways a profoundly new experience, as I address below. Yet despite these changes in where people grow old and who cares for them, the elderly Bengalis studied by Lamb work to maintain certain values of intergenerational reciprocity by likening the forms of care given in the old age home to that which their children provided. In Norwood's chapter on terminal illness and euthanasia in the Netherlands, we similarly see that people's use of official euthanasia policy embodies core values of collective decision making, enabling people to strategically manage the otherwise unruly transition toward death. These examples reveal how people seek to retain aspects of who they are in the face of physical change.

This process of preservation is also selective. As aging people adapt to altered physical capacities, they come to experience their interactions with others and the world around them differently. As they do so, they may reorient themselves toward the norms that shaped their prior behavior. The essays in this volume reveal this point especially with respect to gendered norms of masculinity and femininity. For example, Wentzell argues that Mexican men suffering from decreased sexual function develop a critique of gendered norms of machismo that guided their behavior in their youth. Shea demonstrates that in China, women undergoing *gengnianqi* (the Mandarin word usually translated as menopause) talk about how they become far more irritable and prone to reacting strongly to situations that they might previously have silently endured. Their bodily reactions become part of how they evaluate both their past suffering and their present social circumstances (see also Kleinman and Kleinman 1994). There is, however, safety in these types of selective rejection and recasting because aging women's complaints or impotent men's revisions of machismo can be easily dismissed as sour grapes and thereby emptied of social power.

At the same time, the movement toward old age is a profoundly innovative process. These innovations often occur as people draw on already existing practices and transform them to adapt to new circumstances. We can see such innovation in the older people who continue to work at the Vita Needle factory outside Boston where the median age of the workers is seventy-four. Though it is generally expected that older people in the United States will retire from the workforce, Lynch shows that the employees at Vita Needle have chosen to go back to work, some because they want to, others because they need to. In either case, we see how they actively forge new ways of aging that draw on the importance of work to the creation of self and to the creation of a new stage of life. As they do so, they offer a new way of experiencing that stage (a point that is also true of the Bengalis depicted by Lamb). In Sri Lanka, meanwhile, Gamburd demonstrates that young people's labor migration, paired with a longer life span, have changed the circumstances in which people age. Consequently, as older Sri Lankans try to figure out new ways to honor intergenerational obligations, they debate whether to pass on their inheritance to their children and relatives while they are still living or after their death. Like young people coming of age who meet an existing terrain and transform it, so too old people with their changing personal capacities move across a social and cultural landscape. As they do so, those moving toward old age draw from long-standing ideas about the importance of work and material resources for creating human value. As they deploy them in their new and changing circumstances, they reformulate what it means to be old.

Synoptic illusions of what it means to age centrally shape the movement from adulthood to old age. Arguably, the dominant narrative about old age in many Western contexts is that old people are unable to change and that they epitomize decline. This narrative has deep roots. Mannheim's theory of generational change, for example, is premised on the idea that the old are less open to change simply because they have lived longer and have more of what he calls "ballast." Meanwhile, Lawrence Cohen (1994) notes that aging and the inevitable death it signifies threaten cultural meaning. Many societies symbolically associate *able* adult bodies with the collective social body. Consequently, bodies that age and die represent not just an individual threat, but a threat to cultural meaning and social continuity more generally.

Cultural representations of old age are also closely tied to distinctive ways of figuring the relationship between past, present, and future that emerged in Europe in the nineteenth century. One reason we do not usually think of generational change as occurring as adults move toward old age, even though arguably they do meet new circumstances and have to negotiate them, is because doing so would go against modern conceptions of time that associate progress and youth (Cole and Durham 2008). If our interpretations—whether popular or scholarly—assume that there is no movement or innovation among the elderly, and that we therefore always already know about their experience, then there is no point in attaching a notion of generational change to this group.

Yet clearly dominant representations of loss and decline elide much of the heterogeneity that is as important in old age as it is in any other phase of life. The present essays make clear the importance of such heterogeneity on several different levels. At the broad cultural level, for example, Rodrí-guez-Galán reveals how Puerto Rican women who immigrate to the United States often continue to raise their grandchildren, thereby continuing to occupy the role of "mother" long past when the Anglo majority considers it normative. They not only take pride in their caring labor, but they also gain emotional and social support for themselves. So too Danely teaches us how in Japan, the process of growing older is not figured as decline or atrophy. Rather people grow older in dialogue with unseen spirits and ancestors. As Guyer and Salami's analysis of the "life course of indebtedness" in Nigeria shows, people constantly reframe their intergenerational debts and commitments as they age; they remake the ground on which social life can go forward. Such heterogeneity within dominant representations takes place at the more individual level as well. For example, there is diversity in whether and how the Poles studied by Robbins are able to forefend against loss and negotiate new and positive social relationships in public retirement homes. This variation rests on how successfully particular individuals recreate a sense of home in the new institutional context. In all these examples, we see both the synoptic illusions at work and the actual variation within them.

What accounts for the marked change of valence that differentiates the transition toward adulthood from the movement into old age? Part of the answer lies in the profoundly different meaning of the set of models that the synoptic illusion of aging provides in many societies across the world, and its possible effects. If the synoptic illusion of youth provides a set of circulating models associating youth and change that many young people use to pull themselves toward the future, the dominant figuration of old age as loss becomes a weight against which those moving toward old age push. We can see the power of this representation and how people work against it in almost every essay in this book. It is there in how the workers at Vita Needle factory go out and find new jobs despite the fact that it is neither expected nor easy. It is there as well in the cultural work Bengalis engage in to cast living in an old age home as a sign of their children's nurture rather than abandonment. The many different examples of people suffering bodily impairments and struggling to reconfigure their understandings of themselves and prevalent social and cultural norms further reveal how images of loss and decline pervade their efforts. The negative synoptic illusion widely associated with old age acts, above all, to create a drag on older people's actions. One gets the sense, repeatedly, of the passage of time and the weight of negative social expectation against which the elderly must *push* to make new futures.

Conclusion: Synoptic Illusions among Age Groups and Scholars

Synoptic illusions, of course, are not limited to the analyses of the young or old. They are a feature of all social and cultural life. Only by simplifying and schematizing the infinite variation around us can we make sense of our social worlds. Such models help people to act; they become ways of imagining oneself into the world. Synoptic illusions also frame narrative possibilities. They help create a sense of narrative tension, as when we want to know the rest of a story because we assume we do not know how it turns out.

Synoptic illusions not only shape social and cultural life; they also inflect what scholars choose to analyze and how they approach their objects of study. Consequently, they encourage the mixing of analytic and popular categories. Such mixing occurs in many domains—think, for example, of Donna Haraway's (1989) observation of how conceptions of race and gender among humans inform the science of primatology. But slippage between scholarly and popular categories appears to be particularly frequent with respect to topics that are more easily taken to be universal because they are a highly visible part of our physical make up as human beings. After all, we all are born, grow up, and if we are lucky, reach old age. Consequently, because growing up and growing old are phenomena that we think we know well and we take for granted, the line between folk categories and analytic categories easily blurs.

This blurring of popular and scholarly representations encouraged by synoptic illusions applies to the scholarship on youth as well as that on old age. I have argued elsewhere that there is a tendency to over-privilege rupture in many scholarly analyses of youth (Cole 2010), precisely because we are used to thinking of youth as forging a future that differs radically from the past. Yet despite this general scholarly tendency to interpret youth in keeping with popular conceptions of this phase of life, there has also been, as I suggested earlier, an efflorescence of new work examining young people's constitutive role in social life, more so than for the aged.

To be sure, it is possible that the difference between the two fields reflects a demographic lag—that the numerical presence of youth became visible sooner than that of the elderly, and that scholarly attention simply followed this demographic trend. But I suspect that the different valence of the synoptic illusion relevant to youth and old age may also play a role. The effects of synoptic illusions are arguably as true for the scholarship on youth and aging as they are for the people we study. Perhaps because the valence of the synoptic illusion linked to youth is positive—associating youth with the hope of a new, perhaps better, future—scholars studying youth appear to have more latitude to explore the creative role of youth in social and cultural life. Although this efflorescence does not guarantee that new ideas and ways of conceptualizing youth emerge, the widespread excitement and sense of urgency around the topic may make it easier.

By contrast, scholars working on aging have to work against the negative valence of the synoptic illusion as much as their subjects do. This is especially so because implicitly the synoptic illusions associated with old age create a sense of foreclosure: because we know that old age leads inexorably toward death, we know the outcome, and we interpret it accordingly. The shift in the balance between past and future transforms the horizon of the possible. Like the elderly, so too scholars must exert more effort to create a sense of narrative possibility—a sense that there is, if you look closely, something to discover. Taking up this implicit challenge, the essays presented here make their contribution by striving to move behind the synoptic illusion to examine the diverse, concrete ways that people grow older in dialogue with their predecessors, contemporaries, and successors.

Acknowledgments

Warm thanks to Sarah Lamb, Caitrin Lynch, and Aaron Seaman for their comments on prior drafts of this Afterword; all remaining shortcomings are my own.

Notes

1. On Europe and its aging population, see Greenberg and Muehlebach, 2007. For popular representations of the Arab Spring as a youth movement see Shadid 2011 and Ahmed 2011. For more scholarly treatments see Schwartz 2011. For a discussion of migration from Africa in the popular press see Daley 2011. For academic discussions see Geschiere and Socpa n.d.; Mains 2007; Newell 2005. On "boomerang" children and the changing life course see Cohen 2010 for popular representations; see Newman 2012 for a scholarly treatment.
2. For popular representations of this issue see Achenbach 2011 and Stewart 2010.
3. On the relation of age to specific types of subjects with particular kinds of capacities see Berman 2011; Cole 2010; El Ouardani n.d.; Schildkrout 1978.

CONTRIBUTORS

Mary Catherine Bateson is a cultural anthropologist, linguist, and visiting scholar at Boston College. She has taught at Harvard University, Amherst College, Northeastern University, Spelman College, and George Mason University, from which she retired in 2003, as well as in Iran and the Philippines. She is the author of ten books, including *Composing a Life* (1989) and, most recently, *Composing a Further Life: The Age of Active Wisdom* (2010).

Diana De G. Brown is associate professor of anthropology and co-chair of the anthropology program at Bard College. She is a specialist on Brazil, where she has done field research on Umbanda, an Afro-Brazilian religion, and on the comparative use of health resources. She is currently conducting research on aging, health, and beauty in the southern Brazilian city of Florianopolis. Her publications include *Umbanda: Religion and Politics in Urban Brazil* (Second Edition 1994) and many articles and book chapters in English and Portuguese, published in the U.S. and Brazil.

Jennifer Cole, a cultural anthropologist, is professor in the department of comparative human development at the University of Chicago, and the author of *Sex and Salvation: Imagining the Future in Madagascar* (2010) and *Forget Colonialism? Sacrifice and the Art of Memory in Madagascar* (2001). She is also the co-editor of several books, including *Generations and Globalization: Youth, Age, and Family in the New World Economy* (2007); *Figuring the Future: Globalization and the Temporalities of Children and Youth* (2008); and *Love in Africa* (2009), all of which have examined issues of youth and generations as well as love, gender, and sexuality and their relation to social change in broader comparative perspective.

Jason Danely is assistant professor of anthropology at Rhode Island College. His research focuses on religion and health in Japan as it relates to experiences of aging and the life course. Past work has appeared in the *Journal of Aging, Humanities, and the Arts* (2009) and in the *Journal of Ritual Studies* (2012). His book manuscript, *Departures and Returns: Aging and the*

Creativity of Loss, is based on his ethnographic fieldwork with older adults in Kyoto, Japan and is currently in preparation. Danely's current research looks at the construction of rituals of hope in the context of population aging, economies of care, and elder abandonment.

Michele Ruth Gamburd is professor of anthropology at Portland State University. She is the author of *The Kitchen Spoon's Handle: Transnationalism and Sri Lanka's Migrant Housemaids* (2000) and *Breaking the Ashes: The Culture of Illicit Liquor in Sri Lanka* (2008). She is co-editor (with Dennis B. McGilvray) of *Tsunami Recovery in Sri Lanka: Ethnic and Regional Dimensions* (2010).

Jane I. Guyer is George Armstrong Kelly professor in the department of anthropology at Johns Hopkins University. She has carried out research in Nigeria and Cameroon devoted to questions of agro-ecology, livelihood, economic history, and the management of money, resulting in several monographs and edited collections. The two most recent collections are special issues of *Human Ecology* (2007) devoted to "Time and African Land Use: Ethnography and Remote Sensing" (co-edited with Eric Lambin) and *Anthropological Theory* (2010) devoted to "Number as Inventive Frontier" (co-edited with Naveeda Khan and Juan Obarrio).

Sarah Lamb is professor of anthropology at Brandeis University and co-chair of the South Asian Studies Program. She is the author of *White Saris and Sweet Mangoes: Aging, Gender, and Body in India* (2000) and *Aging and the Indian Diaspora: Cosmopolitan Families in India and Abroad* (2009), and co-editor of *Everyday Life in South Asia* (2002, 2010).

Caitrin Lynch is associate professor of anthropology at Franklin W. Olin College of Engineering and visiting research associate in the department of anthropology at Brandeis University. She is the author of *Juki Girls, Good Girls: Gender and Cultural Politics in Sri Lanka's Global Garment Industry* (2007) and *Retirement on the Line: Age, Work, and Value in an American Factory* (2012). She is also the producer of the documentary film "My Name is Julius" (http://www.juliusfilm.com).

Lindsey Martin is a postdoctoral fellow at the Michael E. DeBakey Veterans Affairs Medical Center, Health Services Research and Development Center of Excellence in Houston, Texas. She is a medical anthropologist with research interests in the study of chronic illness, the life course, aging, medical pluralism, practitioner-patient communication, medical decision-making, and qualitative methods.

Frances Norwood is assistant research professor in the department of anthropology at George Washington University. She conducts research on long-term and end-of-life care for persons with disabilities and persons who are elderly. She is the author of *The Maintenance of Life: Preventing Social Death through Euthanasia Talk and End-of-Life Care* (2009) and winner of the 2011 Margaret Mead Award. She is currently finishing a project on the impact of built forms and spatial practices in innovative long-term care environments in the Netherlands.

Jessica C. Robbins is a PhD candidate in the department of anthropology at the University of Michigan, Ann Arbor. Her dissertation focuses on aging, memory, and personhood in Poland and her broader research interests include gender, kinship studies, medical anthropology, morality, and postsocialism. Previous work has been published in *Anthropology News* and *Michigan Discussions in Anthropology*.

Marta B. Rodríguez-Galán is assistant professor of sociology at St. John Fisher College. Her main research interests are in aging and social gerontology, and Hispanic cultural studies. She has published empirical articles in the *Journal of Aging and Health* and *Activities, Adaptation & Aging*. She is currently working on an ethnographic study of Puerto Rican grandmothers raising grandchildren in Boston, Massachusetts and Rochester, New York.

Kabiru K. Salami is lecturer in the department of sociology, University of Ibadan, Nigeria. He has been involved in community-based social research for over ten years in different parts of Nigeria, including in the community where the chapter for this volume was based. His recent studies have looked at issues of livelihood, career building, and the relevance of the household in the well-being of its members.

Jeanne L. Shea is associate professor in the anthropology department at University of Vermont. A medical and psychological anthropologist, her research interests include cross-cultural perspectives on middle age, menopause, and aging; women's bodily and social experiences of aging in contemporary China; social discourse on romance, sex, and marriage in later life; familial and spousal caregiving of the elderly in China; efficacy and evidence in traditional Chinese medicine; and the negotiation of identity and hybridity in everyday life among Chinese immigrants and Canadian-born Chinese in Montreal. Her research has appeared in *Culture, Medicine, and Psychiatry*; *Modern China*; *Journal of Complementary and Alternative Medicine*; *American Journal of Human Biology*; *Ageing International*; and *Maturitas*.

Emily Wentzell is assistant professor in the department of anthropology at the University of Iowa. Her research combines approaches from medical anthropology, gender studies, and science and technology studies to examine the gendered social consequences of sexual health interventions, and has appeared in journals including *American Ethnologist, Body and Society,* and *Social Science and Medicine.* Her book based on the research project presented here is forthcoming from Duke University Press. She is co-editor of *Medical Anthropology at the Intersections: Histories, Activisms, and Futures* (2012).

BIBLIOGRAPHY

Achenbach, Joel. 2011. "World Population Not Only Grows, But Grows Old." *Washington Post*, 11 October. http://www.washingtonpost.com/national/health-science/world-population-not-only-grows-but-grows-old/2011/10/25/gIQAdt17VM_story.html.

Adler, Shelley R., Jennifer R. Fosket, Marjorie Kagawa-Singer, Sarah A. McGraw, Evaon Wong-Kim, Ellen Gold, and Barbara Sternfeld. 2000. "Conceptualizing Menopause and Midlife: Chinese American and Chinese Women in the US." *Maturitas* 35, no. 4 (April): 11–23.

Ahmed, Amel. 2011. "Yemeni Youth are Guarding the Revolution." *Al Jazeera*, English version, 11 June. http://english.alijazeera.net/indepth/features/2011/01/20116101050.

Alvarez, Sonia E. 2010. "Translating the Global: Effects of Transnational Organizing on Local Feminist Discourses and Practices in Latin America." In *Women, Gender, and Politics: A Reader*, ed. Mona Lena Krook and Sarah Childs. New York: Oxford University Press.

Alves, Andrea Moraes. 2008. "Os Idosos, as Redes de Relações Sociais e as Relações Familiares." In *Idosos no Brasil: Vivências, Desafios e expectativas na Terçeira Idade*, ed. A.L. Neri. São Paulo: Editora Fundação Perceu Abramo e Edicões SESC.

Amoss, Pamela T., and Stevan Harrell, eds. 1981. *Other Ways of Growing Old*. Stanford: Stanford University Press.

Amuchástegui Herrera, Ana. 1996. "El significdo de la virginidad y la iniciación sexual. Un relato de investigación." In *Para Comprender la Subjetividad: Investigación cualitativa en salud reproductiva y sexualidad*, ed. I. Szasz and S. Lerner. México D.F.: El Colegio de México.

Amuchástegui Herrera, Ana. 2008. "La masculinidad como culpa esencial: subjetivación, género y tecnología de sí en un programa de reeducación para hombres violentos." In *II Congreso Nacional Los Estudios de Género de los Hombres en México: Caminos Andados y Nuevos Retos en Investigación y Acción*. Mexico City.

Astuti, Rita. 2007. "Ancestors and the Afterlife." In *Religion, Anthropology, and Cognitive Science*, ed. Harvey Whitehouse and James Laidlaw. Durham: Carolina Academic Press.

Baars, Jan, Dale Dannefer, Chris Phillipson, and Alan Walker, eds. 2006. *Aging, Globalization, and Inequality: The New Critical Gerontology*. Amityville: Baywood Publishing Company.

Baer, Hans. 2004. *Toward an Integrative Medicine: Merging Alternative Therapies with Biomedicine*. Walnut Creek: AltaMira Press.

Baltes, Paul B. 1997. "On the Incomplete Architecture of Human Ontogeny." *American Psychologist* 52, no. 4: 366–380.

Basting, Anne Davis. 2009. *Forget Memory: Creating Better Lives for People with Dementia.* Baltimore: Johns Hopkins University Press.

Bateson, Mary Catherine. 1989. *Composing a Life.* New York: Atlantic Monthly Press.

Bateson, Mary Catherine. 2010. *Composing a Further Life: The Age of Active Wisdom.* New York: Knopf.

Bauer, Brent, ed. 2010. *Mayo Clinic Book of Alternative Medicine,* second edition, New York: Time Inc.

Becker, Gay. 1997. *Disrupted Lives: How People Create Meaning in a Chaotic World.* Berkeley: University of California Press.

Becker, Gay, and Sharon R. Kaufman. 1995. "Managing an Uncertain Illness Trajectory in Old Age: Patients' and Physicians' Views of Stroke." *Medical Anthropology Quarterly* 9, no. 2 (June): 165–187.

Benedict, Ruth. 1934. *Patterns of Culture.* Boston: Houghton Mifflin Company.

Benedict, Ruth. 1946. *The Chrysanthemum and the Sword: Patterns of Japanese Culture.* New York: New American Library.

Berger, Gabriella E. 1999. *Menopause and Culture.* London: Pluto Press.

Berman, Elise. 2011. "The Irony of Immaturity: K'iche' Children as Mediators and Buffers in Adult Social Interactions." *Childhood* 18, no. 2: 274–288.

Bernard, H. Russell. 2011. *Research Methods in Cultural Anthropology,* fifth edition. Lanham: AltaMira Press.

Berry, Sara. 1985. *Fathers Work for their Sons: Accumulation, Mobility, and Class Formation in an Extended Yoruba Community.* Berkeley: University of California Press.

Biggs, Simon, Ariella Lowenstein, and Jon Hendricks, eds. 2003. *The Need For Theory: Critical Approaches to Social Gerontology.* Amityville: Baywood Pub. Co. Inc.

Birdwell-Pheasant, Donna, and Denise Lawrence-Zúñiga, eds. 1999. *House Life: Space, Place, and Family in Europe.* Oxford: Berg.

Blackwood, Evelyn. 2005. "Wedding Bell Blues: Marriage, Missing Men, and Matrifocal Follies." *American Ethnologist* 32, no. 1: 3–19.

Bletzer, Keith V. 2007. "Identity and Resilience Among Persons with HIV: A Rural African American Experience." *Qualitative Health Research* 17, no. 2 (February): 162–175.

Bliss, Katherine Elaine. 2001. *Compromised Positions: Prostitution, Public Health, and Gender Politics in Revolutionary Mexico City.* University Park: Pennsylvania State University Press.

Blowsnake, Sam. 1999 [1926]. *Crashing Thunder: The Autobiography of an American Indian,* ed. Paul Radin. Ann Arbor: University of Michigan Press.

Bourdieu, Pierre. 1977. *Outline of a Theory of Practice,* trans. Richard Nice. Cambridge: Cambridge University Press.

Bourdieu, Pierre. 1990. *The Logic of Practice.* Stanford: Stanford University Press.

Britto da Motta, Alda. 1999. "As dimensões de gênero e classe social na análise do envelhecimento." *Cadernos Pagú* 13: 191–221.

Brodwin, Paul E., ed. 2000. *Biotechnology and Culture: Bodies, Anxieties, and Ethics.* Bloomington: Indiana University Press.

Bulbeck, Chilla. 2001. "Speaking Menopause: Intersections Between Asian and Western Medical Discourses." *Intersections* 5 (May). http://intersections.anu.edu.au/issue5/bulbeck2.html.

Burnette, Denise. 1999. "Custodial Grandparents in Latino Families: Patterns of Service Use and Predictors of Unmet Needs." *Social Work* 44, no. 1: 22–34.

Burr, Jeffrey A., and Mutchler, Jan E. 1992. "The Living Arrangements of Unmarried Elderly Hispanic Females." *Demography* 29, no. 1: 93–112.

Burton, Linda. 1995. "Intergenerational Patterns of Providing Care in African-American Families With Teenage Childbearers: Emergent Patterns in an Ethnographic Study." In *Adult Intergenerational Relations: Effects of Societal Change*, eds. Vern L. Bengston, K. Warner Schaie, and Linda M. Burton. New York: Springer Publishing.

Burton, Linda, Peggye Dilworth-Anderson, and Cynthia Merriwether-deVries. 1994. "Context and Surrogate Parenting Among Contemporary Grandparents." *Marriage and Family Review* 20, no. 3–4: 349–366.

Butler, Robert N. 2008. *The Longevity Revolution: The Benefits and Challenges of Living a Long Life*. New York: Public Affairs Press.

Cachioni, Meire. 2003. *Quem Educa os Idosos: Um estudo sobre professores de Universidades de Terçeira Idade*. Campinas SP: Editora Alínea.

Caldas, Célia Pereira. 2002. "O Idoso em Processo de Demência: o impacto na família." In *Antropologia, Saúde e Envelhecimento*, eds. M. C. de Souza Minayo and C. Coimbra Jr. Rio de Janeiro: Editora Fiocruz.

Caputo, Richard K. 2000. "Second-generation Parenthood: A Panel Study of Grandmother and Grandchild Coresidency among Low-income Families, 1967–1992." *Journal of Sociology and Social Welfare* 27, no. 3: 3–20.

Carillo, Héctor. 2002. *The Night is Young: Sexuality in Mexico in the Time of AIDS*. Chicago: University of Chicago Press.

Carillo, Héctor. 2007. "Imagining Modernity: Sexuality, Policy, and Social Change in Mexico." *Sexuality Research and Social Policy: Journal of NSRC* 4, no. 3: 74–91.

Carsten, Janet, ed. 2000. *Cultures of Relatedness: New Approaches to the Study of Kinship*. New York: Cambridge University Press.

Carsten, Janet, ed. 2007. *Ghosts of Memory: Essays on Remembrance and Relatedness*. Malden: Blackwell.

Casagrande, Joseph B. 1960. *In the Company of Man*. New York: Harper.

Caspi, Opher, Lee Sechrest, Howard C. Pitluk, Carter L. Marshall, Iris R. Bell, and Mark Nichter. 2003. "On the Definition of Complementary, Alternative, and Integrative Medicine: Societal Mega-Stereotypes vs. the Patients' Perspectives." *Alternative Therapies in Health and Medicine* 9, no. 6 (November/December): 58–62.

Centraal Bureau voor de Statistiek (CBS). 2007. *Gezondheid en zorg in cijfers 2007*. The Netherlands: Centraal Bureau voor de Statistiek.

Chaimowitz, Flávio. 1998. *Os Idosos Brasileiros no Seculo XXI: Demografia, Saúde e Sociedade*. Belo. Horizonte MG: Editora Postgraduate Brasil.

Choudhuri, Ajanta. 2003. "*Santāner Bideśe Sthāyibhābe Thākā Ki Kāmya?*" [Is It Desirable If One's Children Settle Permanently Abroad?] *Sangbād Pratidin*. 14 June: 10.

Cieraad, Irene. 1999. "Dutch Windows: Female Virtue and Female Vice." In *At Home: An Anthropology of Domestic Space*, ed. Irene Cieraad. Syracuse: Syracuse University Press.

Clark, Margaret. 1968. "The Anthropology of Aging: A New Area for Studies of Culture and Personality." In *Middle Age and Aging*, ed. Bernice L. Neugarten. Chicago: University of Chicago Press.

Cliggett, Lisa. 2005. *Grains from Grass: Aging, Gender, and Famine in Rural Africa*. Ithaca: Cornell University Press.

Cohen, Gene D. 2005. *The Mature Mind: The Positive Power of the Aging Brain.* New York: Basic Books.

Cohen, Lawrence. 1994. "Old Age: Cultural and Critical Perspectives." *Annual Review of Anthropology* 23: 153–178.

Cohen, Lawrence. 1998. *No Aging in India: Alzheimer's, the Bad Family, and Other Modern Things.* Berkeley: University of California Press.

Cohen, Patricia. 2010. "Long Road to Adulthood is Growing Even Longer." *New York Times,* 12 June. http://www.nytimes.com/2010/06/13/us/13generations.html.

Cole, Jennifer. 2010. *Sex and Salvation: Imagining the Future in Madagascar.* Chicago: University of Chicago Press.

Cole, Jennifer, and Deborah Durham, eds. 2008. *Figuring the Future: Globalization and the Temporalities of Children and Youth.* Santa Fe: School for Advanced Research Press.

Collier, Jane, and Sylvia Yanagisako. 1987. *Kinship and Gender: Essays toward a Unified Analysis.* Stanford: Stanford University Press.

Collins, Daryl. 2009. *Portfolios of the Poor: How The World's Poor Live on $2 a Day.* Princeton: Princeton University Press.

Coontz, Stephanie. 2000. *The Way We Never Were: American Families and the Nostalgia Trap.* New York: Basic Books.

Creighton, Millie R. 1990. "Revisiting Shame and Guilt Cultures: A Forty-Year Pilgrimage." *Ethos* 18, no. 3 (September): 279–307.

Cronk, Lee. 2008. "Reciprocity and the Power of Giving." In *Conformity and Conflict: Readings in Cultural Anthropology,* thirteenth edition, eds. James Spradley and David W. McCurdy. New York: Addison Wesley Longman.

Cruise-O'Brien, Donal B. 1996. "A Lost Generation? Youth Identity and State Decay in West Africa." In *Postcolonial Identities in Africa,* ed. Richard Werbner and Terence Ranger. London: Zed Books.

Csikszentmihalyi, Mihaly. 2008. *Flow: The Psychology of Optimal Experience.* New York: Perennial Modern Classics.

Csordas, Thomas. 1994. "Words From the Holy People: A Case Study in Cultural Phenomenology." In *Embodiment and Experience: The Existential Ground of Culture and Self,* ed. Thomas Csordas. Cambridge: Cambridge University Press.

Daley, Suzanne. 2011. "Chasing Riches from Africa to Europe and Finding Only Squalor." *New York Times,* 25 May. http://www.nytimes.com/2011/05/26/world/europe/26migrants.html.

Daniel, E. Valentine. 1984. *Fluid Signs: Being a Person the Tamil Way.* Berkeley: University of California Press.

Dannefer, Dale, and Casey Miklowski. 2006. "Developments in the Life Course." In *The Futures of Old Age,* eds. John A. Vincent, Chris R. Phillipson, and Murna Downs. Thousand Oaks: Sage Publications.

Dannefer, Dale, and Lynn Falletta. 2007. "Life Course." In *Encyclopedia of Gerontology,* ed. James Birren. Oxford: Elsevier.

Dannefer, Dale, and Antje Daub. 2009. "Extending the Interrogation: Life Span, Life Course, and The Constitution of Human Aging." *Advances in Life Course Research.* (Special Issue: Reconsidering the Linked Lives Principle) 14, no. 1–2: 15–27.

Davis, Dona. 1996. "The Cultural Constructions of the Premenstrual and Menopause Syndromes." In *Gender and Health: An International Perspective,* eds. Carolyn Sargent and Caroline Brettell. Upper Saddle River: Prentice Hall.

de Certeau, Michel. 1984. *The Practice of Everyday Life*, trans. Steven Rendall. Berkeley: University of California Press.

de Certeau, Michel, Luce Giard, and Pierre Mayol. 1998. *The Practice of Everyday Life: Volume 2, Living and Cooking*, trans. Timothy J. Tomasik. Minneapolis: University of Minnesota Press.

de Keijzer, Benno, and Gabriela Rodriguez. 2007. "Hombres Rurales: Nueva generación en un mundo cambiante." In *Sucede que me canso de ser hombre: Relatos y reflexiones sobre hombres y masculinidades en México*, eds. Ana Amuchástegui and Ivonne Szasz. Mexico City: El Colegio de México.

de Silva, W. Indralal. 2007. *Beyond Twenty Million: Projecting the Population of Sri Lanka 2001–2081*. Colombo: Institute of Policy Studies.

Debert, Guita Grin. 1999. *A Reinvenção da Velhice: Socialização e Processo de Reprivatização do Envelhecimento*. São Paulo: EDUSP.

Deng, Yingchao. 1984. "Discussion of How to Handle Women's Climacteric" [Tantan Zenmeyang Duidai Funu Gengnianqi]. *China Woman (Zhongguo Funu)* 40, no. 2: 6.

Dickson, Geri L. 1991. "Menopause: Language, Meaning, and Subjectivity: A Feminist Poststructuralist Analysis." In *Proceedings of the Society for Menstrual Cycle Research, Eighth Conference*, eds. Ann M. Voda and Rosemary Conover. Scottsdale: Society for Menstrual Cycle Research.

Dolbin-MacNab, Megan L. 2006. "Just Like Raising Your Own? Grandmothers' Perceptions of Parenting a Second Time Around." *Family Relations* 55: 564–575.

Dunn, Elizabeth. 2004. *Privatizing Poland: Baby Food, Big Business, and the Remaking of Labor.* Ithaca: Cornell University Press.

Durham, Deborah. 2004. "Disappearing Youth: Youth as Social Shifter in Botswana." *American Ethnologist* 31, no. 4: 589–605.

Durham, Deborah. 2012. "A Lost Continent? Youth and the Loss of Adulthood across Africa." Paper presented at the Association of American Geographers meetings, February. New York.

Dwyer, Jeffrey W., Gary R. Lee, and Thomas B. Jankowski. 1994. "Reciprocity, Elder Satisfaction, and Caregiver Stress and Burden: The Exchange of Aid in the Family Caregiving Relationship." *Journal of Marriage and Family* 56, no. 1: 35–43.

Ehrenreich, Barbara, and Arlie Hochschild. 2002. *Global Woman: Nannies, Maids, and Sex Workers in the New Economy.* New York: Henry Holt and Co.

Ekerdt, David J. 1986. "The Busy Ethic: Moral Continuity Between Work and Retirement." *The Gerontologist* 26: 239–244.

Elder, Glen H., Jr. 1999 [1974]. *Children of the Great Depression: Social Change in Life Experience.* Twenty-fifth anniversary edition. Boulder: Westview Press.

Elder, Glen H., Jr. 1999. "The Life Course and Aging: Some Reflections." American Sociological Association Distinguished Scholar Lecture, Section on Aging, University of North Carolina at Chapel Hill, 10 August. www.unc.edu/~elder/pdf/asa-99talk.pdf.

Elder, Glen H., Jr., Monica Kirkpatrick Johnson, and Robert Crosnoe. 2003. "The Emergence and Development of Life Course Theory," In *Handbook of the Life Course*, eds. Jeylan T. Mortimer and Michael J. Shanahan. New York: Kluwer Academic/Plenum Publishers.

Ellison, Ralph. 1995. *Invisible Man.* New York: Random House, Inc.

El Ouardani, Christine Nutter. Forthcoming. "Acquiring Reason and Cultivating Strength: Growing up in Rural Morocco in a Time of Development," In *Everyday*

Life in the Muslim Middle East, third edition, eds. Donna Lee Bowen, Evelyn A. Early, and Becky L. Schulthies. Bloomington: Indiana University Press.

Erikson, Erik H. 1958. *Young Man Luther: A Study in Psychoanalysis and History.* New York: W.W. Norton & Company.

Erikson, Erik H. 1959. *Identity and the Life Cycle.* New York: W.W. Norton & Company.

Erikson, Erik H. 1963 [1950]. *Childhood and Society.* New York: W.W. Norton & Company.

Erikson, Erik H. 1970. *Gandhi's Truth: On the Origins of Militant Non-Violence.* New York: W.W. Norton & Company.

Erikson, Erik H. 1974. *Dimensions of a New Identity: The 1973 Jefferson Lectures in the Humanities.* New York: W.W. Norton & Company.

Erikson, Erik H. 1997. *The Life Cycle Completed* (extended version with chapters by Joan Erikson). New York: W.W. Norton & Company.

Escobar Latapí, Agustín. 2003. "Men and Their Histories: Restructuring, Gender Inequality, and Life Transitions in Urban Mexico." In *Changing Men and Masculinities in Latin America*, ed. Matthew C. Gutmann. Durham: Duke University Press.

Evans-Pritchard, E. E. 1940. *The Nuer: A Description of the Modes of Livelihood and Political Institutions of a Nilotic People.* Oxford: Oxford University Press.

Fantin, Márcia. 2000. *Cidade Dividida: Dilemas e Disputas Simbólicas em Florianopolis.* Florianopolis: Editora Cidade Futura.

Fass, Paula. 2008. "Childhood and Youth as an American/Global Experience in the Context of the Past." In *Figuring the Future: Globalization and the Temporalities of Children and Youth*, eds. Jennifer Cole and Deborah Durham. Santa Fe: School for Advanced Research Press.

Fehérváry, Krisztina. 2002. "American Kitchens, Luxury Bathrooms, and the Search for a 'Normal' Life in Post-socialist Hungary." *Ethnos* 67, no. 3: 369–400.

Fishman. Ted, C. 2010. *Shock of Gray: The Aging of the World's Population and How it Pits Young against Old, Child against Parent, Worker against Boss, Company against Rival, and Nation against Nation.* New York: Scribner.

Foner, Nancy. 1984. *Ages in Conflict: A Cross-Cultural Perspective on Inequality Between Old and Young.* New York: Columbia University Press.

Fortes, Meyer. 1953. "The Structure of Unilineal Descent Groups." *American Anthropologist* 55: 17–41.

Fortes, Meyer. 1970. *Time and Social Structure and Other Essays.* New York: Humanities Press.

Fortes, Meyer. 1984. "Age, Generation, and Social Structure." In *Age and Anthropological Theory*, eds. David I. Kertzer and Jennie Keith. Ithaca: Cornell University Press.

Fortes, Meyer, and E. E. Evans-Pritchard, eds. 1994 [1940]. *African Political Systems.* Kegan Paul International.

Franklin, Sarah. 2006. "The Cyborg Embryo: Our Path to Transbiology." *Theory, Culture, and Society* 23, no. 7–8: 167–87.

Franklin, Sarah, and Susan McKinnon, eds. 2001a. *Relative Values: Reconfiguring Kinship Studies.* Durham: Duke University Press.

Franklin, Sarah, and Susan McKinnon. 2001b. "Introduction." In *Relative Values: Reconfiguring Kinship Studies*, eds. Sarah Franklin and Susan McKinnon. Durham: Duke University Press.

Freedman, Marc. 1999. *Prime Time: How Baby Boomers will Revolutionize Retirement and Transform America.* New York: Public Affairs Press.

Freedman, Marc. 2005. "The Boomers, Good Work and the Next Stage of Life." *New Face of Work Survey*, June. http://www.encore.org/find/resources/boomers-good-work-and.

Freeman, Carla. 1998. "Femininity and Flexible Labor: Fashioning Class through Gender on the Global Assembly Line." *Critique of Anthropology* 18: 245–262.

Freud, Sigmund. 1961. *Beyond the Pleasure Principle*. New York: W.W. Norton & Company.

Freud, Sigmund. 1962 [1916]. *Three Contributions to the Theory of Sex*. New York: Dutton.

Fry, Christine. L., ed. 1981. *Dimensions: Aging, Culture, and Health*. Brooklyn, New York: Praeger.

Fuller-Thomson, Esme, and Meredith Minkler. 2000. "African American Grandparents Raising Grandchildren: A National Profile of Demographic and Health Characteristics." *Health and Social Work* 25, no. 2: 109–118.

Gamaniratne, Nirosha. 2007. *Population Ageing, Policy Responses and Options to Extend Retirement Coverage: Case Study of Sri Lanka*. Colombo: Institute of Policy Studies.

Gamburd, Geraldine DeNering. 2010. *Discovering the Rights Model: An Analysis of Kinship and Caste in Rural Ceylon*. Colombo: Social Scientists' Association.

Gamburd, Michele Ruth. 2000. *The Kitchen Spoon's Handle: Transnationalism and Sri Lanka's Migrant Housemaids*. Ithaca: Cornell University Press.

Gamburd, Michele Ruth. 2008. "Milk Teeth and Jet Planes: Kin Relations in Families of Sri Lanka's Transnational Domestic Servants." *City and Society* 20, no. 1: 5–31.

Ge, Meiyun, and Meihua Shen. 1994. "Funü Gengnianqi: Jiankang Yu Tiaoshi Fangfa" [Female Climacteric and Methods for Regulating It]. *Funü Yanjiu Luncong* (*Collection of Women's Studies*) 3: 21–6.

Geschiere, Peter, and Antoine Socpa. n.d. "Changing Mobilities, Shifting Futures." In *African Futures*, eds. Brian Goldstone, Juan Obarrio, and Charles Piot. In preparation for University of Chicago Press.

Gibbons, Ann. 1997. "Why Life After Menopause?" *Science* 276, no. 5312 (25 April): 535.

Gillis, John R. 1997. *A World of Their Own Making: Myth, Ritual, and the Quest for Family Values*. Cambridge: Harvard University Press.

Glascock, Anthony P. 1982. "Decrepitude and Death-hastening: The Nature of Old Age in Third World Societies." In *Aging and the Aged in the Third World*, Part I, Volume 22 of *Studies in Third World Societies*, ed. Jay Sokolovsky. Williamsburg: College of William and Mary, Department of Anthropology. December: 43–66.

Glascock, Anthony P., and Susan Feinman. 1981. "Social Asset or Social Burden: An Analysis of the Treatment for the Aged in Non-industrial Societies." In *Dimensions: Aging, Culture, and Health*, ed. Christine L. Fry. New York: Praeger.

Gleckman, Howard. 2009. *Caring for our Parents: Inspiring Stories of Families Seeking New Solutions to America's Most Urgent Health Crisis*. New York: St. Martin's Press.

Goffman, Erving. 1959. *The Presentation of Self in Everyday Life*. Garden City: Doubleday.

Goldin, Ian, Geoffrey Cameron, and Meera Balarajan. 2011. *Exceptional People: How Migration Shaped our World and Will Define our Future*. Princeton: Princeton University Press.

Good, Byron. 1994. *Medicine, Rationality, and Experience: An Anthropological Perspective*. Cambridge: Cambridge University Press.

Good, Mary-Jo DelVecchio, Paul E. Brodwin, Byron J. Good, and Arthur Kleinman, eds. 1992. *Pain as Human Experience: An Anthropological Perspective.* Berkeley: University of California Press.

Goodman, Catherine, and Merril Silverstein. 2002. "Grandmothers Raising Grandchildren: Family Structure and Well-being in Culturally Diverse Families." *Gerontologist* 42, no. 5: 676–689.

Goody, Jack. 1962. *The Developmental Cycle of Domestic Groups.* Cambridge: Cambridge University Press.

Gorer, Geoffrey, and John Rickman. 1950. *The People of Great Russia: A Psychological Study.* New York: Chanticleer Press.

Green, James W. 2008. *Beyond the Good Death: the Anthropology of Modern Dying.* Philadelphia: University of Pennsylvania Press.

Greenberg, Jessica, and Andrea Muehlebach. 2007. "The Old World and its New Economy: Notes on the 'Third Age' in Western Europe Today." In *Generations and Globalization: Youth, Age, and Family in the New World Economy,* eds. Jennifer Cole and Deborah Durham. Bloomington: Indiana University Press.

Greenhalgh, Susan. 2001. *Under the Medical Gaze: Facts and Fictions of Chronic Pain.* Berkeley: University of California Press.

Griffiths, John, Heleen Weyers, and Maurice Adams. 2008. *Euthanasia and Law in Europe.* Portland: Hart Publishing.

Grinstead, Linda Nicholson, Sharon Leder, Susan Jensen, and Linda Bond. 2003. "Review of Research on the Health of Caregiving Grandparents." *Journal of Advanced Nursing* 44, no. 3: 318–326.

Gutmann, Matthew C. 1996. *The Meanings of Macho: Being a Man in Mexico City.* Berkeley: University of California Press.

Guyer, Jane I. 1994. "Lineal Identities and Lateral Networks: Anthropological Approaches to Marital Change, Based on Research in a Rural Yoruba community." In *Nuptiality in Sub-Saharan Africa: Anthropological Approaches to Demographic Change,* eds. Caroline Bledsoe and Gilles Pison. Oxford: Oxford University Press.

Guyer, Jane I. 1997. *An African Niche Economy: Farming to Feed Ibadan, 1968–88.* Edinburgh: Edinburgh University Press for the International African Institute.

Hall, G. Stanley. 1969 [1921]. *Adolescence.* New York: Arno Press.

Hall, G. Stanley. 1922. *Senescence: The Last Half of Life.* New York: D. Appleton and Company.

Hall, Stephen S. 2007. "The Older and Wiser Hypothesis." *New York Times Magazine,* 6 May. http://www.nytimes.com/2007/05/06/magazine/06Wisdom-t.html?pagewanted=all#.

Hallowell, Irving. 1937. "Temporal Orientation in Western Civilization and in Pre-Literate Society." *American Anthropologist* 39, no. 4 (October–December): 647–670.

Han, Carol. 2011. "Symptoms of Another Life: Time, Possibility, and Domestic Relations in Chile's Credit Economy." *Cultural Anthropology* 26, no. 1: 7–32.

Hannay, Michael, and M. H. M. Schrama. 1996. *Van Dale Handwoordenboek, Nederlands-Engels.* Utrecht/Antwerpen: Van Dale Lexicografie.

Hannerz, Ulf. 2000. "Thinking about Culture in Cities." In *Understanding Amsterdam: Essays on Economic Vitality, City Life, and Urban Form,* eds. Leon Deben, Willem Heinemeijer, and Dick van der Vaart. Amsterdam: Het Spinhuis.

Haraway, Donna. 1989. *Primate Visions: Gender, Race, and Nature in the World of Modern Science.* New York: Routledge.

Haraway, Donna. 1991. *Simians, Cyborgs, and Women.* New York: Routledge.

Hareven, Tamara K. 1982. "The Life Course and Aging in Historical Perspective." In *Aging and Life Course Transitions: An Interdisciplinary Perspective,* eds. Tamara K. Hareven and Kathleen J. Adams. New York: Guilford Press.

Hareven, Tamara K. 1994. "Aging and Generational Relations: A Historical and Life Course Perspective." *Annual Review of Sociology* 20: 437–461.

Harevan, Tamara K. 1995. "Changing Images of Aging and the Social Construction of the Life Course." In *Images of Aging: Cultural Representations of Later Life,* eds. Mike Featherstone and Andrew Warnick. London: Routledge.

Hareven, Tamara. K. 2000. "Historical Perspectives on Aging and Family Relations." In *Handbook of Aging and the Social Sciences,* fifth edition, eds. Robert H. Binstock and Linda K. George. San Diego: Academic Press.

Hazan, Haim. 1984. "Continuity and Transformation among the Aged: A Study in the Anthropology of Time." *Current Anthropology* 25, no. 5 (December): 567–78.

Heinz, Walter R., Ansgar Weymann, and Johannes Huinink, eds. 2009. *The Life Course Reader: Individuals and Societies across Time.* New York: Campus Verlag.

Hinojosa, Ramon, Craig Boylstein, Maude Rittman, Melanie Sberna Hinojosa, and Christopher Faircloth. 2008. "Constructions of Continuity after Stroke." *Symbolic Interaction* 31, no. 2 (Spring): 205–224.

Hirsch, Jennifer. 2003. *A Courtship After Marriage: Sexuality and Love in Mexican Transnational Families.* Berkeley: University of California Press.

Hirsch, Jennifer S., and Constance A. Nathanson. 2001. "Some Traditional Methods are More Modern Than Others: Rhythm, Withdrawal, and the Changing Meanings of Sexual Intimacy in Mexican Companionate Marriage." *Culture, Health, and Sexuality* 3, no. 4: 413–428.

Hoagland, Edward. 2009. "Curtain Calls: The Fever Called 'Living' is Conquered at Last." *Harpers Magazine.* March: 31–40.

Hoare, Carol H. 2002. *Erikson on Development in Adulthood: New Insights from the Unpublished Papers.* New York: Oxford University Press.

Hochschild, Arlie Russell. 2001 [1997]. *The Time Bind: When Work Becomes Home and Home Becomes Work.* New York: Holt Paperbacks.

Hollan, Douglas W., and Jane C. Wellenkamp. 1996. *The Thread Of Life: Toraja Reflections on the Life Cycle.* Honolulu: University of Hawai'i Press.

Honwana, Alcinda, and Filip De Boeck, eds. 2005. *Makers and Breakers: Children and Youth in Postcolonial Africa.* Oxford: James Curry.

Horst, Han van der. 2001. *The Low Sky: Understanding the Dutch.* Schiedam: Scriptum Publishers.

Hrdy, Sarah. 2009. "Meet the Alloparents." *Natural History* 118, no. 3 (April): 24–29.

Hussein, Ameena. 2000. *Sometimes There is no Blood: Domestic Violence and Rape in Rural Sri Lanka.* Colombo: International Centre for Ethnic Studies.

Hyland, Richard. 2009. *Gifts: A Study in Comparative Law.* Oxford: Oxford University Press.

Iliffe, John. 2005. *Honour in African History.* Cambridge: Cambridge University Press.

Institute of Medicine. 2011. *Relieving Pain in America: A Blueprint for Transforming Prevention, Care, Education, and Research.* Washington D.C.: Institute of Medicine.

Jackson, Jean E. 2000. *Camp Pain: Talking with Chronic Pain Patients.* Philadelphia: University of Pennsylvania Press.

Jackson, Jean E. 2005. "Stigma, Liminality, and Chronic Pain: Mind-body Borderlands." *American Ethnologist* 32, no. 3 (August): 332–353.

Jamuna, D. 2003. "Issues of Elder Care and Elder Abuse in the Indian Context." In *An Aging India: Perspectives, Prospects, and Policies*, eds. Phoebe S. Liebig and S. Irudaya Rajan. New York: Haworth Press.

Jeffery, Patricia, and Roger Jeffery. 2010. "Allah Gives Both Boys and Girls." In *Everyday Life in South Asia*, second edition, eds. Diane P. Mines and Sarah Lamb. Bloomington: Indiana University Press.

Jiménez Guzman, Lucero. 2003. *Dando Voz a Los Varones: Sexualidad, Reproducción y Paternidad de Algunos Mexicanos*. Cuernavaca, Morelos: Universidad Nacional Autónoma de México, Centro Regional de Investigaciones Multidisciplinarias.

Johnson-Hanks, Jennifer. 2002. "On the Limits of Life Stages in Ethnography: Toward a Theory of Vital Conjunctures." *American Anthropologist* 104, no. 3: 865–880.

Joyce, Kelly, and Laura Mamo. 2006. "Graying the Cyborg: New Directions in Feminist Analyses of Aging, Science, and Technology." In *Age Matters: Realigning Feminist Thinking*, eds. Toni M. Calasanti and Kathleen F. Slevin. New York: Routledge.

Katz, Stephen. 2000. "Busy Bodies: Activity, Aging, and the Management of Everyday Life." *Journal of Aging Studies* 14, no. 2 (June): 135–152.

Kaufert, Patricia. 1982. "Myth and the Menopause." *Sociology of Health and Illness* 4, no. 2: 141–66.

Kaufman, Sharon R. 1986. *The Ageless Self: Sources of Meaning in Later Life*. Madison: University of Wisconsin Press.

Kaufman, Sharon. 2005. *And a Time to Die: How American Hospitals Shape the End of Life*. New York: Scribner.

Keith, Jennie. 1982. *Old People as People: Social and Cultural Influences on Aging and Old Age*. Boston: Little Brown.

Keith, Jennie, Christine L. Fry, Anthony P. Glascock, and Charlotte Ikels. 1994. *The Aging Experience: Diversity and Commonality across Cultures*. Thousand Oaks: Sage.

Kelly, Patty. 2008. *Lydia's Open Door: Inside Mexico's Most Modern Brothel*. Berkeley: University of California Press.

Kertzer, David. 1983. "Generation as a Sociological Problem." *Annual Review of Sociology* 9: 125–149.

Kertzer, David L., and Jennie Keith, eds. 1984. *Age and Anthropological Theory*. Ithaca: Cornell University Press.

Kierkegaard, Søren. 1967. *Stages on Life's Way*, trans. Walter Lowrie. New York: Schocken Books.

Kleinman, Arthur. 1986. *Social Origins of Distress and Disease: Depression, Neurasthenia, and Pain in Modern China*. New Haven: Yale University Press.

Kleinman, Arthur. 1988. *The Illness Narratives: Suffering, Healing, and the Human Condition*. New York: Basic Books.

Kleinman, Arthur. 1992. "Pain and Resistance: The Delegitimation and Relegitimation of Local Worlds." In *Pain as Human Experience: An Anthropological Perspective*, eds. Mary-Jo DelVecchio Good, Paul E. Brodwin, Byron J. Good, and Arthur Kleinman. Berkeley: University of California Press.

Kleinman, Arthur, and Joan Kleinman. 1994. "How Bodies Remember: Social Memory and Bodily Experience of Criticism, Resistance, and Delegitimation Following China's Cultural Revolution." *New Literary History* 25: 707–723.

Kleinman, Arthur, Paul E. Brodwin, Byron J. Good, and Mary-Jo DelVecchio Good. 1992. "Pain as Human Experience: An Introduction." In *Pain as Human Experience: An Anthropological Perspective*, eds. Mary-Jo DelVecchio Good, Paul E. Brodwin, Byron J. Good, and Arthur Kleinman. Berkeley: University of California Press.

Kōseirōdōsho, Abridged Life Tables for Japan. 2009. http://www.mhlw.go.jp/english/database/db-hw/lifetb09/dl/contents.pdf.

Krauss, Stephen E., 2005. "Research Paradigms and Meaning Making: A Primer." *Qualitative Report* 10 (4 December): 758–70.

Kuper, Adam. 2000. *Culture: The Anthropologist's Account*. Cambridge: Harvard University Press.

Lamb, Sarah. 1993. "Growing in the Net of Maya: Persons, Gender, and Life Processes in a Bengali Society." PhD diss., University of Chicago.

Lamb, Sarah. 1997. "The Making and Unmaking of Persons: Notes on Aging and Gender in North India." *Ethos* 25, no. 3: 279–302.

Lamb, Sarah. 2000. *White Saris and Sweet Mangoes: Aging, Gender, and Body in North India*. Berkeley: University of California Press.

Lamb, Sarah. 2001. "Generation in Anthropology." In *International Encyclopedia of the Social and Behavioral Sciences*, eds. Neil J. Smelser and Paul B. Baltes. Oxford: Pergamon Press.

Lamb, Sarah. 2007. "Aging Across Worlds. Modern Seniors in an Indian Diaspora," In *Generations and Globalization: Youth, Age, and Family in the New World Economy*, eds. Jennifer Cole and Deborah L. Durham. Bloomington: University of Indiana Press.

Lamb, Sarah. 2009. *Aging in the Indian Diaspora: Cosmopolitan Families in India and Abroad*. Bloomington: Indiana University Press.

Lambek, Michael. 1996. "The Past Imperfect: Remembering as a Moral Practice." In *Tense Past: Cultural Essays in Trauma and Memory*, eds. Paul Antze and Michael Lambek. New York: Routledge.

Langford, Jean M. 2009. "Gifts Intercepted: Biopolitics and Spirit Debt." *Cultural Anthropology* 24, no. 4: 681–711.

Lasch, Christopher. 1995. *Haven in a Heartless World*. New York: W.W. Norton & Company.

Laslett, Peter. 1987. "The Emergence of the Third Age." *Ageing and Society* 7: 133–160.

Laslett, Peter. 1991. *A Fresh Map of Life: The Emergence of a Third Age*. Cambridge: Harvard University Press.

Leavitt, Stephen. C. 1995. "Seeking Gifts from the Dead: Long-Term Mourning in a Bumbita Arapesh Cargo Narrative." *Ethos* 23, no. 4 (December): 453–473.

Lee, Gary R., and Eugene Ellithorpe. 1982. "Intergenerational Exchange and Subjective Well-Being among the Elderly." *Journal of Marriage and Family* 44, no. 1: 217–224.

Leibing, Annette. 2005. "The Old Lady from Ipanema: Changing Notions of Old Age in Brazil." *Journal of Aging Studies* 19: 15–31.

Leng, Kwok Wei. 1997. "Menopause and the Great Divide: Biomedicine, Feminism, and Cyborg Politics." In *Reinterpreting Menopause: Cultural and Philosophical Issues*, eds. Paul A. Komesaroff, Philipa Rothfield, and Jeanne Daly. New York: Routledge.

Levinson, Daniel J. 1978. *The Seasons of a Man's Life*. New York: Ballantine.

Levy, René, and The Pavie Team. 2005. "Why Look at Life Courses in Interdisciplinary Perspective?" In *Towards an Interdisciplinary Perspective on the Life Course, Advances in Life-Course Research* 10: 3–32.

Lewis, Herbert. 2001. "The Passion of Franz Boas." *American Anthropologist* 103, no. 2: 447–467.

Lewis, Oscar. 1963 [1961]. *The Children of Sanchez: Autobiography of a Mexican Family.* New York: Vintage Books.

Liebig, Phoebe S. 2003. "Old-Age Homes and Services: Old and New Approaches to Aged Care." In *An Aging India: Perspectives, Prospects, and Policies*, eds. Phoebe S. Liebig and S. Irudaya Rajan. New York: Haworth Press.

Lifton, Robert J. 1993. *The Protean Self: Human Resilience in an Age of Fragmentation.* New York: Basic Books.

Lipset, Seymour Martin. 1992. "The Work Ethic, Then and Now." *Journal of Labor Research* 13: 45–54.

Lipsitt, Lewis P. 2003. "Behavioral Aspects of Crib Death: The Rise and Fall of Alternative Hypotheses." *Current Directions in Psychological Science* (31 July).

Livingston, Julie. 2005. *Debility and the Moral Imagination in Botswana.* Bloomington: University of Indiana Press.

Livingston, Julie. 2007. "Maintaining Local Dependencies: Elderly Women and Global Rehabilitation Agendas in Southeastern Botswana." In *Generations and Globalization: Family, Youth, and Age in the New World Economy*, eds. Jennifer Cole and Deborah Durham. Bloomington: Indiana University Press.

Lock, Margaret. 1993. *Encounters with Aging: Mythologies of Menopause in Japan and North America.* Berkeley: University of California Press.

Lock, Margaret. 1998a. "Anomalous Ageing: Managing the Postmenopausal Body." *Body and Society* 4, no. 1: 35–61.

Lock, Margaret. 1998b. "Deconstructing the Change: Female Maturation in Japan and North America." In *Welcome to Middle Age! And Other Cultural Fictions*, ed. Richard A. Shweder. Chicago: University of Chicago Press.

Lock, Margaret, Allan Young, and Alberto Cambrosio, eds. 2000. *Living and Working with the New Medical Technologies: Intersections of Inquiry.* Cambridge: Cambridge University Press.

Lukose, Ritty. 2009. *Liberalization's Children: Gender, Youth, and Consumer Citizenship in Globalizing India.* Durham: Duke University Press.

Lynch, Caitrin. 2012. *Retirement on the Line: Age, Work, and Value in an American Factory.* Ithaca: Cornell University Press.

Mains, Daniel. 2007. "Neoliberal Times: Progress, Boredom, and Shame among Young Men in Urban Ethiopia." *American Ethnologist* 34, no. 4: 659–673.

Mains, Daniel. 2011. *Hope is Cut: Youth, Unemployment, and the Future in Urban Ethiopia.* Philadelphia: Temple University Press.

Magazine, Roger, and Martha Areli Ramirez Sanchez. 2007. "Continuity and Change in San Pedro Tlalcuapan, Mexico: Childhood, Social Reproduction, and Transnational Migration." In *Generations and Globalization: Youth, Age, and Family in the New World Economy*, eds. Jennifer Cole and Deborah Durham. Bloomington: Indiana University Press.

Mak, Geert. 2000. *Amsterdam*, trans. Philipp Blom. Cambridge: Harvard University Press.

Malinowski, Bronislaw. 2001 [1927]. *Sex and Repression in Savage Society.* London: Routledge.

Mandala, Elias. 1990. *Work and Control in a Peasant Economy: A History of the Lower Tchiri Valley in Malawi, 1859–1960.* Madison: University of Wisconsin Press.

Mandelbaum, David G. 1973. "The Study of Life History: Gandhi." *Current Anthropology* 14: 177–206.

Mannheim, Karl. 1993 [1927]. "The Problem of Generations." In *From Karl Mannheim,* ed. Kurt H. Wolff. New Brunswick: Transaction.

Marecek, Jeanne, and Udeni Appuhamilage. 2011. "Present But Unnamed: Feminisms and Psychologies in Sri Lanka." In *Handbook of International Perspectives on Feminism,* eds. Alexandra Rutherford, Rose Capdevila, Vindhya Undurti, and Ingrid Palmary. New York: Springer.

Marglin, Stephen A., and Juliet B. Schor. 1992. *The Golden Age of Capitalism: Reinterpreting the Postwar Experience.* Oxford, U.K.: Oxford University Press.

Markus, Hazel R., and A. Regula Herzog. 1991. "The Role of the Self Concept in Aging." *Annual Review of Gerontology and Geriatrics* 11: 110–143.

Markus, Hazel R., and Paul Nurius. 1986. "Possible Selves." *American Psychologist* 41, no. 9: 954–969.

Marriott, McKim. 1976. "Hindu Transactions: Diversity without Dualism." In *Transaction and Meaning: Directions in the Anthropology of Exchange and Symbolic Behavior,* ed. Bruce Kapferer. Philadelphia: Institute for the Study of Human Issues.

Martin, Emily 1997. "The Woman in the Menopausal Body," In *Reinterpreting Menopause: Cultural and Philosophical Issues,* eds. Paul A. Komesaroff, Philipa Rothfield, and Jeanne Daly. New York: Routledge.

Martin, Emily. 2001 [1987]. *The Woman in the Body: A Cultural Analysis of Reproduction.* Boston: Beacon Press.

Mattingly, Cheryl, and Linda Garro, eds. 2000. *Narrative and the Cultural Construction of Illness and Healing.* Berkeley: University of California Press.

Mauss, Marcel. 1990. *The Gift: The Form and Reason for Exchange in Archaic Societies,* trans. W.D. Halls, London: Routledge.

Maybury-Lewis, David. 1984. "Age and Kinship." In *Age and Anthropological Theory,* eds. David I. Kertzer and Jennie Keith. Ithaca: Cornell University Press.

Mayer, Karl Ulrich. 2009. "New Directions in Life-Course Research." *Annual Review of Sociology* 35: 413–33.

McAdams, Dan P. 2005. "Studying Lives in Time: A Narrative Approach." *Towards an Interdisciplinary Perspective on the Life Course, Advances in Life Course Research* 10: 237–258.

McKee Irwin, Robert, Edward J. McCaughan, and Michelle Rocío Nasser, eds. 2003. *The Famous 41: Sexuality and Social Control in Mexico, c. 1901.* New York: Palgrave Macmillan.

McKee Irwin, Robert. 2003. *Mexican Masculinities.* Minneapolis: University of Minnesota Press.

Mead, Margaret. 1970. *Culture and Commitment: A Study of the Generation Gap.* New York: Natural History Press.

Mead, Margaret. 2001 [1928]. *Coming of Age in Samoa.* New York: HarperCollins Perennials.

Mendes, Patrícia M. Teixeira. 1998 "Cuidadores: heróis anônimos do cotidiano." In *Envelhecimento com dependência: revelando cuidadores,* ed. Ursula Margarida S. Karsch. São Paulo: EDUC.

Miles, Ann. 2010. "Ecuadorian Women's Narratives of Lupus, Suffering and Vulnerability." In *Chronic Conditions, Fluid States: Chronicity and the Anthropology of Ill-*

ness, eds. Lenore Manderson and Carolyn Smith-Morris. New Brunswick: Rutgers University Press.

Minkler, Meredith, and Fuller-Thomson, Esme. 2005. "African American Grandparents Raising Grandchildren: A National Study Using the Census 2000 Supplementary Survey." *Journal of Gerontology* 60B, 2: S82–S92.

Mitteness, Linda S., and Judith C. Barker. 1995. "Stigmatizing a 'Normal' Condition: Urinary Incontinence in Late Life." *Medical Anthropology Quarterly* 9, no. 2 (June): 188–210.

Morgan, Gwyn. 2011. "Youth Unemployment the Kindling that Fuels Unrest." *Globe and Mail*. 11 September. http://www.theglobeandmail.com/report-on-business/commentary/gwyn-morgan/youth-unemployment-the-kindling-that-fuels-un rest/article2161624/.

Morrow-Howell, Nancy, James Hinterlong, and Michael Sherraden. 2001. *Productive Aging: Concepts and Challenges*. Baltimore: Johns Hopkins University Press.

Mortimer, Jeylan T., and Michael J. Shanahan. 2003. *Handbook of the Life Course*. New York: Kluwer Academic/Plenum Publishers.

Motta, Flávia de Mattos. 2002. "Gênero e Reciprocidade: Uma Ilha no Sul do Brasil." Ph.D. diss., State University of Campinas—UNICAMP.

Myerhoff, Barbara 1979. *Number Our Days*. New York: E.P. Dutton.

Myerhoff, Barbara. 1984. "Rites and Signs of Ripening: The Intertwining of Ritual, Time, and Growing Older." In *Age and Anthropological Theory*, eds. David I. Kertzer and Jennie Keith. Ithaca: Cornell University Press.

National Center for Health Statistics. 2006. "Health, United States, 2006: With Chartbook on Trends in the Health of Americans." Hyattsville, Maryland. www.cdc.gov/nchs/data/hus/hus06.pdf.

Neilson, Brett. 2003. "Globalization and the Biopolitics of Aging." *The New Centennial Review* 3, no. 2 (Summer): 161–186.

Nerí, Anita Liberalesso, ed. 2006. *Cuidar de idosos no contexto da família: questões psicológicas e sociais*, second edition. Campinas: Alínea.

Neugarten, Bernice. L., ed. 1968. *Middle Age and Aging*. Chicago: University of Chicago Press.

Newell, Sasha. 2005. "Migratory Modernity and the Cosmology of Consumption in Côte d'Ivoire." In *Migration and Economy: Global and Local Dynamics*, ed. Lillian Trager. Walnut Creek: AltaMira Press.

Newman, Katherine. 1996. "Ethnography, Biography and Cultural History: Generational Paradigms in Human Development." In *Ethnography and Human Development: Context and Meaning in Social Inquiry*, ed. Richard Jessor, Anne Colby, and Richard Shweder. Chicago: University of Chicago Press.

Newman, Katherine. 2012. *The Accordion Family: Boomerang Kids, Anxious Parents, and the Private Toll of Global Competition*. Boston: Beacon Press.

Norimoto, Iino. 1962. "Dōgen's View of Interdependence." *Philosophy East and West* 12, no. 1 (April): 51–57.

Norwood, Frances. 2009. *The Maintenance of Life: Preventing Social Death Through Euthanasia Talk and End-of-Life Care—Lessons from The Netherlands*. Durham: Carolina Academic Press.

Notelovitz, Morris, and Diana Tonnessen. 1994. *Menopause and Midlife Health*. New York: St. Martin's Press.

Oliver, Caroline. 2008. *Retirement Migration: Paradoxes in Ageing*. New York: Routledge.

Onwuteaka-Philipsen, B. D., et al. 2007. *Evaluatie: Wet Toetsing Levensbeëindiging op Verzoek en Hulp bij Zelfdoding* [*Evaluation of the Termination of Life on Request and Assisted Suicide (Review Procedure) Act of 2002*]. The Hague: ZonMw.

Parrenas, Rhacel Salazar. 2005. *Children of Global Migration: Transnational Families and Gendered Woes.* Stanford: Stanford University Press.

Patterson, Thomas C. 1998. "Flexible Accumulation, Flexible Labor, and their Consequences." *Critique of Anthropology* 18: 317–319.

Paz, Octavio. 1985 [1961]. *The Labyrinth of Solitude and other Writings*, trans. Lysander Kemp. New York: Grove Weidenfeld.

Peixoto, Clarice. 2000. "Entre o stigma e a compaixâo e os termos classificatórios: velho, velhote, idoso, terçeira idade." In *Velhice ou Terçeira Idade*, second edition, ed. Myriam Moraes Lins de Barros. Rio de Janeiro: Fundação Getúlio Vargas.

Pendergast, David, John Sherry, Simon Roberts, and Time Plowman. 2009. "Technology and Independent Living." *Anthropology News* (November): 9–10.

Petersen, Peter G. 1999. *Grey Dawn: How the Coming Age Wave Will Transform America—and the World.* New York: Crown Press.

Phillipson, Chris, and Graham Allan. 2004. "Aging and the Life Course." In *The Blackwell Companion to the Sociology of Families*, eds. Jacqueline Scott, Judith Treas, and Martin Richards. Malden: Blackwell Publishing.

Pike, Karen D., and Bengston, Vern L. 1996. "Caring More or Less: Individualistic and Collectivist Systems of Family Eldercare." *Journal of Marriage and the Family* 58, no. 2: 379–392.

Plath, David. 1980. *Long Engagements: Maturity in Modern Japan.* Stanford: Stanford University Press.

Porter-Szücs, Brian. 2011. *Faith and Fatherland: Catholicism, Modernity, and Poland.* New York: Oxford University Press.

Prefeitura Municipal de Florianopolis. n.d. *Terçeira Idade, Escola de Vida: Leis dos Idosos, Municipal, Estadual e Federal.* Florianopolis: Prefeitura Municipal.

Pruchno, Rachel. 1999. "Raising Grandchildren: The Experiences of Black and White Grandmothers." *The Gerontologist* 39, no. 2: 209–221.

Radcliffe-Brown, A. R. 1929. "Age-organisation—Terminology." *Man* 29: 21.

Rajan, S. Irudaya, and Sanjay Kumar. 2003. "Living Arrangements among Indian Elderly: New Evidence from National Family Health Survey." *Economic and Political Weekly* 38: 75–80.

Rajan, S. Irudaya, U. S. Mishra, and P. Sankara Sarma. 1999. *India's Elderly: Burden or Challenge?* New Delhi: Sage Publications.

Ramirez, Josué. 2009. *Against Machismo: Young Adult Voices in Mexico City.* New York: Berghahn Books.

Randall, William. L., and Gary M. Kenyon. 2004. "Time, Story, and Wisdom: Emerging Themes in Narrative Gerontology." *Canadian Journal on Aging* 23, no. 4: 333–346.

Rapoport, Amos. 1969. *House Form and Culture.* Englewood Cliffs: Prentice-Hall.

Rasmussen, Susan J. 1997. *The Poetics and Politics of Tuareg Aging: Life Course and Personal Destiny in Niger.* DeKalb: Northern Illinois University Press.

Reynolds, Frances, and Sarah Prior. 2003. "'Sticking Jewels in Your Life:' Exploring Women's Strategies for Negotiating an Acceptable Quality of Life with Multiple Sclerosis." *Qualitative Health Research* 13, no. 9 (November): 1225–1251.

Rial, Carmen Sílvia. 1988. "Mar-de-Dentro: A Transformação do Espaço Social na Lagoa da Conceiçao." MA thesis, Porto Alegre, UFRGS.

Roe, Kathleen M., Meredith Minkler, Frances Saunders, and Gregg E. Thomson. 1996. "Health of Grandmothers Raising Children of the Crack Cocaine Epidemic." *Medical Care* 34, no. 11: 1072–1084.

Ronald, Richard, and Allison Alexy. 2011. *Home and Family in Japan: Continuity and Transformation.* New York: Routledge.

Rosaldo, Renato. 1976. "The Story of Tukbaw: 'They Listen as He Orates.'" In *The Biographical Process: Studies in the History and Psychology of Religion*, ed. Frank E. Reynolds and Donald Capps. The Hague: Mouton.

Rosaldo, Renato.1980. *Ilongot Headhunting, 1883–1974: A Study in Society and History.* Stanford: Stanford University Press.

Rowe, John W., and Robert L. Kahn. 1998. *Successful Aging.* New York: Random House.

Rybczynski, Witold. 1986. *Home: A Short History of an Idea.* New York: Penguin Books.

Salami, Kabiru K., and William R. Brieger. 2010–11. "Commercial Charcoal Production in the Ibarapa District of Southwestern Nigeria: Forestry Dividends and Welfare Implications." *International Quarterly of Community Health Education* 31, no. 4: 369–85.

Salgero Velásquez, Ma. Alejandra. 2007. "Preguntarse cómo ser padre es también preguntarse cómo ser hombre: reflexiones sobre algunos varones." In *Sucede que me canso de ser hombre: Relatos y reflexiones sobre hombres y masculinidades en México*, eds. Ana Amuchástegui and Ivonne Szasz. Mexico City: El Colegio de México.

Salkeld, Ellen Jackson. 2008. "Integrative Medicine and Clinical Practice: Diagnosis and Treatment Strategies." *Complementary Health Practice Review* 13, no. 1 (January): 21–33.

Sánchez-Ayendez, Melba. 1988. "The Puerto Rican American Family." In *Ethnic Families in America: Patterns and Variations*, eds. Charles H. Mindel, Robert W. Habenstein, and Roosevelt Wright, Jr. New York: Elsevier.

Santos, Sílvia Maria Azevedo dos. 2006. *Idosos, Família e Cultura: Um estudo sobre a construção do papel do Cuidador*, second edition. Campinas SP: Alínea.

Savishinsky, Joel S. 2002. *Breaking the Watch: The Meanings of Retirement in America.* Ithaca: Cornell University Press.

Schama, Simon. 1987. *The Embarrassment of Riches: An Interpretation of Dutch Culture in the Golden Age.* New York: Vintage Books.

Scheer, Jessica, and Mark Luborsky. 1991. "The Cultural Context of Polio Biographies." *Orthopedics* 14, no. 11: 1173–1184.

Scheid, Volker. 2007. "Traditional Chinese Medicine—What Are We Investigating? The Case of Menopause." *Complementary Therapies in Medicine* 15: 54–68.

Scheper-Hughes, Nancy, and Margaret M. Lock. 1987. "The Mindful Body: A Prolegomenon to Future Work in Medical Anthropology." *Medical Anthropology Quarterly* 1, no. 1: 6–41.

Schildkrout, Enid. 1978. "Age and Gender in Hausa Society: Socio-Economic Roles of Children in Urban Kano." In *Sex and Age as Principles of Social Differentiation*, ed. Jean LaFontaine. London: Academic Press.

Schwartz, Stephanie. 2011. "Youth and the 'Arab Spring.'" On the Issues, by Stephanie Schwartz, United States Institute of Peace. April 28. http://www.usip.org/publications/youth-and-the-arab-spring.

Seale, Clive. 1998. *Constructing Death: The Sociology of Dying and Bereavement.* Cambridge: Cambridge University Press.

Seltzer, Mildred M., and Jon Hendriks. 1986. "Explorations in Time." *American Behavioral Scientist* 29, no. 6 (July/August): 653–661.

Setterson, Richard A., and Karl Ulrich Mayer. 1997. "The Measurement of Age, Age-Structuring and the Life Course." *Annual Review of Sociology* 23: 233–61.

Shadid, Anthony. 2011. "Syria's Sons of No One." *New York Times*, 31 August. http://www.nytimes.com/2011/09/04/magazine/syrias-sons-of-no-one.html.

Shea, Jeanne. 2006. "Cross-Cultural Comparison of Women's Midlife Symptom-Reporting: A China Study." *Culture, Medicine, and Psychiatry* 30, no. 3 (September): 331–62.

Sheehy, Gail. 1995. *New Passages: Mapping Your Life.* New York: Random House.

Shen, Rong. 1990 [1982]. "At Middle Age." In *Seven Contemporary Chinese Women Writers*, ed. Gladys Yang. Beijing: Chinese Literature Press.

Shostak, Marjorie. 1983. *Nisa: The Life and Words of a !Kung Woman.* New York: Random House Vintage.

Silveira, Maria Lúcia da. 2000. *O Nervo Cala, O Nervo Fala: a linguagem da doença.* Rio de Janeiro: Editora Fiocruz.

Silverman, Phillip, ed. 1987. *The Elderly as Modern Pioneers.* Bloomington: Indiana University Press.

Simmons, Leo. 1945. *The Role of the Aged in Primitive Societies.* New Haven: Yale University Press.

Simmons, Leo. 1960. "Aging in Preindustrial Societies." In *Handbook of Social Gerontology*, ed. Clark Tibbetts. Chicago: University of Chicago Press.

Smith, Robert. 1974. *Ancestor Worship in Contemporary Japan.* Stanford: Stanford University Press.

Sokolovsky, Jay. 2009a. "Aging, Center Stage: New Life Course Research in Anthropology." *Anthropology News* (November): 5.

Sokolovsky, Jay, ed. 2009b. *The Cultural Context of Aging: Worldwide Perspectives,* third edition. Westport: Praeger.

Solimeo, Samantha. 2009. *With Shaking Hands: Aging with Parkinson's Disease in America's Heartland.* New Brunswick: Rutgers University Press.

Spiro, Melford E. 1983. *Oedipus in the Trobriands.* Chicago: University of Chicago Press.

Sri Lankan Bureau of Foreign Employment (SLBFE). 2009. *Annual Statistical Report of Foreign Employment 2009.* Battaramula: SLBFE.

SSA (Social Security Administration). 2011. "Earnings Limits." Social Security Administration Electronic Fact Sheet, Washington, D.C.: SSA Publication No. 05-10003. January, ICN 451385. http://www.ssa.gov/pubs/10003.html.

Stacey, Judith. 1997. *In the Name of the Family: Rethinking Family Values in the Postmodern Age.* Boston: Beacon Press.

Stack, Carol B. 1970. *All Our Kin: Strategies for Survival in a Black Community.* New York: Harper and Row.

Stevens, Evelyn. 1973. "Marianismo: The Other Face of Machismo in Latin America." In *Female and Male in Latin America*, ed. Ann Pescatello. Pittsburgh: University of Pittsburgh Press.

Stewart, Martha. 2010. "The Other Health Care Crisis—America's Elderly." *Huffington Post*, 20 January. http://www.huffingtonpost.com/martha-stewart/the-other-health-care-cri_b_429968.html.

Stone, Linda. 2010. *Kinship and Gender: An Introduction,* fourth edition. Boulder: Westview Press.

Strathern, Andrew, and Pamela J. Stewart. 2011. *Kinship in Action: Self and Group.* Boston: Prentice Hall.

Stuart-Hamilton, Ian. 2011. *An Introduction to Gerontology.* New York: Cambridge University Press.

Stucci, Deborah. 1994. "Programas de Preparaçao à Aposentadoria e o Mapeamento do Curso da Vida do Trabalhador." MA thesis, UNICAMP (Universidade de Campinas, São Paulo).

Susser, Ida, and Nila Chatterjee. 1998. "Critiquing Flexible Labor." *Critique of Anthropology* 18: 243–244.

Taylor, Janelle S. 2008. "On Recognition, Caring and Dementia." *Medical Anthropology Quarterly* 22, no. 4: 313–335.

Taylor, Richard. 2006. *Alzheimer's from the Inside Out.* Baltimore: Health Professions Press.

Terkel, Studs. 1997. *Working: People Talk About What They Do All Day and How They Feel About What They Do.* New York: The New Press.

Torres, Sandra. 2006. "Culture, Migration, Inequality, and 'Periphery' in a Globalized World: Challenges for Ethno-and Anthropogerontology." In *Aging Globalization and Inequality: The New Critical Gerontology,* eds. Jan Baars, Dale Dannefer, Chris Phillipson, and Alan Walker. Amityville: Baywood Publishing Company.

Traphagan, John W. 2004. *The Practice of Concern: Ritual, Well-Being, and Aging in Rural Japan.* Durham: Carolina Academic Press.

Trawick, Margaret. 1990. *Notes on Love in a Tamil Family.* Berkeley: University of California Press.

Tsuji, Yohko. 1997. "Continuities and Changes in the Conceptions of Old Age in Japan." In *Aging: Asian Concepts and Experiences, Past and Present,* eds. Susanne Formanek and Sepp Linhart. Vienna: Österreichische Akademie der Wissenschaften.

Tsuji, Yohko. 2005. "Time is Not Up: Temporal Complexity of Older American's Lives." *Journal of Cross-Cultural Gerontology* 20, no. 1: 3–26.

Tuljapurkar, Shripad, Nan Li, and Carl Boe. 2000. "A Universal Pattern of Mortality Decline in the G7 Countries." *Nature* 405: 789–792.

Turnbull, Colin M. 1983. *The Human Cycle.* New York: Simon and Schuster-Touchstone.

Tymicki, Krzysztof. 2009. "The Correlates of Infant and Childhood Mortality: A Theoretical Overview and New Evidence from the Analysis of Longitudinal Data of the Bejsce (Poland) Parish Register Reconstitution Study of the 18th–20th Centuries." *Demographic Research* 20: 559–594. doi:10.4054/DemRes.2009.20.23.

Uchitelle, Louis. 2010. "American Dream is Elusive for New Generation." *New York Times,* 6 July. http://www.nytimes.com/2010/07/07/business/economy/07generation.html.

Valle, Ramon, and Helen Cook-Gait. 1998. *Caregiving Across Cultures.* Oxford: Routledge.

Van Wolputte, Steven. 2004. "Hang on to Your Self: Of Bodies, Embodiment, and Selves." *Annual Review of Anthropology* 33: 251–69.

Vatuk, Sylvia. 1990. "To Be a Burden on Others: Dependency Anxiety among the Elderly in India." In *Divine Passions: The Social Construction of Emotion in India,* ed. Owen Lynch. Berkeley: University of California Press.

Vera, Hernan. 1989. "On Dutch Windows." *Qualitative Sociology* 12, no. 2: 215–34.

Veras, Renato, ed. 1997. *Terçeira Idade: Desafios para o Terçeiro Milênio,* second edition. Rio de Janeiro: Fundação Getúlio Vargas.

Voland, Eckart, Athanasios Chasiotis, and Wulf Schiefenhövel, eds. 2005. *Grandmotherhood: The Evolutionary Significance of the Second Half of Female Life*. New Brunswick: Rutgers University Press.

Wal, Gerrit van der, Agnes van der Heide, Bregje D. Onwuteaka-Philipsen, and Paul J. van der Maas. 2003. *Medische besluitvorming aan het einde van het leven: De praktijk en de toetsingsprocedure euthanasie [Medical decision-making at the end of life: the practice and euthanasia reporting procedure]*. Utrecht: de Tijdstroom.

Wanasundera, Leelangi. 2001. *Migrant Women Domestic Workers: Cyprus, Greece, and Italy*. CENWOR: Colombo.

Wardlow, Holly, and Jennifer S. Hirsch. 2006. "Introduction." In *Modern Loves: The Anthropology of Romantic Courtship and Companionate Marriage*, eds. Jennifer S. Hirsch and Holly Wardlow. Ann Arbor: The University of Michigan Press.

Weber, Max. 2002 [1905]. *The Protestant Ethic and the Spirit of Capitalism*. New York: Penguin.

Weibel-Orlando, Joan. 2009. "Grandparenting Styles: The Contemporary American Indian Experience." In *The Cultural Context of Aging: Worldwide Perspectives*, ed. Jay Sokolovsky. Westport: Praeger.

Weismantel, Mary. 1995. "Making Kin: Kinship Theory and Zumbagua Adoptions." *American Ethnologist* 22, no. 4: 685–704.

Weiss, Brad. 2009. *Street Dreams and Hip Hop Barbershops: Global Fantasy in Urban Tanzania*. Bloomington: Indiana University Press.

Weiss, Robert S. 2005. *The Experience of Retirement*. Ithaca: Cornell University Press.

Wentzell, Emily. 2011. "Making 'Male Sexuality': Hybrid Medical Knowledge and Viagra in Mexico." In *Gender and the Science of Difference: Cultural Politics of Contemporary Science and Medicine*, ed. Jill A. Fisher. New Brunswick: Rutgers University Press.

Wentzell, Emily, and Jorge Salmerón. 2009. "You'll 'Get Viagraed': Mexican Men's Preference for Alternative Erectile Dysfunction Treatment." *Social Science and Medicine* 68, no. 10: 1759–1765.

Wentzell, Emily, and Marcia Inhorn. 2011. "The Male Reproductive Body." In *A Companion to the Anthropology of Bodies and Embodiment*, ed. Fran Mascia-Lees. New York: Wiley-Blackwell.

Whitehead, Alfred N. 1929. *Process and Reality: An Essay in Cosmology*. Cambridge: Cambridge University Press.

Whitehead, Alfred N. 1933. *Adventures of Ideas*. New York: The MacMillian Company.

Willis, Paul. 1977. *Learning to Labor: How Working Class Kids Get Working Class Jobs*. New York: Columbia University Press.

Wilson, Monica. 1951. *Good Company: A Study of Nyakusa Age Villages*. London: Oxford University Press.

Wohl, Robert. 1979. *The Generation of 1914*. Cambridge: Cambridge University Press.

Wolf, Margery.1972. *Women and the Family in Rural Taiwan*. Stanford: Sanford University Press.

Woodward, Kathleen. 1991. *Aging and Its Discontents: Freud and other Fictions*. Bloomington: Indiana University Press.

World Bank. 2008. *Sri Lanka: Addressing the Needs of an Aging Population*. Report No. 43396-LK. Human Development Unit, South Asia Region. 28 May. http://go.worldbank.org/I14DRI6CS0.

Yamada, Yoko, and Yoshinobu Kato. 2006. "Images of Circular Time and Spiral Repetition: The Generative Life Cycle Model." In *Culture and Psychology* 12, no. 2: 143–160.

Yamada, Yoko. 2003. "The Generative Life Cycle Model: Integration of Japanese Folk Images and Generativity." In *The Generative Society: Caring for Future Generations*, eds. Ed de St. Aubin, Dan P. McAdams, and Tae Chung Kim. Washington, D.C.: American Psychological Association.

Yamaori, Tetsuo. 1997. "Buddha and *Okina* ('Aged Man'): The Expression of Dying and Maturity." In *Aging Asian Concepts and Experiences Past and Present*, eds. Susanne Formanek and Sepp Linhart. Vienna: Österreichische Akademie der Wissenschaften.

Young, Richard, and Fukui Ikeuchi. 1997. "Geriatric Rituals in Japan." In *Aging Asian Concepts and Experiences Past and Present*, eds. Susanne Formanek and Sepp Linhart. Vienna: Österreichische Akademie der Wissenschaften.

INDEX